The Taming of Education

Rob Creasy

The Taming of Education

Evaluating Contemporary Approaches to Learning and Teaching

palgrave
macmillan

Rob Creasy
School of Psychological & Social Science
York St John University
York, UK

ISBN 978-3-319-62246-0   ISBN 978-3-319-62247-7   (eBook)
DOI 10.1007/978-3-319-62247-7

Library of Congress Control Number: 2017951721

Cover design by Samantha Johnson

Printed on acid-free paper

This Palgrave Macmillan imprint is published by Springer Nature
The registered company is Springer International Publishing AG
The registered company address is: Gewerbestrasse 11, 6330 Cham, Switzerland

As with all books, there are many people who have made contributions to a greater and lesser degree. Fiona takes a lot of credit for providing support at home. At work a good number of people have helped enormously to make this book happen and I know that I will overlook some in naming just a few. To those who do get named, many thanks go to Mike Bottery, Julian Stern, Matthew Clarke, Paul Smith and Tony Leach. There's quite a few acronyms used in this book so here are two that go beyond home and work. For those who join me at Hillsborough, UTO, WAWAW!

Contents

LIST OF TABLES

CHAPTER 1

Seeing Education as a Process

1.1   Introduction

Education is an integral part of societies across the globe. Although there may be differences with respect to how it is provided, the fact remains that pupils and students around the world are often required to attend compulsory education and are then able, required even in some countries, to study for qualifications at increasingly higher levels. In the English-speaking world, it is common to find references to compulsory education comprising primary and secondary education, followed by Tertiary Education, which may be referred to as Continuing or Further Education, and then Higher Education. What is also evident is that education does not just exist within society in a neutral sense; it is always the product of a range of social and political forces. Education may appear to be axiomatic but it is always subject to a range of ways of understanding it. Because of this it is subject to a number of forces which act upon it. Some of these forces may be said to be internal in that they appear to be rooted within education itself, but very often they are external to it. In this way education can be seen within formalised institutions as well as within a much broader and more informal context. Education, at whatever level, however, is not apart from society, it is a part of society and social forces are rarely simple.

There may be lots of commentators and educationalists who would propose that education is a right but this has not always been the case

© The Author(s) 2018
R. Creasy, *The Taming of Education*,
DOI 10.1007/978-3-319-62247-7_1

(Wrigley 2009). As such, contrasting debates about the value and purposes of education can be identified (Pring 2004). Biesta's (2009) argument that education meets three functions, qualification, socialisation and subjectification, is an illustration of this. One way of considering education is to consider the intrinsic and extrinsic value that it has. This can be seen in ideas about education which reflect a humanist tradition espousing education as having its own value, and being a key component with respect to personal development, but this approach can be juxtaposed with a utilitarian approach towards education. From the utilitarian perspective, education exists to serve a purpose that is extrinsic to the individual. There are links to a neoliberal perspective within the utilitarian approach. From a neoliberal perspective, the purpose of education is seen as being the way in which it contributes to the economy or, at least, to the way in which it facilitates an individual's contribution to the economy which in turn is argued to be reflected in the rewards that individuals receive. This reflects the idea of human capital in which investment in education on an individual's part will increase the rewards that they can expect in terms of income (Hartog and Oosterbeek 2007). However, a consideration of income differentials with respect to varying occupations illustrates that this is not a strong argument.

This human capital argument may have had more relevance in the past when, in industrialised countries in particular, education could provide advantages within the labour market, but to echo the argument that Blacker (2013) presents, the rate of return on education can be seen to have been falling over the past 50 years. Blacker presents a rather pessimistic view of the role of education within contemporary society in which he argues that technological and economic developments suggest that for many of the population, there is little to be educated for. Although his argument has some merit with respect to economic developments and the experience of work, I would argue that it maybe makes the mistake of accepting the neoliberal argument regarding education existing to provide for the economy as a given, something which I am certain Blacker would not have intended. Instead it could be argued that the falling demand for education that arises because of automation within the economy actually reiterates the importance of education having value in its own right with respect to self-development.

Within this book I adopt a critical perspective on the way in which education is organised and experienced, and although the focus is on England, the arguments that will be made have resonance across the globe. I start from the position that education must be fit for purpose, whatever that purpose may be. However, I will suggest that the forces which are acting upon education may be seen as creating educational provision which is not fit for purpose. I propose that this position applies whether or not one adheres to either a utilitarian or a self-developmental view of education. I do this by arguing that education is being increasingly tamed when what is required for each position is education that is wicked. Chapter 2 will illustrate and explain what is meant by wicked and tame in this context.

1.2 Education as a Process

A key factor that contributes to the taming of education is that it is increasingly being seen as a process. This concept may be seen as underpinning much that applies to education and, in some ways, there are aspects of education which give the impression that this is the case. For example, it would be hard to argue that education does not change individuals. Not only does education change individuals, one of the main reasons for education is precisely that. We want to change people. Education exists for that very reason. Indeed, it is when education does not appear to have changed an individual that we consider it to have failed. For that reason, we can see that it is unsurprising that we view education as a process. However, we can always be certain that individuals will change over time and so being able to attribute any change to education is maybe not as simple as it first seems.

So, in that respect we have a situation wherein we can establish both an original state, that is, before education, and an end state, that is, after education, but the extent to which it is education that has caused the change is not as simple as it first appears. Irrespective of this concern, considerations of education tend to assume a causal relationship with change and with assessing the extent of change. The question then turns to the nature of the process itself and how we might establish an understanding of what the process has produced. It is at this point that it is important to recognise that how we provide education is social. There is no inevitable structure to education, nor is there any intrinsic characteristic of it which means that education can only be structured and provided for in any one way. However, what will be argued is that not only has education come to be seen as a process, there are forces that act upon education which operate in ways which mean that ever-increasing aspects of control have been brought to bear upon it. Importantly though the consequences of increasing control are not in our long-term interests.

It is also pertinent to note that I am concerned with formal systems of education. It is irrelevant, in one sense, if education is being provided for publicly, organised by the State, or privately, such as a private school or college. The important thing here is that a system has been set up to provide education. As such, we can draw an immediate distinction between learning and education because one thing that we can always be certain of is that individuals will always learn. So, the key thing to consider here is that this book is focused upon structures and systems that are established with a view towards particular aspects of learning which can generally be characterised by the idea of a curriculum. In that sense the curriculum provides some degree of formality towards what should be or is expected to be learnt. In turn, this then provides the possibility of the measurement of such learning.

So, following from this we can see how educational systems include providers of education, in terms of organisations such as schools, colleges and universities, and in respect of individuals who teach and where this means that the work of such organisations and teachers may be measured. This is not to presume that such measurement is either accurate or useful, only to point out that it is used with increasing importance in terms of consequences. As well as organisations and teachers being measured, pupils and students are being measured also.

1.3   STRUCTURE OF THE BOOK

In presenting arguments that relate to the concept of wicked and tame, Chap. 2 draws significantly from the original concept of wicked problems as put forward by Rittel and Webber (1973). As will be argued in Chap. 2, the value of this conceptual framework is that Rittel and Webber articulate the problems faced by individuals who work with complex issues. This resonates with education. However, the original idea can be seen as a dichotomy wherein any particular issue is either seen as wicked or tame. I see this as a useful starting point but one which does not really go far enough; indeed it could be argued that the initial concept as proposed by Rittel and Webber is itself tame. For this reason the concept is developed further so that it is wickedity and tameness which are brought to the fore in a manner whereby education can be seen as more wicked or more tame.

The concept of wicked and tame is useful when considering education because issues relating to teaching and learning are always complex. In addition to this, a key part of education, especially within the Higher

Education sector, is that it seeks to develop new knowledge rather than just mastering what is already known. It seeks creativity and originality (Hussey and Smith 2010). The argument that is presented here adopts the position that if creativity and originality are valued as part of the remit of education, then we need to establish ways of accommodating this. This impacts upon how we carry out assessment of education and because of this assessment will often be referred to as a key part of understanding education practices. For example, if creativity and originality are important, and are something to be valued, then an approach to assessment which is able to capture this is required. This would be wicked assessment as opposed to assessment which is tame. In establishing tameness though, we are drawn into a consideration of control, something that is explored within Chap. 3.

A key part of the argument is that creativity and originality are things that we need to generate as part of education but recent developments suppress these. One reason for the suppression of creativity and originality may be seen as the increasing levels of control being exercised over teachers at all levels. This is considered in Chap. 3 and is presented as representing a shift away from the ability of teachers to exercise control over their work. In particular Chap. 3 considers the ways in which the State has come to impose greater levels of control on the educational sector.

This is developed further in Chap. 4. The key factor behind the actions of the State is presented as being the rise of neoliberal politics. Neoliberalism has had an increasing influence across the globe and operates in ways which shape education in line with its own discourse. A major aspect of this is the promotion of education as being a competitive exercise as well as seeing the benefits of education as providing private advantage within an economic context. The idea of New Public Management will be presented as a strategy by which neoliberalism has achieved change within education to the disadvantage of teachers, as will the role of standardisation.

The ways in which education has come to be organised and structured are the focus of Chap. 5. In particular it will be considered that the economic concerns and demands of society influence the ways in which education is provided. Ideas about the so-called knowledge society will be used to demonstrate the way in which originality and creativity are increasing in importance as we move into a post-industrial economy. This is very important for promoting the argument that education needs to be wicked in that wickedity is bound up with creativity and originality. What will be demonstrated through a consideration of Further and Higher Education in particular though is that there has been a growing importance placed upon credentials but where educational developments aimed at reducing uncertainty, and so, increasing credentials, may act to squeeze out creativity and originality. As such, although creativity and originality is said to be increasing in importance, educational systems, not just in England, are developing in ways which suppress this.

The idea of education being understood and approached as if it were a process is considered within Chap. 6. It is argued that coming to see education as a process lays the foundations for adopting approaches which will remove uncertainty from what happens within education. A key part of this is a move towards the use of learning outcomes which can be seen as a consequence of a managerialist discourse which seeks control over educational processes (Lorenz 2012). In turn, it is argued that this contributes to education being tamed. In a similar vein, the contemporary discourse of education as a means by which children and young people can reach their potential will also be considered as a way in which the process model of education comes to be accepted.

Having developed the argument that education has been subject to forces which have tamed it, Chap. 7 investigates the extent to which this can be evidenced and will set out to provide an illustration of how the concept of tameness and wickedity can be mobilised as an evaluative tool for teachers. It does this by focusing on contemporary assessment practices within Higher Education, an area of education with which I am currently engaged.

Changes within Higher Education has seen Higher Education Institutions (HEIs) being increasingly managed as though they were businesses (Reid 2009). This means that academic activities are managed through strategic control. A major feature of this control involves the measurement of outputs. Within Higher Education there are a range of outputs but an important one may be seen as the awards that students leave with. Such awards invariably rest upon a process of assessment of their learning and development, but assessing the extent of a student's learning and development does not sit easily with the managerial prerogative for control. As such the development of a learning outcomes approach to Higher Education can be seen as facilitating control over the learning process.

In considering whether or not education is wicked or tame, my argument is that tameness contributes to an impoverished experience of education. In contrast to tame approaches, I argue that effective education would be a system that is able to benefit from being a practice which can incorporate wickedity in a number of ways. In the case study presented within Chap. 7, I make the case that wicked assessment will be more able to reward creativity and originality, but it may also contribute to greater levels of student engagement and provide benefits for both teachers and for society as a whole in terms of how this contributes to economic activity.

Chapter 8 sets out to establish where we are now with respect to the contemporary landscape in education and to draw the issues raised in previous chapters together to suggest ways in which we can move away from tameness in education and towards wickedity. The value of critically considering practices within education through the lens of tameness and wickedity is that tameness can be seen as having the potential to undermine education. This argument reflects the work of Biesta (2013) who provides a critical account of developments within education in general based on both the individualisation of education and its repositioning as a duty within a market economy. Similarly, Hussey and Smith (2010) point to the way in which what is being assessed often ends up as representing only a part of what a student has learnt or only particular aspects of their overall development. The use of learning outcomes contributes to this problem by focusing attention upon predetermined aspects of learning and development. In this way originality may be unrewarded when it does not correspond to the stated learning outcomes. Such an approach also reduces the professional expertise of teachers and acts against rewarding applied learning or of originality in a student's work.

The main argument that is being developed however rests upon the argument that Rittel and Webber's concept of wicked problems can be used to understand how education may be understood as becoming increasingly tame. In doing this Chap. 8 will also provide critical discussions of the ways in which education has developed in a manner which becomes distracted into a consideration of issues that are peripheral to teaching such as the idea of therapeutic education (Ecclestone and Hayes 2009). Such developments can be seen as the outcome of a process of depoliticalisation within education (Clarke 2012; Clarke and Phelan 2017). Depoliticalisation though brings individualism to the fore and promotes an understanding of education which is focused upon what institutions and teachers do and/or the readiness or ability of individuals to learn. The depoliticalisation of education supports a turn towards

therapeutic education, reflective practice and a focus on learning as typified in the readily accepted myth of learning styles as each represents an
individualised aspect of education, decoupled from the social and political
context.

Chapter 9 closes the book by considering the need for risk within education and by emphasising some of the ways in which tameness can be
resisted such as a reconsideration of the values and purpose of education.
It concludes by providing a manifesto for wicked education, a summary of
the issues that have been raised throughout the book as a call for wickedity. The aim throughout the book is to reiterate that education is for a
purpose and, irrespective of whether you see education from an idealistic
or a utilitarian perspective, education has to be fit for purpose. A combination of factors however is changing education in a number of ways and
increasingly taming it. The problem is that tame education is impoverished education, it is not fit for purpose.

REFERENCES

Biesta, Gert. 2009. Good Education in an Age of Measurement: On the Need to
    Reconnect with the Question of Purpose in Education. *Educational Assessment,
    Evaluation & Accountability* 21 (1): 33–46. doi:10.1007/s11092-008-9064-9.
    ———. 2013. *The Beautiful Risk of Education*. Boulder, CO: Paradigm Publishers.
Blacker, D.J. 2013. *The Falling Rate of Learning and the Neoliberal Endgame*.
    Winchester: Zero Books.
Clarke, Matthew. 2012. The (Absent) Politics of Neo-Liberal Education Policy.
    Critical Studies in Education 53 (3): 297–310. doi:10.1080/17508487.2012
    .703139.
Clarke, M., and A. Phelan. 2017. *Teacher Education and the Political: The Power of
    Negative Thinking*. London: Routledge.
Ecclestone, K., and D. Hayes. 2009. *The Dangerous Rise of Therapeutic Education*.
    London: Routledge.
Hartog, Joop, and Hessel Oosterbeek. 2007. What Should You Know About the
    Private Returns to Education? In *Human Capital: Advances in Theory and
    Evidence*, ed. Joop Hartog and Henriëtte Maassen van den Brink, 7–20.
    Cambridge: Cambridge University Press.
Hussey, Trevor, and Patrick Smith. 2010. *The Trouble with Higher Education*.
    Abingdon: Routledge.
Lorenz, Chris. 2012. If You're So Smart, Why Are You Under Surveillance?
    Universities, Neoliberalism, and New Public Management. *Critical Inquiry* 38
    (3): 599–629. doi:10.1086/664553.

Pring, Richard. 2004. *Philosophy of Education: Aims, Theory, Common Sense and Research.* London: Continuum.

Reid, Ian C. 2009. The Contradictory Managerialism of University Quality Assurance. *Journal of Education Policy* 24 (5): 575–593. doi:10.1080/02680930903131242.

Rittel, Horst W.J., and M. Melvin Webber. 1973. Dilemmas in a General Theory of Planning. *Policy Sciences* 4 (2): 155–169.

Wrigley, T. 2009. Rethinking Education in the Era of Globalization. In *Contesting Neo-Liberal Education: Public Resistance and Collective Advance*, ed. D. Hill. Abingdon: Routledge.

CHAPTER 2

Education: Wicked or Tame?

2.1 INTRODUCTION

This chapter opens by introducing the concept of wicked and tame. It then moves on to demonstrate the value of employing this concept with respect to education through substituting wicked and tame for the more nuanced concepts of wickedity and tameness. The underlying concept of wicked and tame is rooted in the work of Rittel and Webber (1973), and although in many contemporary debates the focus tends to be on wicked problems, this can only really be understood through a recognition of what a tame problem is. Rittel and Webber introduced the idea of wicked problems so as to illustrate the complexity of some situations and the problems that this poses for practitioners engaged in roles that are not characterised by routine solutions being used to deal with routine problems. As such, the concepts of wicked and tame will be established. It will be argued, however, that although the original concept of wicked and tame problems presents a useful framework for approaching assessment, it falls into the trap of presenting a clear dichotomy which is not evident in practice.

What this means for education is then explored. A particular focus of the chapter will be concerned with aspects of assessment. Here, the argument that assessment policies may be tame and, as such, fail to assess the full extent of learning will be explored. The implication of this is that education becomes impoverished, to an extent, because assessment practices are limited. To develop this argument further, Chap. 6 presents a

© The Author(s) 2018
R. Creasy, *The Taming of Education*,
DOI 10.1007/978-3-319-62247-7_2

discussion of learning outcomes as this will demonstrate how contemporary assessment practices reflect the idea of education as a process but where the tendency is to adopt a reductionist position regarding what is being assessed. The development and adoption of learning outcomes is presented as part of the process by which one part of education, assessment, becomes tame.

2.2   CONCEPTUALISING ISSUES AS WICKED OR TAME

The concept that is central to this book is rooted in that of problems being either wicked or tame. This section will consider the concept of wicked and tame problems as first outlined by Rittel and Webber (1973). It will then consider how this may be developed further. The idea that problems can be defined as either wicked or tame originally emerged in the work of Rittel and Webber (1973) in response to issues related to urban planning. It has since been applied to diverse concerns such as health (Blackman et al. 2006), business strategy (Camillus 2008), marine policy (Jentoft and Chuenpagdee 2009), education (Bore and Wright 2009; Knight and Page 2007; Wright 2011; Jordan et al. 2014) and social policy (Hayden and Jenkins 2014). The growing use of this conceptual approach provides an indication of its value in understanding contemporary issues with a simple library search resulting in numerous journal articles drawing upon the concept of wicked problems. As such, it is reasonable to conclude that the concept of wicked problems has become established as a way of approaching and understanding complex social issues, and because of this it provides a critical response to solutions which draw upon techno-rational approaches. At the heart of the concept is the idea that some problems have clear or obvious outcomes whilst others are far less straightforward. For Rittel and Webber, tame problems are found in the type of issues where outcomes are obviously right or wrong. Wicked problems, however, reflect complexity and relativity.

This does not mean that tame problems are simple, as Bottery (2016, 37) makes clear: "they may be, but they may also be technically quite complex, being distinguished from 'wicked' problems by being embedded within clear rules of procedure, clear definitions of the problem, and strong agreement on—or strong imposition of—what is believed to be a successful solution".

For example, in engineering, although a project may pose challenges, it can be seen how the issue is often a tame one in the approach taken by

Rittel and Webber. This is because there is a certainty that can be known regarding the physical properties of materials. So, if I was tasked with constructing a table that would be suitable for my classroom, I could ascertain the weights and stresses that are likely to be applied to it and, knowing the properties of certain materials, construct a workable table. In itself this is not only tame, it is also simple. If the task was to process nuclear materials, the physical properties still lead to the problem being tame in that they are known, and therefore the problem is still subject to procedures with an obvious end result even though there is a degree of complexity that was absent within the first example.

For Rittel and Webber, the examples may differ in complexity but they remain tame, something that can be seen as applying to all problems that are accommodated within a scientific perspective. It could be argued that science, as an approach, seeks tameness if we see the term tameness as reflecting certainty. When it comes to matters that are rooted in social behaviours, however, there is a degree of complexity and uncertainty that accompanies such concerns and which means that tameness becomes elusive. Following Rittel and Webber, any social policy issue is inevitably a wicked problem as will be explained further below. As such, issues to do with how we engage in the practice of education, such as teaching and assessment, are wicked because of the range of factors involved. An approach that may work effectively with one cohort, or in one subject, may not work as well with other cohorts or within other disciplines. Similarly, what is appropriate, or works well with one age group, may not be at all successful with a different age group.

Bottery (2016) adds to our understanding of wicked problems in pointing out that in areas such as social policy, indeed any issue which involves social behaviour, there is often a degree of complexity which means that understanding problems in causal ways, such as is found within scientific problems, is often insufficient. In spite of increasing levels of bureaucracy and the establishment of standardised practices, human activities are generally characterised by both unexpected and unintended consequences. Significant time and effort may be put into reducing unexpected and unintended outcomes, for example, by the increased levels of management experienced within such as education, and which will be discussed in Chap. 3 which follows, but humans are not automatons and their behaviour is often at odds with what may have been anticipated or planned. Part of this problem is that individuals may not be in agreement regarding the matters that are under scrutiny.

The problem, from Rittel and Webber's perspective, is that the aims of social policy are now often associated with values or intentions which may not be shared, problems which may not be self-evident and matters such as equity which may not consensual. However, what can be seen is that those professionals charged with addressing such policy issues have often taken direction from a scientific paradigm, a paradigm which works well when materials are inanimate but which is evidently inappropriate in situations where plurality and reflexivity are intrinsic features of the parties involved. At this point it is worth considering just what we mean by the term paradigms as it can be argued that what Rittel and Webber are engaged in is making a case against adopting a paradigmatical approach which is inappropriate.

2.3   Paradigms

The concept of paradigms has its origins within studies of science in the seminal work of Kuhn (1996). For Kuhn a paradigm may be understood as an organising principle. This is generally used to make sense of what happens with respect to research in a way which establishes any particular research method as valid (Plowright 2011). It should be noted though that in this case Rittel and Webber are not using it to justify an approach with respect to research, but are, instead, using it to make sense of approaches to planning. In research, the epistemological position adopted by a researcher can mean that the validity ascribed to one method then has the effect of invalidating alternative methods. In planning it can be seen how an approach that has been shaped by a scientific perspective may be seen as problematic when dealing with social issues. As such, Rittel and Webber are clearly drawing upon Kuhn's distinction between normative and revolutionary science (Wexler 2009).

Brew (2001) illustrates the ways in which Kuhn's concept of paradigms may impact upon social practices in considering how individuals, working within disciplines, come to develop communities of practice which share ontological and epistemological approaches with reference to the practice of research. She recognises the importance of the relationship between communities of practice and the creation and/or acceptance of knowledge. In doing this she points out that not only have ideas about knowledge, and the methods used to generate knowledge, changed over time, there may be ongoing struggles which privilege some methods whilst reducing the impact of others. It is the privileging of a scientific approach that Rittel and Webber see as problematic, particularly where this is applied to situations that do not follow the logic of science such as matters of social policy. In essence, the argument that Rittel and Webber put forward reflects the ontological and epistemological arguments that are evident within debates about research. Such an idea is at the heart of what Gage (2007) has called "the paradigm wars". This refers to the tensions which exist between those engaged in quantitative and qualitative research wherein each constitutes a separate paradigm. What Rittel and Webber are doing is drawing attention to how scientific approaches, which work well with what they refer to as tame problems, are inappropriate when applied to situations which are social in nature. This is because social issues, as has been argued, involve complexity in a manner that undermines a tame solution.

However, what Rittel and Webber argue is that the successes of projects within town planning, such as the provision of utilities, or the establishment of paved roads is essentially tame. Problems such as these, however, can be seen to be qualitatively different from problems which are linked to social behaviours. However, the success of approaches to town planning issues which may be seen as focused on utilities has led to reliance upon such approaches even when the nature of the problem has changed. For Rittel and Webber, the fact that some approaches end up being adopted more readily than others leads to a situation whereby some projects will inevitably fail because of the mistaken belief that social problems can be tackled in the same way that scientific problems can be tackled.

I might add here though that scientific approaches towards problems are often quite seductive. They have often produced results which have had significant, and positive, impacts upon our lives. Rittel and Webber acknowledge this, pointing to how clean water and power are provided to urban areas, how many diseases have been effectively eradicated as a consequence, and how thousands of individuals are moved around towns and cities smoothly. In light of this, and given that education is generally accepted as being important, it is not surprising that some may seek an approach to education which is able to replicate the successes of a scientific approach. As a consequence it is possible to see how political discourse may favour particular approaches even where the problem itself has now changed and where the subject matter is not inanimate materials but individuals. This can be illustrated by considering the scientifically based research movement in the USA (Denzin and Lincoln 2008) and the rise of evidence-based practice within the UK (Hammersley 2007). In both cases, this has emerged out of disciplines such as medicine where it may be seen as wholly appropriate but has since been gaining ground in areas where such certainties are far less obvious.

Arguments in support of evidence-based practice in education are neatly summarised by Ravitch (1998) who draws upon her own experience of being admitted to hospital and uses this experience to contrast the ways in which the medical profession draws upon research compared to what happens within education. In this comparison the certainties of medicine are clearly presented favourably and as something which education could learn from. In doing this though Ravitch overlooks the very real differences in respect of the subject that is being researched in that although human biology does not always respond to medicine in uniform ways, there is clearly a much greater degree of certainty than with respect to how different individuals respond to teaching.

Hargreaves (2007) offers a similar argument, claiming that the adoption of qualitative methods within educational research has not been of practical use because of the inevitable nature of such research being small scale and having problems in respect of generalisation. This position appears to take a rather narrow view of education which ignores the complexity that is evident when considering the social and cultural contexts within which education takes place. For Hargreaves, education seems to be being understood as a process which can be dealt with in a way that is analogous to other forms of production processes. It is the view of education as being analogous to a process that will be shown to have contributed significantly to the taming of education.

Where Hargreaves' argument falls down is that, in general, the problems faced by the medical profession are far tamer than the problems faced by teachers. In one sense the concerns of medicine, the concern to affect a cure, have no correspondence in education. Teachers are not seeking to cure their pupils or students. However, it could be argued that it is the seductiveness of certainty which makes it easy to overlook this. Consideration of the subject matter faced by each profession illustrates the complexity of education when compared to medicine and illustrates that education is rarely ever going to be tame in the way that Rittel and Webber use the concept.

2.4   THE TEN PROPERTIES OF WICKED PROBLEMS

From Rittel and Webber's original conception we can see that they considered that a wicked problem lacks the clarity that is evident within tame problems. The wicked problem has no obvious end state, nor a solution that is intrinsically right or wrong. It is not that the solution has been arrived at; generally it is that a solution has been arrived at, possibly because of time or financial constraints. Importantly, there is no intrinsic quality to the problem by which it is characterised; rather, the problem is defined by the perspectives of the individuals who are engaged with it. As such, the problem itself, ideas about how to address it and even what is accepted as a satisfactory outcome can all be contested in a way which demonstrates the political nature of evidence. Importantly though, when planners get it wrong, there are real consequences for individuals, and it is for this reason that they argue that when it comes to wicked problems, there can be no right to arriving at the wrong solution. For Rittel and Webber, most social and public policy issues address wicked problems. In sum, they present the defining characteristics of wicked problems in a ten-point model as thus:

1. Wicked problems have no definitive formulation.
2. Wicked problems have no stopping rules.
3. Solutions to wicked problems cannot be true or false, only good or bad.
4. There is no immediate and no ultimate test of a solution to a wicked problem.
5. Every solution to a wicked problem is a "one-shot" operation; because there is no opportunity to learn by trial and error, every attempt counts significantly.
6. Wicked problems do not have an enumerable (or an exhaustively describable) set of potential solutions, nor is there a well-described set of permissible operations that may be incorporated into the plan.
7. Every wicked problem is essentially unique.
8. Every wicked problem can be considered to be a symptom of another problem.
9. The existence of a discrepancy representing a wicked problem can be explained in numerous ways. The choice of explanation determines the nature of the problem's resolution.
10. The planner has no right to be wrong.

2.5   WICKEDITY AS A CONTINUUM

Rittel and Webber's ten characteristics of wicked problems have been very influential, as has been demonstrated earlier, and seem to becoming more so. They may, however, be seen to imply that the concept of wicked and tame problems is embedded within a clear dichotomy as some, such as Wexler (2009, 533), have suggested. Wexler presents the distinction between tame and wicked problems in tabular form as follows (Table 2.1):

In this approach Wexler adopts the dichotomy that is intrinsic to the manner in which wicked and tame problems were initially formulated but in doing so the complexity of many issues is overlooked. As Bottery (2016, 45) states, "it would in some ways be attractive if it were always possible to distinguish between simple and tame problems, and so to always know with certainty with which kind one was dealing. But this is unlikely to be the case, as many problems are likely to be mixtures of tame and wicked issues, and separating them out will be extremely problematic, and on some occasions even impossible". A more useful model is provided if we

Table 2.1   The distinction between tame and wicked problems as per Wexler (2009)

Tame problems	Wicked problems
Relatively easy to define and can be treated as separate from other problems and the environment	Relatively difficult to define and cannot be easily separated from other problems and the environment
Information needed to solve or make sense of the problem is readily available, well structured and easy to put into use	Information needed to solve or make sense of the problem is ill-structured, changing and difficult to put into use
There is a consensus not only amongst problem solvers over what is the best method but also those with the problem accept and agree with the legitimate problem solvers	There is neither a consensus amongst problem solvers over what is the best method or a clear agreement over who is and is not a legitimate problem solver
This class of problems has precedents from which one can learn or take advice from others in order to become a "bona fide" problem solver	These problems are unique and changeable; therefore attempts to solve them make learning difficult and progress towards a solution erratic
Stakeholders to the problem defer to the expertise of the problem solver and seek little or no say in the process beyond that requested	Stakeholders to the problem join the problem solvers in possessing conflicting views of the problem, its solution and the degree of involvement of the problem stakeholders

see wicked and tame as two ends of a continuum whereby wickedity falls at one end and tameness at the other. To see wicked and tame as part of a continuum helps to transform the concept from something which is essentially descriptive into something which is evaluative. For example, if we take the first of Wexler's issues and apply it to the issue of the assessment of learning within education:

Relatively easy to define and can be treated as separate from other problems and the environment	Relatively difficult to define and cannot be easily separated from other problems and the environment

We might consider that assessment within education could be viewed as tame in that it is relatively easy to define as well as often being treated as being separate from other problems and, very often, the context in which it takes place. To adopt this position though would be to adopt a limited or superficial consideration, of what assessment seeks to do.

So, where Rittel and Webber provide us with the original concept of problems as being wicked or tame, I propose that the real value of their work lies in it being reconceptualised as wickedity or tameness as alluded to above. This allows us to liberate the approach from something that is focused on particular problems and repositions it as a characteristic of any system or provision. Tameness is quite easy to understand. It is a system whereby there is uniformity, there are certainties. Wickedity encompasses complexity and uncertainty. It represents a system whereby not only are uniformity and certainty not present it may also be that they are not wanted. This is because wickedity in the manner in which it is being proposed here encompasses both creativity and originality, qualities which contribute to both a dynamic society and a dynamic economy.

Furthermore, the argument being presented here is that if both wickedity and tameness can be understood as characteristics of systems, we can then use this to evaluate the outcomes or consequences of education as a whole. In such an evaluation though, it is important to establish that from my perspective wickedity is seen as desirable and tameness is seen as undesirable. Why that is the case has already been suggested, tame education is impoverished. Tame education can be seen to be limited with respect to where it takes us. Wicked education is desirable because it accommodates creativity and originality.

2.6   THE VALUE OF CONSIDERING WICKEDITY AND TAMENESS

The analytical value of considering wickedity and tameness means that it may be applied to different aspects of educational provisions. What follows from this is that we can see that as the individual progresses through the levels within education we are concerned with tasks and challenges of differing levels of complexity. It may well be that in some situations the need to learn specific things or where a concern with internalising key concepts means that tameness poses less of a problem but that does not mean that this is the case throughout education or that this just applies to some levels.

For example, when I was at junior school, I, along with other members of my class, was expected to learn our times tables, which in the UK meant up to the 12 times table (in 1970 the UK monetary system still had 12 pennies in a shilling and the system of measurement had 12 inches in a foot. Because of this 12 was quite a significant number and it was quite understandable to learn the 12 times table). We were assessed on our learning by standing in front of the class and reciting any one of the multiplication tables that we were being expected to learn and which we were volunteering to be tested on. In that sense the problem of conceptualising my learning and adequately assessing my learning was quite straightforward. It could be said to have been tame. Both learning and the assessment of it were unambiguous. There was a clear structure to what was required and agreement as to whether or not learning had been demonstrated was not an issue.

Such an approach echoes the idea of the recitation script approach to education (Tharp and Gallimore 1988) but it is an approach that has limitations. By the time it came to me demonstrating that I understood the concept of ontology, or of discourse, the problem of assessing my learning had become much more difficult, especially as such concepts are often assessed as part of a quite extensive assessment task. Now, in this second example, the problem of how to assess my learning is still relatively easy to define but I would say that it is far more difficult to achieve. Similarly, to establish what I was being required to learn may appear to be straightforward, but the complexity of each concept means that reaching a judgement about the extent of my learning is much less easy than with respect to when I was learning multiplication tables.

In part, the problem identified above arises as a consequence of the differences between levels of education but it is not confined to this. More will be said about the differences between levels of education in later chapters, but what is evident is that the education for young children is generally more concerned with ensuring that they have the skills to engage in society and to engage with education itself. As such it makes sense to focus upon learning how to read and write or to carry out arithmetic because these are so essential to our everyday lives. Education at this level then appears to be much more concrete, but it would be wrong to give the impression that teaching at primary school does not involve exposure to, and the understanding of, abstract concepts. Both numerals and the alphabet are abstract systems. Furthermore, primary teachers will be very familiar with the creative capacities of young children.

I would argue that the goal of education should always be the nurturing of creativity and originality, irrespective of the level, but it is often at the level of Higher Education that more is expected of students in terms of what they can do with what they have learnt. At the same time, the content of Higher Education can be seen to be more complex in respect of how teachers are able to assess it in some aspects. However, if creativity and originality are to be valued, an approach to education which is able to promote and nurture this is required.

In the introduction though, it was suggested that education has increasingly been seen as a process. One of the consequences of treating education as a process, however, is that the education sector is in danger of losing the ability to nurture and promote originality and creativity as strategies and practices are adopted which have the effect of taming education. The students who enter Higher Education in England generally do so after 14 or 15 years in other educational establishments such as schools and colleges. What happens to children and young people within schools and colleges will inevitably shape how they engage with Higher Education but as Hargreaves (2003, 1) warns:

> ...instead of fostering creativity and ingenuity, more and more school systems have become obsessed with imposing and micromanaging curricular uniformity. In place of ambitious missions of compassion and community, schools and teachers have been squeezed into the tunnel vision of test scores, achievement targets, and league tables of accountability.

Hargreaves is not alone in considering that such an approach is becoming firmly established throughout education and this is not just in England (Macfarlane 2017; Ball 2016; Hardy 2015; Roberts-Holmes 2015).

When considering concerns such as these, concerns that are rooted within national educational policies, two concepts can be seen as pertinent: post-industrialisation and the knowledge society. Both resonate with the idea of wickedity and tameness as it is being used here. During the 1970s writers such as Bell (1976) and Touraine (1974) were arguing that Western industrial societies were transforming as a consequence of primary and secondary industries diminishing in importance and being replaced by new types of economic activity. In many ways both Bell and Touraine were demonstrating significant foresight when their arguments are viewed from the standpoint of the twenty-first century. Although they both argued that changes in modern Western societies were coming, they could not have foreseen the way deindustrialisation happened so rapidly within the UK during the 1980s. Within 10 years of the publication of the books by Bell and Touraine, the predictions that they were making were coming to pass within the UK as deindustrialisation changed the socio-economic landscape.

Deindustrialisation, however, was accompanied by two other economic developments, the rise of the service sector and the establishment of what was then referred to as new technology, now generally referred to as Information and Communication Technologies (ICT). This has seen a significant change in terms of economic activity within the UK. Many traditional industries have declined or been lost, and manufacturing in particular is far less labour intensive than it was only 40 years ago. Unskilled and semi-skilled jobs in manufacturing in particular have been lost, and the application and uses of computerised systems within the economy have changed many types of work. These developments may be seen to have validated the extent to which Bell and Touraine had argued for the increased importance of information within this change. This, in turn, set the scene for what has come to be referred to as a knowledge society and for arguments which assert the need for lifelong learning to support upskilling or reskilling as the economy develops.

Almost synonymous with the idea of a knowledge society though is the term knowledge economy (Finn 2015), both of which may be seen as simple abstractions of complex societies. The differences may not appear profound, but in distinguishing between a knowledge society and a knowledge economy, it can be argued that a knowledge society can be best understood as the type of society that is shaped by a knowledge economy (Gudanescu and Cristea 2009). For Gudenescu and Cristea, a knowledge society results in a much greater level of importance being placed upon human capital. In relation to this, human capital theory puts forward the idea that it is the skills which individuals possess which shape their ability to secure work and achieve higher earnings than had they not achieved a specified level of education or training. As a consequence of this is the basic idea that individuals are able to use education and training to invest in themselves (Hartog and Maassen van den Brink 2007). This is pertinent because of the changed conditions of economic activity that follow from both globalisation and post-industrialism and which makes education more important.

Although the impact of forces such as globalisation will be considered more fully within Chap. 3, it is worth noting that in general education is seen as responding to social and political developments rather than driving them. So, in terms of the idea of a knowledge economy or a knowledge society, there is the understanding that changes in the economic sphere exert pressure upon education. The social and economic conditions of twenty-first century England can be seen to be very different when compared to the immediate post-Second World War period, a difference that would be recognised in very many countries. Not only has work become more precarious for many people, the nature of the work available requires very different skills. What can be seen, however, is that the human capital approach that was referred to above reflects an individualistic understanding of education. From a neoliberal perspective, individuals have a duty to become educated or skilled so that they may contribute to the economy and maintain or secure a decent standard of living for themselves. If we do adopt the position that individuals invest in themselves with respect to their education, then, in turn, this reflects the argument that will be put forward in Chap. 6, regarding the ways in which inequalities come to be viewed as the outcome of poor choices made by individuals.

However, if the general argument regarding the transformation of the economy is accepted, with an acknowledgement that society has become a knowledge society, then the importance of creativity and originality becomes self-evident. It means that economic activity comes to rely more heavily on individuals who can be creative. This means that it is important for education to be able to nurture this. What will be argued, however, is that for a number of different reasons, developments within education, not only within the UK, are acting to subdue creativity and originality.

Education is being tamed. The long-term consequences for society, of tame education, will restrict or hinder our abilities to develop in positive ways by reducing the academic potential of pupils and students. What is required is for education to accommodate wickedity. The question may then be how we have ended up in a situation whereby education is increasingly coming to be tame. As will be demonstrated throughout the book, there are significant forces acting upon education as a social practice which are increasingly taming it.

2.7   Conclusion

In conclusion, this chapter has illustrated the way in which the original conceptualisation of wicked problems (Rittel and Webber 1973) can be developed as an evaluative tool through which to approach any issue. The concerns of this book are that we use the concept of wicked and tame to assess the extent to which education reflects one or the other. There is no intention of claiming, however, that all aspects of education will reflect this in a uniform manner but at the same time general conclusions will be drawn. As far as this book is concerned, the general conclusion is that developments in policy and practice have increased the tameness of education.

The chapter has also demonstrated why this is of concern. The social and economic context has and is changing. The fact that England has experienced a process of deindustrialisation is not in dispute. As a consequence of this, the nature of work and the possibilities for securing work have changed. The idea of a knowledge economy having developed is not a new one and is something that is intrinsic to numerous policy approaches coming from consecutive governments. As part of this there is a greater need for individuals to leave the education system with the ability to be creative and original. If, as has been argued, we can see creativity and originality as being bound up with wickedity, then an education system must be able to nurture this if it is to be fit for purpose. What will be demonstrated throughout the book, however, is that education is developing in ways which is making this increasingly less possible. Education is becoming tame and within a knowledge economy tame education is not fit for purpose.

It is important to note, however, that the argument being presented here is not one which rests upon a privileging of economic factors. I would argue that the economy is important in terms of how it contributes to the wellbeing and living standards of society though at the same time how we organise the economy is also of concern. Alongside economic concerns though, there are also more idealistic concerns when it comes to education as were raised in Chap. 1. Individual development is also intrinsically linked to education and although an increasing focus on employability may suggest that individual development has been reduced in significance that is not to say that it has no value. However, just as tame education is not fit for purpose in economic terms, so it will be argued that it is not fit for purpose in developmental terms. The type of tame education which positions education as a process and which dehumanises all those who are involved in it plays no part in developing autonomous citizens.

Because of concerns such as these, both idealistic and pragmatic, the argument remains. The concept of evaluating wickedity and tameness is one that is valid if we want to establish an education system that works for the benefit of society.

REFERENCES

Ball, Stephen J. 2016. Neoliberal Education? Confronting the Slouching Beast. *Policy Futures in Education* 14 (8): 13.

Bell, D. 1976. *The Coming of Post-Industrial Society.* New York: Basic Books.

Blackman, T., E. Elliott, A. Greene, B. Harrington, D. Hunter, L. Marks, L. McKee, and G. Williams. 2006. Performance Assessment and Wicked Problems: The Case of Health Inequalities. *Public Policy and Administration* 21 (2): 66–80.

Bore, Anne, and Nigel Wright. 2009. The Wicked and Complex in Education: Developing a Transdisciplinary Perspective for Policy Formulation, Implementation and Professional Practice. *Journal of Education for Teaching* 35 (3): 241–256. doi:10.1080/02607470903091286.

Bottery, M. 2016. *Educational Leadership for a More Sustainable World.* London: Bloomsbury.

Brew, Angela. 2001. *The Nature of Research: Inquiry in Academic Contexts.* London: Routledge.

Camillus, J.C. 2008. Strategy as a Wicked Problem. *Harvard Business Review* 86 (5): 96–105.

Denzin, Norman K., and Yvonna S. Lincoln. 2008. Introduction: The Discipline and Practice of Qualitative Research. In *Strategies of Qualitative Enquiry*, ed. Norman K. Denzin and Yvonna S. Lincoln. London: Sage.

Finn, Mike. 2015. Education Beyond the Gove Legacy. In *The Gove Legacy*, ed. Mike Finn, 14. Basingstoke: Palgrave Macmillan.

Gage, N. 2007. The Paradigm Wars and their Aftermath: A 'Historical' Sketch of Research on Teaching Since 1989. In *Educational Research and Evidence-Based Practice*, ed. M. Hammersley. London: Sage.

Gudanescu, N., and A. Cristea. 2009. Education and Life Long Learning: Argument for the Development of Knowledge Based Economy and Society. *Lex et Scientia* 16 (1): 430–441.

Hammersley, Martin. 2007. *Educational Research and Evidence-Based Practice*. London: Sage/The Open University.

Hardy, Ian. 2015. A Logic of Enumeration: The Nature and Effects of National Literacy and Numeracy Testing in Australia. *Journal of Education Policy* 30 (3): 335–362. doi:10.1080/02680939.2014.945964.

Hargreaves, A. 2003. *Teaching in the Knowledge Society: Education in the Age of Insecurity*. New York: Teachers College Press.

Hargreaves, D.H. 2007. Teaching as a Research-Based Profession: Possibilities and Prospects. In *Educational Research and Evidence-Based Practice*, ed. Martin Hammersley. London: Sage.

Hartog, Joop, and Henriëtte Maassen van den Brink. 2007. Epilogue: Some Reflections on Educational Policies. In *Human Capital: Advances in Theory and Evidence*, ed. Joop Hartog and Henriëtte Maassen van den Brink, 233–235. Cambridge: Cambridge University Press.

Hayden, Carol, and Craig Jenkins. 2014. 'Troubled Families' Programme in England: 'Wicked Problems' and Policy-Based Evidence. *Policy Studies* 35 (6): 631–649. doi:10.1080/01442872.2014.971732.

Jentoft, S., and R. Chuenpagdee. 2009. Fisheries and Coastal Governance as a Wicked Problem. *Marine Policy* 33 (4): 553–560.

Jordan, Michelle E., Robert C. Kleinsasser, and Mary F. Roe. 2014. Wicked Problems: Inescapable Wickedity. *Journal of Education for Teaching* 40 (4): 415–430. doi:10.1080/02607476.2014.929381.

Knight, Peter, and C. Anna Page. 2007. *The Assessment of 'Wicked' Competences*. Milton Keynes: Open University Practice-Based Professional Learning Centre.

Kuhn, T. 1996. *The Structure of Scientific Revolutions*. 3rd ed. Chicago, IL: University of Chicago Press.

Macfarlane, B. 2017. *Freedom to Learn: The Threat to Student Academic Freedom and Why It Needs to Be Reclaimed*. Abingdon: Routledge.

Plowright, David. 2011. *Using Mixed Methods: Frameworks for an Integrated Methodology*. London: Sage.

Ravitch, D. 1998. What If Research Really Mattered? *Education Week* 18 (16): 33.

Rittel, Horst W.J., and M. Melvin Webber. 1973. Dilemmas in a General Theory of Planning. *Policy Sciences* 4 (2): 155–169.

Roberts-Holmes, Guy. 2015. The 'Datafication' of Early Years Pedagogy: If the Teaching Is Good, the Data Should Be Good and If There's Bad Teaching,

There Is Bad Data. *Journal of Education Policy* 30 (3): 302–315. doi:10.1080 /02680939.2014.924561.

Tharp, R.G., and R. Gallimore. 1988. *Rousing Minds to Life: Teaching, Learning, and Schooling in Social Context.* Cambridge: Cambridge University Press.

Touraine, A. 1974. *The Post-Industrial Society.* London: Wildwood House.

Wexler, M. 2009. Exploring the Moral Dimension of Wicked Problems. *International Journal of Sociology and Social Policy* 29 (9–10): 531–542.

Wright, Nigel. 2011. Between 'Bastard' and 'Wicked' Leadership? School Leadership and the Emerging Policies of the UK Coalition Government. *Journal of Educational Administration and History* 43 (4): 17.

CHAPTER 3

Control Over Teaching: Taming Teachers

3.1   INTRODUCTION

In the introduction it was argued that the ways in which education is organised, provided and experienced does not just happen. There are a number of factors which act to shape education. One of these factors relates to control over what happens within education. Control can be seen in two ways, as both epistemological and practical, namely, the ways in which disciplines of study are defined and how teaching staff engage in practices relating to such disciplines. Control can also be seen as a site of tension between parties who may view education differently. Where teachers may see education in terms of academic issues, governments may see education in terms of what it produces. For government then there may be a much stronger concern with exerting control in ways which tame education. How governments may achieve influence within education will differ in accordance with different levels of education. At the level of compulsory and Further Education within England, control has been located in government to a much greater extent than is the case within Higher Education for a number of decades. The Education Reform Act 1988 can be seen as a key policy change within compulsory education in how it acted to standardise the work of schools, but later developments such as the numeracy and literacy hour were far more prescriptive approaches to controlling education, at least as far as education provided by the State is concerned.

© The Author(s) 2018
R. Creasy, *The Taming of Education*,
DOI 10.1007/978-3-319-62247-7_3

It should already be obvious that in considering what shapes education, it is difficult to point to any single factor. This chapter is focused on establishing that there is a struggle between those who teach and the State, though this may be more or less obvious depending upon the government that is in power at any given time. However, where this struggle may be seen as being concerned with vested interests, manifest as human actions on a political stage, other factors may be seen as being more abstract or discursive. For example, it was argued above that the Education Reform Act 1988 established a degree of standardisation. What is important is to recognise that a discursive concept such as standardisation itself can be seen as shaping education when it becomes accepted as a valid and desirable principle.

3.2   Academic Control Over Education

The issue of control within education becomes pertinent when it is seen as a process and where particular outcomes are both required and expected. In considering control over education, it can be seen that there are similarities at all levels of education, but that in recent decades, teachers within Higher Education have been able to preserve a level of autonomy and self-determination to a much greater extent than teachers in compulsory or Further Education. This is not to suggest that teachers within compulsory or Further Education cannot regain professional power, nor that teachers within Higher Education will necessarily keep their autonomy. For example, what is evident is that in recent decades, teachers within the compulsory education sector have been under significant pressure with respect to what they teach and how they teach it. Debates over how to teach phonics, what should be in curricula and how pupils' behaviour should be managed can be seen as examples of ways in which the State is able to exercise control over the compulsory education sector in a manner that would seem highly unlikely within Higher Education. A teacher teaching in the 1960s may have considered it inconceivable that in 1998 the State would insist that all State schools introduce a literacy hour for pupils aged 5–11 and then determine how many minutes within that hour would be allocated to different activities such as 10–15 minutes for whole class reading (Department for Education and Skills 2002; Beard 2000).

In securing control over education as a whole, debates regarding the curriculum illustrate that there are differences relating to how disciplines can be understood. In establishing what constitutes a discipline, it can also be argued that this also involves determining what students should know and how they can be assessed. Although the boundaries between disciplines may be seen as well-established and quite strong, in some cases there may also be times when there is a degree of ambiguity in relation to the boundaries of disciplines. It is always the case however that academic disciplines may be seen as having been constructed by, and existing within, the actions of those academics engaged within them and, of course, those who are engaged to teach them. The boundaries of such disciplines then may be seen as subject to change if they exist as an outcome of social activities.

Although the primary concern is with how teaching staff approach disciplines, this is also affected to an extent by the actions of professional bodies (Becher and Trowler 2001; Becher 1999; Barnett 1990). The concerns of professional bodies will often overlap with the concerns of academics in respect of the boundaries and validity of knowledge. As such disciplines are shaped by what academics or practitioners see as important. This feeds into ideas about how students should be assessed and what they should be assessed on.

This illustrates the way in which all forms of knowledge are, in some form, ideological as they are shaped by competing discourses, though academic concerns may have traditionally dominated and represent the idea of producer capture, that is, the way in which academics within universities, as producers of new knowledge, maintain power over it (Barnett 2003). The epistemological position adopted in this process is bound up with academic work in that knowledge is prized in itself as is the matter of what to research with a view to developing new knowledge. This is often referred to as academic freedom: something that is generally associated with ideas about professionalism when applied to academics (Barnett 2005). This can be contrasted with the ways in which managerialism in the Further Education sector promotes allegiance to the employer rather than towards academic principles (Feather 2016). In addition, Barnett is clear to point out that within Higher Education such an idealised position is waning. Although academics may seek to retain control over knowledge, their ability to do so is less secure than it once was. The discussion of struggles with respect to skill that follows and with managerialism as will be discussed in Chap. 4 will demonstrate some of the issues as to why this is the case.

In general, teaching within Higher Education has been subject to what has been referred to as doctrinalism (Rochford 2008). This reflects the concept of producer capture, as introduced above, in that what is taught is shaped by those staff involved in producing the knowledge. In other words "educational institutions are cultural sites where knowledge gets defined" (Tierny and Rhoads 1995). There is inevitably a political aspect to this. Although the complexity of learning and the difficulties in establishing just what can be learnt or even what can be assessed raises some challenges, teaching has traditionally focused on transferring what the academic knows, and what texts contain, to the student. Although more recent approaches towards teaching may challenge this, it is important to acknowledge that very often, this approach is what students expect. This might not be surprising; if we argue that academics are experts, then it seems reasonable that this leads to expectations that such experts will impart their knowledge. In turn this invests them with the power to determine what is important and, with respect to assessment, whether or not students have understood the subject that they are studying. At the same time though, the expectations on the part of students, that teaching staff will be experts, reinforces the power that teaching staff have to establish what is valid. As all teaching rests upon relationships, it can be seen that the relationship is not an equal one.

If the nature of any academic discipline is shaped by those who are working within that discipline, it can be argued that what these practitioners deem to be important does, in turn, become largely what students learn about. In the case of teachers within Higher Education though, this can be taken further in that they will be concerned not only with what students should learn about, but they will also have opinions as to how the students' learning can be assessed and, importantly, what should be assessed. Raelin (2007) demonstrates this in arguing for an epistemology of practice so as to demonstrate the usefulness of theory rather than just knowing about it. In doing so, he implicitly supports the idea that learning within Higher Education should be wicked rather than tame. It is also a reminder of the point made in Chap. 2 regarding complexity.

The idea that control is contested demonstrates competing interests and contributes to the complexity of education. It means also that control over education can be seen as dynamic. Similarly, control is not just a matter of competition between teachers and the State. In recent decades, managerial groups have become much more powerful within education. For example, within Higher Education, control by academics, rather than control by university structures of governance, was at its peak during the early part of the twentieth century, but more recent developments have seen the decline of what Halsey (1982) has called donnish dominance. In part this is because, traditionally, professionals were seen as socially benign (Bottery 2008). As such, professional educators were able to exert control over the curriculum. Their control was accepted because of two factors; firstly because of their perceived expertise vis-à-vis the discipline or subject matter and secondly because they were seen as acting in ways that are in support of what is seen as being socially good rather than in their own interests. To some extent this is indicative of a positivist view typical of modernity wherein the academic is the expert (Raelin 2007). The emergence of post-modernist and constructivist positions however provide the basis for a critique of this position as will be illustrated in the following section.

The idea that professionals act in ways that are to the benefit of society rather than because of their own vested interests underpins and explains the trust and status that professionals had traditionally been afforded. Although professionalism is a contested concept, it is one which is often used with respect to individuals engaged in education.

In considering professionalism within education, it is not being argued that this has always developed in a planned way. There are accidental or unintended outcomes of processes which arise whereby power has been exercised. However, such power always reflects vested interests to some degree. It is certainly not surprising then that other vested interests may see professional power and control very differently. From the perspective of Public Choice Theory, part of the canon of neoliberalism, the idea that bureaucrats and public servants are engaged in working for the common good is seen as misguided; they are pursuing their own interests (Olssen 2016). Indeed, for adherents of Public Choice Theory, the very idea of an identifiable public good is a myth. Drawing on this perspective, teachers, at whatever level they work, may be seen to be engaged in activities which serve to maximise their own interests (Olssen 2016). The consequence of this is that it provides both an academic and ideological justification for reducing professional power.

Of course, if professional power is reduced, then this will have an impact upon those groups of workers who have laid claim to it. Groups who have been able to achieve professional status have generally secured autonomy. Autonomy can be seen as being associated with control, and it can be seen that increasing control over groups who have claimed professional status makes them more vulnerable to being tamed.

In recent decades, the autonomy afforded to professional groups has come to be viewed as less desirable, partly because of the neoliberal critique of professionalism as being akin to any collective enterprise such as that carried out by a Trades Union, but also as a consequence of general social changes relating to trust (Macfarlane 2017; Bottery 2004; Bottery 2003). In recent decades, trust in professionals has declined and, in turn, this has led to actions being taken by, or on behalf of, governments so as to move power away from professionals. This throws up a noticeable contradiction in that since the early 1980s, although governments have espoused policies of deregulation, public sector professional groups in particular have experienced the opposite as regulatory powers have been introduced which curtail their freedoms (Becher 1999). This increase in regulation may be seen as a proxy measure of a lack of trust. If trust in professionals was high there would be no need, nor any will, to increase regulation. That regulation has increased illustrates the decline, or erosion, of trust.

3.3   STATE CONTROL OVER HIGHER EDUCATION

The previous section dealt with the way in which academics have established the boundaries and concerns of particular disciplines. In doing this, it was argued that this involved the establishment of control over their own work. The ways in which the State can come to exert greater control over education can be seen by considering Higher Education. Within the compulsory education sector provision was traditionally provided by the State, and although the contemporary landscape of compulsory education appears to be fragmented, it is still the case that the State determines to a significant degree what is provided and how. Within the Higher Education sector State control was traditionally more limited but that has been changing. This section deals with ways in which the State has sought to influence Higher Education as an example of how control may be shifted by the actions of governments. Although in recent decades it appears as though this is because of an overriding concern with economic issues, a consideration of State involvement during the 1960s demonstrates that although governments may seek control for economic reasons, they also have other concerns such as national security or values relating to citizenship.

For example, the political concerns which drove the expansion of Higher Education during the 1960s were not detached from economic concerns, but they were also influenced by egalitarian ideas. As such we can see how egalitarian ideas as had become current by the late 1950s and which were driving the move towards comprehensivisation within schools were also impacting upon ideas regarding access to Higher Education (Graham 2008). This reflected the idea that talent was being wasted as a consequence of the educational system that had been established in the late 1940s (Jones 2003). Up until the 1960s, entry to Higher Education was somewhat limited (Hussey and Smith 2010). The Robbins Committee Report in 1963 (Ainley 1994) can be seen as being the impetus behind the shift from Higher Education in England being an elitist system to it becoming a mass system. Although it could be argued that the State saw some economic value in expanding Higher Education activities, there was also the recognition that access to Higher Education reflected the way in which social class in particular restricted opportunities for some. The Robbins report addressed this concern. The expansion of polytechnics accompanied more general changes with regard to Higher Education such as the establishment of new universities. Along with the development of new universities, the Robbins report promoted the idea that Higher Education should be available for all, though this was qualified by selective intakes. The idea that Higher Education should be open to all who can benefit from it however was important in changing the landscape of Higher Education in England and led to significant expansion.

From the 1980s however the State seemed to change its focus with respect to what was happening in the Higher Education sector and started to demonstrate a concern with the role and work of academics. This was being driven in large part by ideas associated with neoliberalism. Prior to the 1980s, different professional groups working within the public sector had been able to use professionalism as a basis for resistance to challenges to their autonomy (Exworthy and Halford 1999). During the 1980s however, political pressures brought to bear upon professional groups increased significantly, partly as a consequence of the antipathy of neoliberal thought to professionalism. The neoliberal critique of professionalism however can be seen against the backdrop of a general trend in recent decades wherein academic control over Higher Education has declined (Brown and Carasson 2013), corresponding with an increased level of State control reflecting the point made previously by Halsey (1982) regarding the decline of donnish dominion.

Part of the increased pressure on professional groups has resulted from the concern of successive governments since 1979 to prioritise demand rather than supply with respect to services. One consequence of seeking to emphasise demand-led services is that employers gain more power to define the types of skills and services that are both valid and desirable (Copnell 2010). Copnell is concerned with changes to Allied Health Professionals resulting from a competence–based framework, but this has resonance with Higher Education, as parallels can be drawn with the Professional Standards Framework as introduced by the Higher Education Academy. Importantly, the impetus for this was the White Paper "The Future of Higher Education" (2003). Along with the development of the Institute for Learning and Teaching in Higher Education, which emerged out of the Dearing report (1997), these two developments are indicative of how UK governments have taken an active interest in exerting control over the work of academics and the nature of Higher Education in recent decades. In particular though, this reflects a move towards codifying professional skills in a way that seeks to make the tacit knowledge claimed by professional groups explicit. In turn this development supports contemporary arguments, often originating within the government, relating to the need for professional groups to be accountable.

3.4   TAME TEACHERS

What has been argued then is that the State has increased control over education in recent decades. As will be demonstrated within the following chapter though, it is not sufficient to claim that there is any overriding factor which has driven this. Rather, it is the case that a number of forces align in ways which mean that power has moved away from those who practise education and towards the State, or, as will be shown later, towards those who manage education. As before though, it can be seen that control fits easily with an understanding of education as a process if we have concerns about what is being produced. This chapter now moves on to consider what such a change means for teachers with respect to their work. In particular it will consider the relevance of skill with respect to teaching.

It has already been argued that education can be seen as analogous to a process and that this influences the way in which it is organised and the ways in which teachers work. Some of these practices may appear innocuous and can be seen as providing a degree of structure that is, indeed, welcome and necessary. One thing that students never appear to appreciate are classes and courses which have little structure and the covering of topics or issues which seem irrelevant. The classic example of this is the teacher who introduces a topic by prefacing it with "this will not be assessed/on the exam but we have to cover it". It might be a fair question to ask if it will definitely not be assessed then why is there a need to cover it but of course, this assumes a somewhat utilitarian approach whereby only topics or issues that are assessed are valid.

Teaching can be seen as an interesting and rewarding profession, possibly because of the unpredictability of each class but also because it provides for some degree of creativity on the part of the teacher. This is not something that is evident in all classes. In arguing that education as a system is becoming tame, it can also be seen that many teachers are themselves becoming tame.

It is common to hear of teaching to the test, and although many might see this as undesirable, in the compulsory sector it may not be surprising. Schools are under significant pressures to achieve particular results and, just like in business with respect to profits, achieving comparable results over a number of years is fast becoming a sign of failure. The idea that a school which maintains educational achievements over a number of years is, in some way, failing, can be seen in comments from UK government ministers regarding coasting schools (Wiggins 2015; Philips 1999). This may be seen as a further way in which the discourse of business and management has come to colonise education. Comments about coasting schools echo, to some extent, the directives of continuous quality improvement. The implication is that schools should not be content with what have previously been seen as good results but should, instead, be constantly striving to achieve better results. Pressures to constantly achieve better results are evident in comments from both Ofsted and the government, though this can sometimes lead to embarrassing slip-ups as when Sir Michael Wilshaw, Head of Ofsted "condemned the fact that that one in five pupils are leaving primary school without reaching the 'national average' in English" (Curtis 2012, np).

In a situation whereby good results are not good enough, it can be seen how the focus of the educational process has moved from what pupils and students learn towards what they are able to demonstrate within formal assessments. What is evident though is that in any process that involves people, there is an inevitable element of risk. Because of this, strategies which remove such risks, which, by implication means increasing control of the process, may come to be viewed as beneficial.

Considerations relating to the work of teachers at all levels are not new and can be seen as being rooted in ideas regarding the part that they play within education in general. If we return to the idea that education can be seen as a process, then the output of teachers' work is the extent to which their subject matter, the pupil or student, has been changed because of their engagement with education. It could be argued that it is what the pupil or student can do or understand, or what they know as a consequence of the teaching that they have received that is the output, but in practice it comes to be the qualification that is awarded or the test result that is achieved which is accepted as such. As has already been considered though, this is not so straightforward. We cannot always know the actual extent of learning, and the role of the teacher is also subject to debate given that the subject, the pupil or student also has to take part in their own education.

It may be fairly obvious to state that some teachers are more effective than others, but the extent to which any teacher is effective can, generally, only be measured partially or by proxy. However, the work of teachers takes place within a political context which requires that some desired outcomes are produced as a consequence of the resources that are devoted to it. It also takes place within a social context wherein other parties, such as parents, students and employers, also desire a particular outcome. Because of these two pressures, it can be seen that the proxy measure of education that is the educational qualification becomes quite significant. As a consequence of this, significant pressure is brought to bear upon what we expect of teachers and the ways in which we train or educate them. Subsequently it also changes what teachers become after their period of initial teacher education (Bottery 2008).

For Bottery this can see teachers being educated to be critical professionals, or it can see them being trained to become craft workers delivering education and putting policies into practice as they work with other professionals. This scenario may be transformed by an increasing privatisation of education to produce the branded technician. Though Bottery puts this forward as a possibility within the schools sector, it may be seen as being established within Early Years education where Early Years workers generally wear an identifiable, branded, uniform.

The concept of teachers as critical professionals conjures up an understanding of them as engaged with their work and with the capacity to reflect upon and instigate change, but the undermining of professionalism

in recent decades acts against the possibility of this. The idea of reflective practice that is intrinsic to the critical professional is another idea that
has come to have significant currency in twenty-first-century education.
It presents an image of individuals who are striving to develop their practice and, in doing so, to enhance quality and improve standards. It is a
concept however, that rests upon trust; trust that such professionals will
work diligently to achieve their best for those that they are teaching;
something that has already been considered as declining in recent years.
It is also the case that it rests upon a degree of organisational autonomy.
In this sense it sees such teachers as being able to make changes to their
work. As was indicated earlier, however, the pressure to perform, to
achieve certain outcomes, acts against this freedom for when professionals seek to change how they work, they introduce the possibility of failure
to achieve what was intended or the possibility of seeing unintended
outcomes.

In considering the educational landscape, within the compulsory and
Further Education sectors in particular then, what is more likely is that
teachers are not really being cast as critical professionals at all, but, rather,
are being shaped as branded technicians. The evidence that can be seen as
supporting this claim rests in how teachers are being required to work and
how they are being prepared for this work. How teachers are educated or
trained is important as this will impact upon not only how they teach but
also how they understand their role as a teacher. Typically, teachers intending to enter the compulsory sector in England have been educated to
degree level for a number of decades. This has included both the development of pedagogical techniques but also a range of theoretical approaches
such as sociology and psychology which inform the practice of teaching.
This teaching has been led by universities in partnership with local authorities and schools. Recent developments however, have seen changes which
can be seen as undermining the role of the university sector in the education and training of teachers and with moves to establish teacher training
within schools.

An overview of policy changes with regard to what is generally referred
to in England as Initial Teacher Education suggests that the Coalition
Government of the UK (from 2010 to 2015) was critical and suspicious of
the involvement of universities with initial teacher education and that they
acted to relocate teacher education out of the Higher Education sector
and into schools (Browne and Reid 2012). The argument being offered

by Browne and Reid is essentially pessimistic and draws upon the 2010 White Paper "The schools white paper: The importance of teaching" to claim that:

> The White Paper represents a craft model of teacher training for England which significantly reduces the scope of the profession and the professional teacher. Models of training, as proposed, limit teacher training to the acquisition of skills confined to the traditional context of the classroom. (Brown and Reid 2012: 498)

The changes encapsulated within the White Paper (DfE 2010) reflect a particular view of education which fits well with the idea that it is a process though it also represents developments which may be seen as reflecting attempts to assure tameness. Tameness is achieved, or made more likely, by increasing levels of control over what teachers do. It certainly seems clear from the current and previous UK governments that teaching is being seen as something that rests upon training rather than education. It is worth considering the implications of this perspective and what will this mean for teaching. Typically the distinction between education and training rests upon the idea that one is trained to be able to carry out a specific task. This fits with routine tasks and roles and where either unexpected occurrences are not expected or where it will be someone else's role to deal with them. Education on the other hand is much broader and does more to prepare the individual for the unexpected, for contingencies. So, training fits very well with tame processes but education is required to deal with the complexity that is inherent within wickedity. Consequently it appears as though the actions of the UK government in 2010 would reinforce a perspective of education as being a tame process.

In one sense the Coalition Government of 2010–2015 offered a persuasive argument regarding the skills that teachers need to be effective within the classroom, but it could be argued that by focusing upon practical skills, and squeezing out reflexive professional skills, this approach reduces the overall role of the teacher as concerned with the classroom rather than having any concerns for the way in which education is provided for. There is certainly a strong argument in support of equipping teachers for the issues that they will face when teaching a lesson, but might it be the case that in privileging the skills of teachers we impoverish their education? With this in mind a consideration of skill, especially with respect to arguments regarding deskilling, is pertinent.

3.5   EXERCISING SKILL

As a job, teaching, at all levels, is in many ways quite opaque. Although it is often the case that teachers are no longer the sole adult within the classroom, particularly in compulsory education, it is still not a job that is routinely observed by others, whether they be colleagues or otherwise. This inevitably creates problems for those who may wish to exert control and to determine how teachers teach. One approach to establishing control and in making the work of teachers more transparent is in the adoption of a competency-based approach. Recent developments in Scotland, which have established standards with respect to teaching, have been presented as a more effective way of achieving better outcomes (Kennedy 2015). What Kennedy also makes clear though is that there is little in the way of evidence which demonstrates the effectiveness of adopting a standards-based approach with respect to achieving the better outcomes that are promised. However, in spite of the lack of evidence, the adoption of standards has become accepted as orthodoxy, and it is taken for granted that educational outcomes will improve because of the adoption of standards.

In some ways both a competencies-based approach and a standards-based approach contribute to formalising the skill set that is employed and utilised by any given group of workers. Skills are very often presented as essential, especially in an economic context. The concept of a knowledge-based economy illustrates the importance given to skills with respect to equipping any society for successful engagement with such an economy. However, as with standards, the concept of skill can be seen to be something which is rarely questioned. Skill is, by definition, a juxtaposition of two or more states. Being skilled, or possessing skills, can always be juxtaposed with not being skilled though discussions regarding increasing skills also points to the fact that skill tends to be understood as a continuum rather than a dichotomy. However skill is often accepted as a taken for granted variable that is found in increasing levels according to occupational position and income level (Vallas 1990).

The relevance to the argument regarding wickedity and tameness is reflected in the claim that "positivists equate certainty in outcome with a lack of skill, often indicated by the routinization of the work process. Conversely, uncertainty is equated with problem solving, lack of routine, and therefore with skill" (Attewell 1990, 438). From this position skill requires the worker to be engaged with the task and to make judgements regarding it. As such, skill may be seen as being present when there is no effective technique or technological process in place to produce the desired outcome. The focus upon certainty of outcomes in this approach is highly relevant to teaching especially when considered in the light of discussions offered above regarding the increasing pressure to establish it as a process.

Such a concern can be seen as pertinent to the place of skill within the work of the teacher now. Skill may appear to be axiomatic, but it is clearly socially constructed. Some abilities and techniques come to be defined as skilled whilst others do not, and judgements are often made about levels of skill. If so, then it can be accepted that skills are not static. The skills inherent within the role of the teacher in the twenty-first century will certainly differ when compared to previous decades. This is not just because the technologies employed within teaching have changed but also because the individuals being educated have also changed and that both exist within a changed policy context. Because of this it would not be surprising to find that in some ways, the work of teachers, at all levels, has been subject to the development of new skills which may be understood as a process of upskilling. For example, the introduction of Information and Communication Technologies such as interactive whiteboards and Virtual Learning Environments have seen teachers at all levels acquire new skills. At the same time though, there have been developments, as have been alluded to which have had, or are having, the opposite effect, and as a consequence of this, teachers are finding their work changing in a way which could be described as having seen them being deskilled.

Although it may be erroneous to claim that teachers have been subject to deskilling in absolute terms, they can be seen to have experienced a certain degree of deskilling in aspects of their work, and this could be understood as being an ongoing process. The crucial element here is that any understanding of deskilling is not the result of a change in perception which has led to the task of teaching as being seen as less skilled, but rather that there has been developments within education which have effectively reduced the overall skills of teachers. This is as a consequence of limiting the parameters of the task of teaching.

It is necessary to define what a teacher does if we are to make any sense of the arguments that teachers now have less scope for the exercising of skills. As such it may be fruitful to re-establish why teachers may be seen as skilled workers.

1. That there is little certainty of outcomes within the process of teaching.
2. That teaching includes acts of both planning and execution.

Teachers may plan and execute within the educational process, but at the same time they are expected to deal with a myriad of obstacles which face them as a consequence of the fact that they are in effect working upon altering animate objects, namely, pupils/students. Importantly though they carry out this process within various constraints.

Teachers engage in much more than teaching alone, but the measure of teaching is always seen as the award that is made with respect to whatever form of assessment is being adopted. So, although the act of teaching is somewhat intangible, because we cannot see learning, this intangibility is given substance by the process of certification. As such, the rhetoric of teaching (the development and nurturing of knowledge and understanding) is subsumed under the reality of certification. In a manner reminiscent of Marx's notion of fetishisation then it can be seen how a subsidiary outcome of education (certification) becomes more important than the processes leading up to it to all intents and purposes. It is perfectly possible to be educated yet not possess qualifications.

The awarding of qualifications can be seen to rest upon concerns regarding trust with awarding bodies emerging as quality control systems to ensure, or guarantee, that the holder of an award can be trusted. Of course, qualifications may also be seen as reflecting positional goods which act to exclude non-holders from a range of social and employment-related positions. In this way the qualification may be seen as acting upon those providing education and those doing the teaching in a different way to those being taught.

Ultimately though we now have a situation in England whereby both government and regulatory bodies seem to be adopting a position whereby teaching is being cast as a labour process. The outcome of such a labour process may be seen as the production of pupils and students who not only have the ability to achieve the award of a certificate, which may be held up as the proof of the worth of teaching, but also as tangible proof of the skill of the teacher. In the case of Higher Education though, a much more ambiguous correlation is being established in that the Teaching Excellence Framework deems that one key measure of good teaching is the jobs that graduates enter after graduating (DfE 2016; Ashwin 2016).

The Marxist concept of the labour process can be summed up as arguing that the skills of workers may generally be seen as an obstacle to the full utilisation of the means of production by Capital (Braverman 1974). If we accept that education has come to be viewed as a productive process, then certification becomes the object which is produced by the labour of teachers. From this we may understand why it might be desirable to deskill teachers. This leads the State, which is after all an employer in this respect, to adopt strategies which will control the labour process within teaching. If teachers can be controlled in such a way as to increase the certainty of the outcome of teaching (certification), then it may be seen that in production terms the efficiency of the teacher, or of the education process, has been increased.

What is important to consider here though is that increased levels of certification may not necessarily demonstrate the skills of the teachers. In respect of this it may be useful to consider the claims made by Kenneth Clarke, Minister for Education, when presented with improved GCSE results, who pointed to a drop in standards by the examining boards as the reason for improvements rather than giving credit to either teachers or pupils/student (Chitty and Simon 1993). This is an argument which has often been rolled out during August when national examination results are announced. Such a statement illustrates how changes in the administration and certification of educational courses may affect the outcomes of the process.

It could be argued then that it may be beneficial to direct the skills of the teachers towards certification rather than the development of understanding. If so it may be seen as prudent to focus upon the certification process as the primary concern of education.

Furthermore, in political terms, increasing certification has a number of attractions in that it may be seen as a positive outcome of a government's policies. If we then place this argument within the context of educational developments within England since the early 1980s, it can be seen how the trend towards quantifiable educational results would make the reduction in the uncertainty of outcomes within teaching very attractive as this should have the effect of increasing certification.

3.6   THE DESKILLING OF TEACHERS

The concept of deskilling was traditionally something that was used to evaluate changes within the work of the working classes in respect of changes to manual labour, especially skilled manual labour. As a concept it rose to prominence with the publication of Harry Braverman's 1974 book, *Labor and Monopoly Capital: The Degradation of Work in the Twentieth Century*. Basically, Braverman's argument draws on Marxist theory to argue that as Capital attempts to achieve the real subordination of labour, it adopts an ongoing process of deskilling. The reason for doing this is to enable Capital to achieve control over the labour process (Braverman 1974). The focus of the argument is on those workers who are classed as being productive. This poses a problem when considering the work of teachers for teachers are not generally accepted as productive workers. Teachers may never have been considered to have been part of the working classes, and increasing the productivity of teachers is very often unlikely to generate a rise in profits. However, when looking at developments within education from the perspective of the early twenty-first century, it can be seen that these arguments do not preclude teachers from being deskilled in accordance with the theoretical arguments put forward by Braverman.

In the case of white-collar workers, Braverman argued that control over the labour process would be achieved through increased supervisory control and an increased division of labour. In addition, changes to the economy, particularly as a consequence of the introduction of new technology, can be seen as breaking the linkage between manual labour and productive work in a way that means that the manual/non-manual divide no longer equates with a distinction between productive and non-productive work (Smith et al. 1991, 1). Within a modern economy then, a labour process does not depend upon the production of a material product. If workers generate an exchange and surplus value, then they can be safely regarded as being located within a labour process, and moreover, if they are paid in wages a value less than the value of the services they provide, then they are clearly being exploited.

Of course this immediately raises a problem in determining the value of services provided within the public sector as a whole and within teaching in particular. However it can be seen that the services provided within the public sector act to the benefit of the private sector, and therefore it can be accepted that private sector interests appropriate some of the surplus value generated by the work that is carried out within the public sector. For example, it is accepted that without an educated and literate workforce, then the private sector would suffer. In addition we have already seen how certification is often seen as the end product of teaching, and it can be accepted that most employers use certification as an integral part of their selection processes.

Therefore if we accept the essence of the deskilling thesis as a trend within the labour process as a whole, we can see that this can legitimately be applied to any situation where work is carried out and as we have already seen, non-manual work can be located within a labour process. As such Braverman (1974) does not preclude white-collar occupations from his thesis. He does refer to what he calls intermediate groups such as teachers being increasingly more likely to experience work in the same way that the working class experience work. This is something which has certainly come to pass in the decades since the publication of his work.

Consequently it seems plausible that if in the case of manual work, the strategies for deskilling are more apparent due to the nature of manual work, so, conversely, it should not be implausible that the more abstract nature of many forms of non-manual work, such as teaching, should be subject to a form of deskilling which is more abstract and consequently less apparent. As Knights and Wilmott (1990) point out, increased control over the labour process will not necessarily be manifested in the application of technology to work but may also be realised through bureaucratic structures, and this can be seen to apply in the case of teaching.

Though it has been criticised, Braverman's thesis, that the skills possessed by workers are normally an obstacle to the full utilisation of the means of production by Capital, does shed significant light upon the objective experiences of work. In addition although Braverman focused upon the craft worker, it may be argued that Capital, in the search for further control, will inevitably seek to widen the scope of its influence to encompass non-manual work such as teaching for not dissimilar reasons. In the late 1980s Jenny Ozga (1988) was arguing that it is in times of economic crisis that the State has a greater need to control aspects of the organisation of teaching. She was pointing to the economic conditions being experienced in the latter stages of the twentieth century as being precisely the sort of conditions which would see the State seek to increase control over education. The era of austerity ushered in by the Coalition Government of 2010 in the wake of the economic crash of 2008 offers a more recent example of a situation within which the State would act, but in reality there is evidence of an ongoing drift towards State control over education rather than a situation whereby this is just a reaction to external events. Though governments may deny that they seek to extend control over the teaching profession, it can be argued that the trends in government policies reflect precisely that. In the language of the argument being put forward here the cumulative effects of such changes are to progressively tame education.

In considering the deskilling of teaching, attention must be focused upon the strategies used. Braverman's thesis can be seen as being based upon strategies such as Taylorism (Stoller 2015; Au 2011). Although there are limitations to the effectiveness of Taylorism, it did legitimise a style of control based upon deskilling. Central to Taylorism is the separation of planning and execution. In one sense, planning and execution within teaching may be seen as indivisible which implies that the arguments around the deskilling of teaching will be limited. This does not mean however that control cannot be exerted on teachers and which has had the effect of deskilling them. A number of commentators have documented both the deskilling, and the proletarianisation, of teachers at all levels. For example, with respect to the schools sector, see Browne and Reid (2012), Buyruk (2014), Ozga (1988). In Further Education see Hodgkinson (1990), Randle and Brady (1997a, b), and in Higher Education see Ellis et al. (2013, 2014); Wilson (1991).

Nevertheless there are problems in controlling the process of teaching itself. Teachers do tend to work in isolation as has been said, and the nature of teaching involves an interaction between a large number of actors with different relationships. The organisational demands of schools, colleges and universities are such that physical control over individual teachers is problematic, and as such any consideration of control must therefore be concerned with more abstract issues such as the example of professionalisation or with the nature of the curriculum.

As in any labour process though, there are two sides to consider. Employers seek to increase control, and employees seek to resist control. Within education, it may be fair to say that there is a further complication in that the nature of the product is also contested which is made possible by the nature of its intangibility, though this is addressed to a large degree by the argument put forward earlier that qualifications have become a de facto product. That said, the strategies that are aimed at deskilling which are adopted will be shaped to some extent by the sector of education that is being considered.

For example, within compulsory education, the curriculum is able to be employed as a strategy of control by the State in a way that is less applicable to Further and Higher education. As such, resistance from teachers may be portrayed as being evidence of producer capture with government-led changes being put forward by the government as a significant improvement over previous curricula for the benefit of pupils/students.

3.7   CONCLUSION

This chapter has focused on struggles over the control of education to illustrate some of the ways in which education is shaped. One particular aspect of this has been a consideration of skill as part of the work or teaching and the way in which teachers may be deskilled. There is a general relationship between skill and power which suggests that a reduction in skill sees a corresponding reduction in power. So, if it is the case that the work of teachers is changed in ways that sees teachers being deskilled, then we can also expect that the power that teachers hold over education is also reduced.

In spite of significant rhetoric about how education is focused on learning, and the way that learning has come to dominate the discourse of education (Biesta 2013), in many ways education has come to be seen as a policy problem (Cochran-Smith 2005), whereby the focus is on finding ways to ensure that teachers produce the outcomes that are required. This sees the concern for learning as being incorporated into a stronger concern for certification. Within contemporary education then, at all levels, in all sectors, what ultimately takes precedence is the certification that is achieved by pupils and students. Recognising this illustrates the way in which education has become seen as a process. As such, where education is accepted as a process, it may be somewhat inevitable that attention is drawn to reducing uncertainty. This increases pressures with regard to how control may be achieved.

Although this chapter has focused on issues relating to who has control over education though, there are other factors which also shape how education is provided for and practised. As such the following chapter considers four other factors: neoliberalism, New Public Management, standardisation and internationalisation. However, although these are presented as discrete drivers of social change, each of which impacts upon education, this is to simplify the issues. They are presented as such to make the argument accessible. Some may be more influential in relation to particular levels of education or of particular aspects of it. Similarly, and as will be evident, there are ways in which the factors overlap. Connections can be made between them. It must also be recognised that each of the factors that will be considered are, in themselves, dynamic and all exist as part of wider social, cultural and political relationships. As such, general trends can be discerned, but there is unlikely to be one defining factor underpinning any particular change.

References

Ainley, P. 1994. *Degrees of Difference: Higher Education in the 1990s*. London: Lawrence & Wishart.

Ashwin, Paul. 2016. 'Bizarre' TEF Metrics Overlook So Much About Teaching Excellence. *Times Higher Education Supplement*. https://www.timeshighereducation.com/blog/bizarre-tef-metrics-overlook-so-much-about-teaching-excellence

Attewell, Paul. 1990. What Is Skill? *Work and Occupations* 17 (4): 26.

Au, Wayne. 2011. Teaching Under the New Taylorism: High-Stakes Testing and the Standardization of the 21st Century Curriculum. *Journal of Curriculum Studies* 43 (1): 25–45.

Barnett, R. 1990. *The Idea of Higher Education*. Buckingham: SRHE & Open University Press.

———. 2003. *Beyond all Reason: Living with Ideology in the University*. Buckingham: Open University Press with Society for Research into Higher Education.

———. 2005. *Reshaping the University: New Relationships Between Research, Scholarship and Teaching*. Maidenhead: Open University Press.

Beard, R. 2000. Research and the National Literacy Strategy. *Oxford Review of Education* 26 (3–4): 15.

Becher, T. 1999. *Professional Practices: Commitment and Capability in a Changing Environment*. New Brunswick, NJ: Transaction Publishers.

Becher, T., and P. Trowler. 2001. *Academic Tribes and Territories: Intellectual Enquiry and the Cultures of Disciplines*. Buckingham: Open University Press.

Biesta, Gert. 2013. *The Beautiful Risk of Education*. Boulder, CO: Paradigm Publishers.

Bottery, Mike. 2003. The Management and Mismanagement of Trust. *Educational Management Administration & Leadership* 31 (3): 245–261.

Bottery, M. 2004. *The Challenges of Educational Leadership*. London: Sage.

———. 2008. Critical Professional or Branded Technician: Changing Conceptions of the Education Worker. In *NZEALS International Educational Leadership*, Auckland, NZ.

Braverman, H. 1974. *Labour and Monopoly Capital*. New York: Monthly Review Press.

Brown, R., and H. Carasson. 2013. *Everything for Sale? The Marketisation of UK Higher Education*. Abingdon: Routledge/Society for Research into Higher Education.

Browne, Liz, and Jay Reid. 2012. Changing Localities for Teacher Training: The Potential Impact on Professional Formation and the University Sector Response. *Journal of Education for Teaching* 38 (4): 497–508. doi:10.1080/0 2607476.2012.709747.

Buyruk, Halil. 2014. "Professionalization" or "Proletarianization": Which Concept Defines the Changes in Teachers' Work? *Procedia—Social and Behavioral Sciences* 116: 1709–1714. doi:10.1016/j.sbspro.2014.01.460.

Chitty, C., and B. Simon. 1993. *Education Answers Back: Critical Responses to Government Policy*. London: Lawrence & Wishart.

Cochran-Smith, Marilyn. 2005. The New Teacher Education: For Better or for Worse? *Educational Researcher* 34 (7): 3–17. doi:10.3102/00131 89X034007003.

Copnell, Graham. 2010. Modernising Allied Health Professions Careers: Attacking the Foundations of the Professions? *Journal of Interprofessional Care* 24 (1): 63–69. doi:10.3109/13561820902946115.

Curtis, B. 2012. How the Ofsted Chief got His Maths Wrong on Sats. *The Guardian*.

Dearing, Ron. 1997. *Higher Education in the Learning Society*. Norwich: HMSO. National Committee of Inquiry into Higher Education.

Department for Education and Skills. 2002. *Building on Improvement. The National Literacy and Numeracy Strategies*. London: Department for Education and Skills. p. 18.

DfE. 2010. *The Importance of Teaching: The Schools White Paper*. Norwich: The Stationary Office. Edited by Department for Education.

———. 2016. *Teaching Excellence Framework: Year Two Specification*. London: HM Govt. Edited by Department for Education.

DfES. 2003. *The Future of Higher Education*. Norwich: HMSC. Edited by Dept For Education and Skills.

Ellis, Viv, Melissa Glackin, Deb Heighes, Mel Norman, Sandra Nicol, Kath Norris, Ingrid Spencer, and Jane McNicholl. 2013. A Difficult Realisation: The Proletarianisation of Higher Education-Based Teacher Educators. *Journal of Education for Teaching* 39 (3): 266–280. doi:10.1080/02607476.2013.799845.

Ellis, Viv, Jane McNicholl, Allan Blake, and Jim McNally. 2014. Academic Work and Proletarianisation: A Study of Higher Education-Based Teacher Educators. *Teaching and Teacher Education* 40: 33–43. doi:10.1016/j.tate.2014.01.008.

Exworthy, M., and S. Halford. 1999. Professionals and Managers in a Changing Public Sector: Conflict, Compromise and Collaboration. In *Professionals and the New Managerialism in the Public Sector*, ed. M. Exworthy and S. Halford. Buckingham: Open University Press.

Feather, Denis. 2016. Organisational Culture of Further Education Colleges Delivering Higher Education Business Programmes: Developing a Culture of 'HEness'—What Next? *Research in Post-Compulsory Education* 21 (1–2): 98–115. doi:10.1080/13596748.2015.1125669.

Graham, G. 2008. *Universities: The Recovery of an Idea*. Exeter: Imprint Academic.

Halsey, A.H. 1982. The Decline of Donnish Dominion. *Oxford Review of Education* 8 (3): 215–219.

Hodgkinson, Peter John. 1990. *A Content-Theoretical Model of Educational Change: The Case of the New Vocationalism.* UCL Institute of Education (IOE).

Hussey, Trevor, and Patrick Smith. 2010. *The Trouble with Higher Education.* Abingdon: Routledge.

Jones, K. 2003. *Education in Britain: 1944 to the Present.* Cambridge: Polity Press.

Kennedy, Aileen. 2015. What Do Professional learning Policies Say About Purposes of Teacher Education? *Asia-Pacific Journal of Teacher Education* 43 (3): 183–194. doi:10.1080/1359866x.2014.940279.

Knights, D., and H. Willmott. 1990. *Labour Process Theory.* Basingstoke: Palgrave Macmillan.

Macfarlane, B. 2017. *Freedom to Learn: The Threat to Student Academic Freedom and Why It Needs to Be Reclaimed.* Abingdon: Routledge.

Olssen, Mark. 2016. Neoliberal Competition in Higher Education Today: Research, Accountability And Impact. *British Journal of Sociology of Education* 37 (1): 129–148.

Ozga, J. 1988. *Schoolwork: Approaches to the Labour Process of Teaching.* Maidenhead: Open University Press.

Philips, Jane. 1999. Not Learning, But Coasting. *Checklist for School Governors in Great Britain* 4309: 30–30.

Raelin, J.A. 2007. Toward an Epistemology of Practice. *Academy Of Management Learning & Education* 6 (4): 495–519.

Randle, Keith, and Norman Brady. 1997a. Further Education and the New Managerialism. *Journal of Further & Higher Education* 21 (2): 229.

———. 1997b. Managerialism and Professionalism in the 'Cinderella Service'. *Journal of Vocational Education & Training* 49 (1): 121–139. doi:10.1080/13636829700200007.

Rochford, F. 2008. The Contested Product of a University Education. *Journal of Higher Education Policy & Management* 30 (1): 41–52.

Smith, C., D. Knights, and H. Willmott. 1991. *White-Collar Work: The Non-Manual Labour Process.* Basingstoke: Macmillan.

Stoller, Aaron. 2015. Taylorism and the Logic of Learning Outcomes. *Journal of Curriculum Studies* 47 (3): 317–333.

Tierny, W.G., and A. Rhoads. 1995. The Culture of Assessment. In *Academic Work*, ed. R. Smyth. Buckingham: SRHE and Open University Press.

Vallas, Steven Peter. 1990. The Concept of Skill: A Critical Review. *Work and Occupations* 17 (4): 19.

Wiggins, Kaye. 2015. 'Good' schools may be 'coasting', too. Times Educational Supplement, 3 July 2015, 1.

Wilson, Tom. 1991. The Proletarianisation of Academic Labour. *Industrial Relations Journal* 22 (4): 250–262.

CHAPTER 4

Shaping the Landscape of Education

4.1 INTRODUCTION

In one sense the arguments and examples that have been given already may be seen as leading up to an argument wherein the changes catalogued are the result of one defining feature of society or the economy. This is not the case. What becomes obvious when one considers the contemporary landscape of education, and seeks to find reasons for the ongoing taming of education, is that there is no overriding factor. For example, although the argument offered in the previous chapter reflecting Braverman's application of Marxist theory to the labour process may be compelling, the scope of the argument is not sufficient to explain how education has been tamed. Indeed, the major criticism of Marxism is that it offers an account of society that is economically deterministic. So, although I would argue for the value of considering how workers are subject to deskilling within the labour process, I would certainly not want to say that this is the sole determinant by which we can explain the taming of education.

A similarly reductionist argument is often offered in respect of how all recent social and economic changes can be boiled down to the impact of neoliberalism. There is no doubt that the political project that can be summed up as neoliberalism has had an impact on many aspects of social life, and I find it hard not to agree that many of these changes have not been socially beneficial. However, as will be argued below, it is difficult to assert that all changes can be attributed to neoliberalism. This is partly

© The Author(s) 2018
R. Creasy, *The Taming of Education,*
DOI 10.1007/978-3-319-62247-7_4

because neoliberalism as practised can be seen to be a somewhat distorted version of the ideology and because other factors, such as rationalisation, have a much longer history and that they also exert an influence which acts to tame education.

Instead, I want to argue that the landscape of contemporary education in England is subject to a range of factors, each of which has greater or lesser influence. Two of these factors, both of which share a concern with considering the issue of control, have already been considered in Chap. 3:

1. The actions of teachers and academics which are concerned with controlling the scope of their work. This involves the definition of disciplines and curricula and may be seen as both epistemological in how education is conceived and understood and practical with respect to how it is organised and practised.

2. Actions by the State. In particular government actions which may be seen as having the aim of weakening the control that teachers and academics have. The concern to weaken the power of those who are engaged in the teaching profession may be seen as a means to an end, in that within a global economy, the role of education becomes more important. As such there is a concern on the part of the government that education produces outputs which reflect political concerns. For example, the habit of Michael Gove, when Secretary of State for Education, to refer to the administrative functions of existing education services as "the blob" can be seen as a condescending approach to those who work in education (Waters 2015). What it does though is to undermine the efforts of educational administrators in a way which legitimises challenges to them.

This chapter introduces and discusses four other factors. These are each important when considering how education is organised and experienced. In turn, these are:

1. Neoliberalism. The political ideology of neoliberalism can be seen as having a significant influence on policy and practice within education. This is often bound up with economic considerations especially with an understanding of education as being seen solely in relation to how it serves economic interests as well as with respect to how it can be organised in ways which are analogous to a market. As such a consideration of neoliberalism will be an important element of this chapter.

2. New Public Management. This is presented here as both a strategy employed by governments to wrest control from professional groups and as being an ideological force in itself, in the way that it privileges the role and scope of management. A key element of management however is with respect to control and it has already been shown how control is likely to reduce wickedity and increase tameness.
3. Standardisation. The general trend towards increasing standardisation is typified by Weber's arguments relating to rationalisation and Ritzer's contemporary reworking of this into the concept of McDonaldization. Standardisation can be seen as doing much to reduce wickedity and establish tameness within education.
4. Internationalisation. This is also presented as an important factor with respect to education. This may be seen as particularly pertinent within Higher Education in England but this does not mean that it has no impact upon education as a whole.

This is not to say that no other issues have the ability to shape the landscape of education rather that these six factors (the four within this chapter and the two considered previously) are presented as the most influential and most relevant at this time.

4.2   Neoliberalism: Markets, Competition and Choice

Although there may be more general political concerns which impact upon the landscape of education, and which have seen the State seek to reduce the power of academics, a general concern with the role that education can play in respect of national economic performance is also important. In recent decades such a trend has not been rooted in any particular UK political party. What is evident is that all parties have adopted the position that, if left to its own devices, the education sector as a whole would not contribute as much to the needs of the economy as it would if it were managed. Such a concern with economics, although not exclusive to neoliberalism, lies at the heart of it and it can be argued that all UK governments since 1979 have, to greater or lesser extent, been influenced by some of the key tenets of this political ideology (Jenkins 2006).

In part, this rest on ideas about how global and national economies have developed over time, and it is important for the argument being put forward, to reiterate the argument that tame education impoverishes education. The concept of a knowledge economy was introduced earlier.

To reiterate, contemporary economic practices, located within a globalised world, mean that economic advantage now tends to rest with innovation (Bottery 2004; Hargreaves 2003). This increases the importance of generating and controlling ideas rather than controlling physical property and can be used to explain why it is that governments are drawn into taking increased control over education because of a concern for more general economic issues.

A concern for more general issues may indeed be the case but how governments intervene is subject to ideological beliefs about how modern economies are best organised, and since the 1980s, education has been subject to significant change as a consequence of the adoption of neoliberalism. It is pertinent to note that although education generally exists within England as a national system, it is also subject to wider, pan-European and global forces which contribute to a neoliberal perspective. For example, the annual publication of national educational performance in a league table format can be seen as establishing an understanding of education as being bound up with competition. In turn a consideration of global forces can be seen to rest upon the global influence of neoliberalism (Peters 2004). The basis of this perspective is that neoliberalism has become an endemic political force on a global scale and is bound up with a particular view of economics which privileges market forces. As such, neoliberalism provides a framework for understanding developments within education. Since the 1970s the neoliberal project has achieved a degree of hegemony with respect to the ways in which the logic of markets has come to shape politics. So much so that in the UK, political parties which would not consider themselves to be neoliberal have also promoted markets, competition and choice.

This concern with neoliberalism is not at all unusual in commentaries regarding contemporary societies and political developments but very often the concept of neoliberalism is presented as axiomatic. It is not. Writers such as Davies (2014), Turner (2011), Amable (2011), and Mirowski and Plehwe (2009) make the point that there is a great deal of confusion concerning just what neoliberalism is. So, although the term neoliberalism is in common use, it is not the case that it is unproblematic. Because of this there is no unambiguous definition that can be offered for it. The various positions which contribute to the neoliberal canon make confusion an almost inevitable outcome. In light of this confusion, it might be best seen as operating as a thought collective (Dean 2014; Mirowski and Plehwe 2009). What makes neoliberalism even more problematic though is the manner in which it is denied as a valid concept, or left unspoken, by many (Mirowski 2014). From a Foucauldian perspective, it can be argued that this denial, or lack of voicing, is the very thing which makes neoliberalism so powerful.

Neoliberalism began as a reaction to what some were seeing as the unwelcome growth of the State (Peck 2010), but it has not seen the demise of the State. In particular neoliberalism may be seen as having an overarching concern with the efficacy of free markets (Clarke 2010), but a commonly held idea that neoliberalism is characterised by a laissez faire approach is clearly misguided.

The concern with a laissez faire approach to society can be seen as being rooted in the work of Hayek, though he is cautious about the value of the term (Hayek 2013 [1973, 1976, 1979]). Hayek is generally recognised as providing a major basis of the intellectual argument of neoliberalism, especially with regard to what he sees as the problems of collective action and with providing justification for a laissez faire approach. To privilege an understanding of neoliberalism as laissez faire however can be seen as incomplete. It certainly does not represent the approach of recent governments who have clearly been influenced by neoliberalism in the late twentieth and early twenty-first century (Davies 2014). The opposite is more accurate; neoliberal governments can be seen as presiding over very active States. Hayek's faith in a self-regulating market can be positioned as being a liberal argument (Olssen 2016). However, rather than adopting a laissez faire approach towards markets, Olssen draws on the work of Buchanan to explain why, within neoliberalism, there is an ongoing need for conscious political intervention so as to ensure that markets work. This is a much more accurate way of understanding the ways in which the State operates as part of neoliberalism. Rather than adopting the laissez faire approach that is usually associated with Hayek, the contemporary neoliberal state may be seen to take on the role of both enforcer, recommodifying services that have been previously been decommodified by introducing competition, and safety net, stepping in to provide support for market systems when they fail (Davies 2014).

In presenting neoliberalism as a factor which shapes education, I echo the work of Davies (2014) in seeing it as an approach wherein the logic of markets is privileged not only within economics but also within politics and, crucially, in the sphere of social and public policy. What this means for social policy is that the State acts to establish forms of service provision which seek to replicate the ways in which real markets work. This sees a concern to introduce competition and choice, and to encourage service users to act as though they are consumers, something which has been termed quasi-markets (Le Grand and Bartlett 1993). This can be seen to be evident in the way in which, since 1979, UK governments have tended to introduce an element of marketisation into a range of policy areas such as education.

For example, this can be seen in developments within Higher Education (Finn 2015) and is evident within the UK government report Higher Ambitions (Dept for Business 2009). Higher Ambitions takes the existence of a knowledge economy as its starting point and positions Higher Education within a consumer-oriented model linked to the development of skills and knowledge relevant to employment.

Although "Higher Ambitions" specifically declares that Higher Education is not seen by the government as only mattering for its economic contribution (p. 41), the main thrust of the document demonstrates that there is an overriding concern with how the Higher Education sector as a whole can contribute to the national economy. For example, it is stated that "the creation of the new Department of Business, Innovation and Skills ..... signals the central role that the Government envisages for Higher Education in contributing to our economic strength and competitive potential" (p. 41). Recent debates regarding the role that Higher Education should play in terms of providing workers is also encapsulated in ideas about employability. The concern that graduates should be employable is revealed in the comment "employers ... report a lack of 'employability' skills in graduates such as business-awareness and self-management" (p. 42). Throughout the document there is a focus upon how Higher Education can supply employers with skills and how students will become more employable. This is contextualised within the idea that the UK operates within a globally competitive market. If Higher Education is to supply graduates with particular skills, it can be seen that these are skills which the State, along with business, and the market, values. These will not necessarily be those which academics value. As such there is pressure on teaching staff to assess for things with which they have not traditionally been concerned with.

The developing discourse of markets in relation to Higher Education which is evident within "Higher Ambitions" is clearly important in understanding policy developments. It can be seen in the partial adoption by the government of the Browne report (2010), together with significant funding cuts as detailed in the comprehensive spending review of October

2010. This change reinforces the concept of the student as consumer by changing the funding of Higher Education programmes so that students pay significantly more than previously. This does not imply that the full costs of Higher Education have been shifted to the student but significant costs have been imposed upon them.

The intention was that Higher Education Institutions would charge varying fees and so students would choose a programme in a manner that was analogous to making any other purchase. This reflects the general approach that has been taken by governments in the UK which have aimed to create, or replicate, markets within sectors where a market was seen to be absent (Brown and Carasson 2013). This approach sees governments acting to impose the logic of the market to areas which appear to exist outside of the market economy by virtue of being part of the public sector. Although government action in this way seems to run counter to the critical approach adopted by neoliberals towards State intervention, it does not undermine the neoliberal argument. Neoliberalism readily accommodates State intervention as being necessary where goods and services are provided for outside of a market environment if the aim of that intervention is to facilitate the move towards a free market (Olssen 2016; Hayek 2013; Turner 2011). This is not the same, however, as arguing that a free market exists as a consequence of such actions. However, although there may be doubts as to the extent that a market has been created, Hughes (2007, 12) demonstrates the extent to which the discourse of markets has become embedded within the sector when she writes:

> Today's UK university students buy a degree. Some also buy a university education. We live in a consumer economy. Education purchases are no different. Those coming into higher education, and those who support them, are buying something. They are arguably little different from consumers walking into shops.

In considering this development, it can also be seen how the privileging of markets has consequences for individuals in that it reconfigures our own understanding of self in a way that impacts upon how we may come to behave. Although Hughes may be overstating the case when she refers to students being analogous to customers within shops, what is important is that individuals behave as though they exist within a free market (Marginson 2009) and, even, that educational staff believe that they are working within a market. The evidence that students behave as consumers with respect to Higher Education is not convincing, but the discourse of markets is present within the Higher Education sector and this does have some effect on the ways in which staff employed within Higher Education act. For example, Higher Education Institutions are increasingly being organised in ways which reflect both markets and business interests; marketing staff within Higher Education will often refer to the institution as a brand; and even some teaching staff will voice the argument that their students are buying a qualification.

Because of this it is important to consider the argument that neoliberalism acts as a discourse within education, shaping what happens within it. Within England, in spite of the presentation of schools in a league table format and the idea of choice, State education at compulsory levels does not involve a market transaction per se, but developments in education policy have created a system wherein the logic of the market has been introduced. Compulsory State-provided education is not paid for by users but is, instead, funded through taxation. At the same time, some courses in the Further Education sector do incur fees, as do most courses within the Higher Education sector. This is not enough to assert that a market exists but that is not necessarily what is important. What is important is the ability of neoliberalism to recast how education is understood.

In one sense it is not difficult to critique the argument that Hughes presented. It may be the case that some forms of education have been recast along market lines through the imposition of student fees, but is this sufficient to say that a market has been established? If, as Hughes argues, Higher Education students buy a degree, we must consider the process that enables them to buy it. Unlike a conventional customer, that is, Hughes' shop customer, students do not simply buy the award. They are compelled to enter into a process which leads to the award being made. In general, this involves the submission of work for judgement and the assessment of that work. The requirement that students submit work for assessment is a practice that has long been a feature of education and may be seen as constituting the traditional practices of education. It can also be seen however as strong evidence that a market transaction is not present within education. Instead, it can be seen that education continues to be shaped by the development of knowledge within disciplines which is then assessed according to what is valued by academics working within those disciplines and which rests upon professional judgements being made. Access to an institution may be paid for, but that is not the same as the claim that an award is being bought.

Unlike Hughes' shop customer, the student that pays fees to "buy" a degree is unable to return their education for a refund should they find that the quality is not what they expected or if they find that there is little use value in the way that they expected. Although, within the discourse of economisation, there is an understanding that education is a commodity, it is not. It may be that education has some similarities with commodities but that is not sufficient grounds with which to assert that it is one. An education cannot be bought twice nor can it be sold on. Importantly though, education has to be engaged with and this implies some activity on the part of the buyer which inevitably introduces a degree of uncertainty into education when it is viewed as a process.

Such an argument will be irrelevant however if the context of Higher Education shifts to the extent that students do see themselves as customers as this will influence their understanding of their place within the system. Alongside this Higher Education Institutions have seemingly accepted the idea of competition as being intrinsic to their work, whether that be competition over students or competition over outputs because of the ways in which research has come to be judged.

This returns us to the discussion of education offered previously in respect of how there is a need to establish an output if education is to be recast as a process. In turn it reiterates a concern with how certainty impacts upon processes. The output, as argued above, can be seen as certification but in spite of this the level of engagement, or of ability, on the part of the pupil or student will clearly impact upon the output that is produced. This introduces a lack of certainty which can cause some consternation for some but it is hard to see how this is not inevitable. There is a further aspect of uncertainty which can be seen to impact upon certification though, this is the actions of those individuals who are charged with making a judgement about students' work. This will be considered in more depth later but it can be seen as being related to the introduction of learning outcomes across education. The emergence and adoption of learning outcomes goes some way to making the assessment of student work a tamer process in the way that it predetermines what is expected. It may be seen that this sits easily with a concern to recast education as a market. In Higher Education the introduction of course fees, ostensibly paid by students, goes only partway to establishing a market. The uncertainty that surrounds the outcomes of taking a course acts as a countermeasure to any argument that a market does exist. Because of this actions which tame Higher Education should have the consequence of removing uncertainty and strengthening the argument that a market really does exist. Of course, if the outcomes of Higher Education, that is to say, the awards for which certificates are granted were ever to become the product of a real market, something which is bought, then we might also see that the value of such awards dissipates.

It is readily accepted that one feature of educational awards is in relation to how this contributes to decision-making as part of recruitment. It was established above that education operates in ways which supports the activity of organisations. Educational certification can provide some evidence relating to job suitability where the award has some correspondence to ability. If education is tamed to such an extent that outcomes become more homogenous and where degrees are bought, the value must be cast into doubt. If such a situation were to be reached, it could be argued that a great deal of the current value of the Higher Education system would have been lost. A market transaction would afford entry to the system but tame education would almost guarantee an outcome. As such Higher Education could be seen to have been impoverished through the establishment of certainty.

So, in conclusion, a consideration of neoliberalism as a force which has shaped education is relevant. This will be demonstrated later by a consideration of how neoliberal reforms within the Further Education sector have had significant consequences. However, although it would be hard to deny the impact that neoliberal thought has had on education, I am not convinced that it is sufficient to be identified as the sole determinant of the ways in which education has developed. Neoliberalism is clearly important and influential when considering education policy but neoliberalism alone is not what is shaping education. One factor that sits easily alongside neoliberalism though is the development and introduction of New Public Management. The next section in this chapter then will consider how work within education has been subjected to increased forms of managerial control.

4.3   THE CONSEQUENCES OF NEW PUBLIC MANAGEMENT

An important theme that will be seen throughout this book is that of control over processes. This tends to follow the reasoning that increased control over a process equates to that process being tame or tamer. Where control is not evident and therefore where uncertainty is the key characteristic of a process, so this can be equated with wickedity. My general

argument is that within education, especially if we accept the premise that
we are living in a knowledge economy, wickedity is more desirable than
tameness. As has been argued above, a situation wherein certainty is
assured in Higher Education is unlikely to be in anyone's long-term interest. This is not to say that I am arguing for anarchy or chaos, far from it,
but we should be aware that total control over education is unlikely to
produce the sort of individual that will contribute to progress. This section focuses upon one particular approach to managing public services
and seeks to demonstrate how this has impacted upon education, often in
ways that are detrimental.

In the previous chapter, it was argued that in terms of control it can be
seen that in recent decades the State has demonstrated an increasing concern with the extent to which educational professionals have, or had, control over education. It has been suggested that governments have
increasingly sought to increase the control which they have which in turn
reduces the control held by educationalists. This is not necessarily a specific intention. It is more plausible to see the control of those who work in
education as part of a strategy by which the output of education overall is
controlled and that this is driven by a combination of political and economic concerns. In considering the tensions that exist between professional control and the increasing levels of state control over education, this
chapter is concerned with identifying particular factors which shape education. However, a further question arises: how has the State been able to
appropriate control over education? Most commentators within England
would concur that the State does now have significant control over the
provision of education but how has this been achieved? What strategy or
mechanism has moved power away from teachers?

This section considers the development of an approach to control
which has been referred to as New Public Management (NPM) or managerialism. NPM can be seen as one way in which neoliberalism becomes
embedded within public services such as education (Ball 2016). The central aspect of this approach involves increasing the control that managers
exert. Although it will be evident as to how NPM overlaps with both
aspects of State control, as have been introduced, and aspects of standardisation, as will follow, NPM will be discussed as exerting a force upon
education in a way which sees it as being more than just a strategy to be
adopted. Importantly then, NPM is presented as being influential in its
own right. It can also be seen that NPM sits easily with neoliberalism as
there is a strong theme of adopting business-like principles or the types of

practices that reflect business principles within NPM. Consequently, this section will give an overview of what NPM is and illustrate how aspects of NPM are relevant to understanding issues relating to education. What will be argued is that particular practices which relate to NPM have changed educational practice in ways which reduce the professional elements of teachers work at all levels and in all sectors.

In echoing the concerns raised above regarding neoliberalism though, caution is necessary before asserting that NPM is a neoliberal strategy. Although we might associate NPM with neoliberal governments, it has clearly been adopted by governments that would not be seen as neoliberal. Hood (1991) charts the development of NPM since the mid-1970s and in doing so demonstrates that NPM predates neoliberalism (if we date neo-liberalism within the UK from the election of Margaret Thatcher's Conservative Government in May 1979). In considering what NPM is, Hood (1991, 4–5) presents seven doctrinal components of the approach as follows:

1. Greater "hands-on" management
2. Explicit standards and measures of performance
3. Greater emphasis on output controls
4. "Disaggregation" of units in the public sector
5. Greater competition in the public sector
6. Stress on private sector styles of management practice
7. Stress on greater discipline and parsimony in resource use

Importantly though, although the term NPM is used in a manner that is unambiguous, it is not a unified approach and variations of NPM do exist, both nationally and globally (Deem and Brehony 2005; Hood 2000; Deem 1998; Dunleavy and Hood 1994). What is also important however is that in the move towards NPM, it is not suggested that organisations will necessarily adopt each doctrine in equal measures. NPM should be seen as a general trend. As NPM brings pressure to bear upon how any sector or provider of education is organised, some of these doctrines will have a greater influence than others. This is the consequences of path dependency combined with the way that working practices become cul-tural forms which, in turn, mediate developments (Hood 2000). Path dependency refers to the ways in which historical patterns of organisational form are difficult to change not only because individuals working within them develop particular approaches to their work but also because of the ways in which others also have expectations as to what they are expected to do. It may also be considered as a consequence of how some professional groups are able to resist change.

So, the historical concerns of Higher Education which have their origins in academic freedom and a concern with learning for its own sake may prove resistant to competing ideas regarding the purpose and nature of Higher Education, and academics, as operating within a market. At the same time, staff within the Further Education sector where significant changes to working practices were introduced may have initially seen NPM as less threatening or been less able to resist it. What is evident is that of the three main education sectors within England, NPM has become more deeply entrenched within Further Education Colleges since incorporation in 1993 than in other sectors. What will be demonstrated in Chap. 5 is that there has been widespread and significant changes in the management of Further Education Colleges with Gleeson (2001, 192) arguing that "the effects of deregulation, marketization and managerialism have impacted on FE in an intense fashion". In explaining why this has been the case, Bryan and Hayes (2007) consider the ways in which these changes can be seen as the consequence of adopting NPM within a context wherein teaching staff are deprofessionalised and undervalued. For Bryan and Hayes, the result is the transformation of Further Education in a way that can be seen as McDonaldization, a concept that is explored more fully in the next section.

Although the Further Education Sector will be shown to have been the sector of education to have been changed the most by the introduction of NPM, it would be difficult to say that NPM has not influenced developments across education as a whole or that NPM is solely directed at the education sector. Changes within a range of public services have seen a decline in the role of traditional bureaucratic and professional models of governance and the emergence of a managerial perspective (Clarke et al. 2000; Clarke and Newman 1997). Hood (2000, 8) however notes that it would be erroneous to think that previous models of organisation and control were unambiguous arguing that "cultural, institutional and power-distribution characteristics" within different societies lead to a diverse range of organisational forms. In addition, managerialism also has different forms (Becher and Trowler 2001). As such, although NPM may be influential within contemporary society, particular aspects have greater or lesser influence as will be seen.

Although NPM is a descriptive term relating to approaches towards the social organisation of work, it can be seen that it fits easily with the discourse of neoliberalism. Indeed concerns regarding the economic performance of industrial workers within the UK in the 1970s, along with concerns about Trades Union activity, may be seen as giving rise to calls for the rights of managers to manage. The first Thatcher government in particular did much to promote management as a legitimate and necessary strategy for improving economic productivity and drew on Hayek's arguments (2007 [1960]) to legitimise an attack on the collective actions of Trades Unions. The rhetoric around the rights of managers to manage that was evident within the 1970s and 1980s did much to establish the difference between those who work and those who manage. This is not to identify with, or agree with this argument, but it can be seen to have consequences for the success or form of NPM within occupational areas where militant Trades Union activity was not a key characteristic.

The idea then that managerialism is bound up with a social division between types of worker, and where one is privileged, is perhaps strongest within the Further Education sector, but it can be seen in recent developments with Higher Education also. As such it is possible to consider NPM as a politicised form of the management of what has been referred to as the bureaucratic university (Barnett 2011; Furedi 2002). Within this, bureaucratic procedures are generally developed by non-academic staff but are used to manage academic work. In this way administrative and management staff usurp control over academic activities. In doing so, academic freedom is reduced as a consequence of being required to engage with systems and procedures designed for managerial rather than academic purposes. In practice increasing levels of control come to be held by non-academics both within and outside of the university. It is the ideological impetus behind such control which is at the heart of NPM and which contributes to the decline of donnish dominion. Where NPM enhances control, then we can also recognise that NPM contributes significantly to the taming of education.

However, although NPM has come to be recognised as a descriptive term, it is not unproblematic. There is no unitary version of such managerialism and variations exist. At the same time, management is not a neutral activity and it should be recognised as a political form (Clarke et al. 2000). As such it is pertinent to note that although NPM is being referred to within this chapter as a major influencing factor within education, this should be taken as a general movement rather than a specified form. What is important though is the way in which NPM acts upon the formation and practice of education. Education has been subject to forms of NPM in similar ways to other public services but this has not been even across educational organisations or sectors. However, although the impact of NPM may have been different within different sections, it can be seen to have acted in practical and discursive ways as has been suggested and education as a whole has been changed by NPM.

One aspect of this is that managerialism can be understood as a cultural formation which carries with it both ideological meanings and practices that are relevant in respect of the impact than that it has in establishing a much greater sense now that teachers within all sectors of education are, and expect to be, managed. NPM then is bound up not only with an approach to a given situation, as well as some notion of how this must be addressed; it also acts in a manner which is self-serving. Management itself is seen as a desirable outcome albeit within a context of an emergent political settlement that reflects the move towards a market society as has been supported by successive governments in recent decades (Clarke and Newman 1997). Crucially though, NPM operates independently of government on an ideological and discursive basis.

This can be seen in the way in which managerialism shapes language (McGuigan 2005). For example, the adoption of the term learning outcomes reflects a process of production rather than of learning. In a similar vein, arguments about quality assurance processes within Further and Higher Education often draw upon ideas about "value for money" in a manner that reflects the economic concerns of business (Singh 2010). What can be seen from this is that the discourse of managerialism is shaping the way in which forms of organisational structure and management are understood. In turn this feeds into the working practices of teachers and academics by exerting a normative force upon them. Alongside the abstract influence of discourse is the reality of a new landscape of education.

However, although NPM may be one way in which education comes to be organised differently, it can be seen as overlapping to an extent with a more widespread general trend that is presented within the next section as standardisation and which has clear implications for the taming of education.

4.4   STANDARDISATION

Standardisation is a process that is concerned with the ordering of goods or services in ways that make them increasingly homogenous. The reasons offered for this are that it affords a degree of interchangeability and eases comparisons. Such a process has had an impact upon education. For example, in Higher Education, standardisation may be seen in the adoption of semesterised programmes built up of modules of equal standing. Such approaches are not restricted to England and provide further evidence of how factors may overlap or intersect. The Bologna approach to Higher Education within the European Union seeks to rationalise Higher Education in a manner that facilitates a European market within Higher Education. However, the Bologna agreement itself did not emerge out of academic concerns but was a political agreement between member states of the European Union (Hussey and Smith 2010). To achieve the harmonisation required by the Bologna agreement however requires the type of bureaucratic rationalisation that Barnett (2011) refers to and which is then subject to political control.

The Bologna process is often presented as a process of harmonising Higher Education across the European Union but the goal of harmonisation must be seen as resting upon a process of standardisation. The end result of such standardisation is that it will enable more accurate comparisons to be made regarding Higher Education within the European Union and facilitate student mobility between Higher Education Institutions. This fits well with the move towards economising Higher Education and establishing a market, but it is not sufficient to explain it (Furedi 2002). Standardisation, however, is not new and may be seen as a key component of rationalisation, something which is most clearly articulated within the work of Weber (Gerth and Wright-Mills 1948), Habermas (1984) and Ritzer (2011). As such, a consideration of rationalisation is pertinent to understanding the moves towards standardisation.

Rationality as a process or driver is closely bound up with ideas about efficiency and outcomes, and this can be seen as being echoed in discussions of both processes and markets with respect to how social and economic activities are best organised. Neoliberal concerns regarding how to organise social and economic activities can be seen to rest upon the idea that private sector businesses are intrinsically more efficient than providers of services who are not subject to the pressures of the market place. Such a claim is often presented as axiomatic and rarely opened up to scrutiny. In these cases efficiency is seen as synonymous with effectiveness. That is not necessarily the case. Even so, organisations, such as those engaged in the provision of education, are exhorted to be more business-like in respect of how they organise their operations.

This can be seen as reflecting the political imperatives of the State in recent decades and can also be seen as fitting comfortably with the practices that are bound up with NPM. Again, this reiterates the point made earlier, that each of these factors does not operate independently at all times. Although, as will be seen, standardisation has a long history, recent developments mean that there is greater pressure to apply it within education.

For Weber (1948) rationality, as found within modern, Western societies, represents a feature of enlightenment thinking wherein the drive to exert control over the natural world is applied to control over social activities, especially with regard to economic and administrative activities. For Weber, this represents formal rationality and is to be distinguished from other forms of rationality as found in other societies and other historical periods. Rationalisation forms a major plank of Weber's writings but it is a concept that has been developed by others.

As such, Habermas (1984) develops Weber's concern with rationality referring to "cognitive-instrumental" rationality as being concerned with the efficient means of achieving ends or goals. Given that a period of study for educational purposes can be seen as having a particular end or goal, his concern with how that should be organised has some resonance. In particular he emphasises the relationship between rationality, knowledge and behaviour. In doing so Habermas draws attention to the way in which forms of social organisation shape the knowledge which individuals hold about the world, which in turn may shape behaviour. In establishing this relationship, Habermas recognises, and emphasises, the extent to which knowledge may be unreliable. As such it can be argued that this promotes the development of rational systems and procedures where the aim is to formalise the subject.

A further development of rationality is found within Ritzer's concept of McDonaldization (2011). This may be criticised as being a simple repackaging of Weber's theory of rationality but the focus on consumption and consumers gives it resonance within contemporary society. In presenting McDonaldization as the contemporary iteration of Weber's work, Ritzer draws out four aspects of rationality which form the drivers of the process: efficiency, calculability, predictability and control. All these may be said to have some relevance in the way that education is currently organised and with the ways in which the uncertainty that is characteristic of wickedity is tamed through the imposition of rational systems.

Ritzer (2002) has considered how McDonaldization has impacted upon the university in negative ways but this can also be seen within colleges and schools. As part of the process of McDonaldization, bureaucratisation transforms the relationship between staff and students in ways which emphasise a transactional contract (Furedi 2002). This move towards standardisation can be seen to dehumanise relationships. I argued earlier that teaching always rests upon a relationship but a consideration of standardisation illustrates that there are varying types of relationship. Relationships within McDonaldized settings, I would argue, will always be less humane because within McDonaldization the worker becomes more of an automaton and less autonomous.

Similarly, Bryan and Hayes (2007) make a strong case to demonstrate that Further Education Colleges have become sites for McDonaldization but actually argue that in some ways the sector can be seen to have gone beyond McDonaldization through the adoption of an overwhelming amount of bureaucracy. This is the consequence of being bound up with an approach to management that is focused on risk management. The result of this is that bureaucratisation has had the effect of reducing the efficiencies that are normally found within McDonaldization, illustrating the irrationality of rationality as warned about by Weber.

Weber (1948, 240) is particularly useful if we turn our attention to focusing upon the ways in which rationality influences the organisation or provision of education. He argues that "a rational bureaucratic structure of domination, as such, develops quite independently of the areas in which it takes hold". This underpins the discussion of how other aspects of the social world come to exert influence over practices within education. For Weber, centres of education become drawn into providing particular types of education and, increasingly, in particular rationalised ways. In doing so, the organisers of educational systems turn their focus onto producing what Weber classes as a "specialist type of man" rather than a "cultivated" man. In arguing this it is clear that Weber regards the "specialist" as inferior, or restricted, when compared to the "cultured man" but this is hidden, he says, under the conditions of bureaucracy and rationality that drives it. Weber is suggesting here that a rationally structured education in some way impoverishes the potential that education has to transform and develop individuals. This idea resonates with the claim that tameness may impoverish the experience and outcomes of education.

It is pertinent to note though that Weber may be overstating the driving force of rationality when he makes such a claim but this is an issue where different factors overlap. It was stated in the previous chapter that for differing reasons the State, as the government, may seek to take control from teachers and academics. The individuals who constitute those engaged in governing, however, also are subject to the forces and principles of rationality in the same way that teaching staff are, but it may be that the State, in the form of the government, is more inclined to promote rationality within education. As such the introduction of Ofsted within the compulsory sectors of education, and of the Quality Assurance Agency in Higher Education, can be seen as the creation of regulatory bodies which not only have power over education, they articulate this power through rational principles in a way that promotes standardisation. The increasing scope of auditing can be seen as being linked to these developments (Hussey and Smith 2010; Power 2003).

For example, Higher Education saw major changes taking place during the 1990s in many universities, each of which represents aspects of standardisation. These changes are manifest, for example, as semesterised patterns of teaching and in guidelines relating to how assessment is to be carried out, such as word restrictions for written work or timings for presentations and exams. Similarly, learning outcomes at both programme and module level with a credit value being assigned in both cases became the standard practice. This was encouraged significantly by the actions of the QAA in establishing guidelines which were said to represent markers of quality and standards. Over time approaches to the organisation of education have gradually become formalised in a way that has become remarkably similar across the Higher Education sector.

There is a danger here, however, of suggesting that rationalisation is imposed upon the education sector by bodies that are external to it such as the State. This is achieved through regulatory agencies as indicated above or by managers who seek to change how teachers work in ways which reflect the aims and concerns of others. In arguing this though, we would be overlooking the fact that teaching staff do not exist outside of society. Rationalisation is something which has come to permeate society. It is not that rationalisation is a force that teachers will somehow naturally resist, but rather, it is a force which many of us go along with. This is because in living in a social world that is subject to rationalised practices and structures, we come to see this as normal and, very often, as beneficial. The professional concerns of teachers may provide a basis from which they approach the activities of education but this is not from a starting point that is divorced from wider society. As such, although some aspects of regulatory bodies such as Ofsted and the QAA may be resisted by staff, this may well rest on a feeling of a loss of control rather than a deep antipathy towards the rational principles which underpin what these bodies present as best practice.

This reflects Ritzer's argument regarding the attractiveness of rationality. As workloads increase across education, through the intensification of work and alongside reduced levels of funding, the ability to cope in an increasingly difficult job can be made easier through the adoption or acceptance of standardised approaches to work. As such a rational approach to teaching and assessment may be welcomed by many. At the same time, many teaching staff will have only worked under the type of rationalised and standardised system described above. For them, this is simply how education is organised.

4.5   INTERNATIONALISATION

Although the argument up to now has been to establish the factors that shape education, it is possible to consider that these are particular to England. However, the form and character of educational provision within England does not exist in a vacuum and it is pertinent to consider the consequences for education of developments in respect of internationalisation.

It should be noted at this point that internationalisation is not synonymous with globalisation, and, importantly, both are concepts that can be contested. I am adopting the position that it is internationalisation, rather than globalisation, which is of greater concern with respect to how this affects education though I am suggesting that it impacts upon Higher Education to a greater extent than it does other sectors. Maringe (2009, 557) offers a useful account of why internationalisation is more appropriate than globalisation and summarises by noting that "while globalisation focuses on competition between nations, internationalisation tends to seek the strengthening of international cooperation". In doing so, though, he reflects the general view of internationalisation which sees it optimistically. Within this view, internationalisation is seen as being bound up with collaborative work which promotes understanding. This is echoed by Robson (2011) who, in focusing upon Higher Education, sees the internationalisation agenda as providing the possibility for a transforming of Higher Education. For him this would be a positive change. As such, although forces related to globalisation may be seen as similar to internationalisation, they are not the same.

Indeed, globalisation as an idea may be seen as a necessary myth within which the preconditions for economic and political change are made possible (Held and McGrew 2000). Globalisation is often seen as being synonymous with economic forces and in this sense politics means the neoliberal agenda (Peters 2004). Globalisation though can be seen to operate in a number of ways or to take on a number of forms (Bottery 2006). Of these varying forms, however, it is economic and political forms which have the potential to affect education the most (Bottery 2000). That the neoliberal agenda is sometimes referred to as the "Washington Consensus" illustrates the strong link between economic and political globalisation (Mirowski 2014; Wolf 2005; Peters 2004; Held 2002; Held and McGrew 2000). From this it can be argued that the forces referred to above with respect to how the discourse of markets have been applied to education are strongly linked to one aspect of neoliberalism, but this does not mean that this can be reduced to neoliberalism.

At the supra-national level, various organisations act to reinforce the basic tenets of the Washington Consensus of free-trade and deregulated markets. However, although it has previously been acknowledged that neoliberalism places some pressure upon education, it has already been established that this in itself is not sufficient to account for how education has developed as a whole. The emphasis upon neoliberalism within globalisation is one reason for seeing internationalisation as more important than globalisation. Even then it would be wrong to see internationalisation purely as the consequence of recent developments. For example, with respect to Higher Education, both Humfrey (2011) and Maringe (2009) refer to the manner within which universities originated as international, but became national institutions. As such, the internationalisation agenda sees a re-emergence of themes that have a long history. It is also the case that internationalisation is not a recent development within England (Humfrey 2011). Geopolitical ties, such as the British Commonwealth, have had a long impact upon Higher Education in England, and the development of the European Union illustrates how more recent international developments have had some impact upon how universities within the UK operate. Of course we are yet to fully see what the UK's decision to leave the European Union will mean for education. It is likely though that there will be increased demands placed upon the Further Education sector to provide skills training should access to skilled workers from mainland Europe be restricted.

By the early twenty-first century, internationalisation had become a major aspect of the way that Higher Education is managed, planned and delivered within the UK (Jiang and Carpenter 2013). In turn, the internationalisation agenda demonstrates the way in which the factors referred to previously overlap. For example, the Sorbonne Declaration (1998) aimed to facilitate the movement of students between European universities through a process of harmonisation in respect of the value and lengths of undergraduate and postgraduate programmes (King 2004). This was followed by the Bologna Declaration (1999). Although the Bologna Declaration does not seek to establish a European system of standardisation per se, its aims do reflect this in how it seeks to establish a European arena for Higher Education by establishing systems which facilitate the movement of students throughout Europe. This can only be possible though by establishing agreed standards. In turn the Bologna Declaration reflects economic concerns in that it inevitably undermines national policies in establishing a supra-national approach which is amenable to the idea of a market within education.

Internationalisation is not restricted to European issues though as has been suggested, and the economic factors which impact upon the Higher Education sector can be seen as driving Higher Education Institutions to both seek international students and to establish a presence outside of the UK. This reflects the impact of markets as was considered above. In sum then, although internationalisation is presented as a key strategy within the Higher Education sector (Maringe 2009), it may be argued that this is as a consequence of economic factors (Robson 2011).

4.6   Conclusion

The intention of this chapter has been to demonstrate that the provision and practice of education is shaped by a number of factors and to demonstrate that it is insufficient to point to any one factor as being the sole determinant of what happens within education. It is the case that at any given time one factor may appear to be more influential than others, but it has also been demonstrated that in many ways factors overlap, that it is difficult to disaggregate them. It has not, however, been the intention to claim that these are the only factors that shape education. In many ways the discussion of control over the work of teachers can also be seen as important in shaping what happens in different sectors of the education system.

In one way factors such as those considered here, alongside the issue of control as discussed within Chap. 3, may be seen as co-dependant rather than independent. A change within one factor may very well have implications for other factors. In presenting this argument, it should be recognised that the social, political and economic context of education is always complex and what was established within Chap. 2 was that complexity is a key characteristic of wickedity. In that sense the context of education is always wicked. It is a context that is always dynamic and always subject to influences which are both intrinsic and extrinsic. However, although it is being argued that the taming of education is not the consequence of any one factor, it is the case that education is being increasingly tamed and, as has been argued previously, tame education is not fit for purpose.

Having put forward a number of factors which shape the way in which education is provided and practised, the following chapters will do more to consider what this means with respect to wickedity and tameness. I do recognise though that the argument regarding the taming of education may be seen as abstract. Chapter 7, which follows later, seeks to do more to demonstrate the way in which the concepts of tameness and wickedity may be used as an evaluative tool by applying it to one aspect of education that is bound up with a view of education as being a process, assessment, before the final chapters make a case for what might be done to resist tameness and to promote wickedity.

REFERENCES

Amable, Bruno. 2011. Morals and Politics in the Ideology of Neo-Liberalism. *Socio-Economic Review* 9 (1): 3–30. doi:10.1093/ser/mwq015.

Ball, Stephen J. 2016. Neoliberal Education? Confronting the Slouching Beast. *Policy Futures in Education* 14 (8): 13.

Barnett, R. 2011. *Being a University*. Abingdon: Routledge.

Becher, T., and P. Trowler. 2001. *Academic Tribes and Territories: Intellectual Enquiry and the Cultures of Disciplines*. Buckingham: Open University Press.

Bottery, M. 2000. *Education, Policy and Ethics*. London: Continuum.

———. 2004. *The Challenges of Educational Leadership*. London: Sage.

Bottery, Mike. 2006. Education and Globalization: Redefining the Role of the Educational Professional. *Educational Review* 58 (1): 95–113.

Brown, R., and H. Carasson. 2013. *Everything for Sale? The Marketisation of UK Higher Education*. Abingdon: Routledge/Society for Research into Higher Education.

Browne, J. 2010. Securing a Sustainable Future for Higher Education: An Independent Review of Higher Education Funding and Student Finance. http://hereview.independent.gov.uk/hereview/

Bryan, J., and D. Hayes. 2007. The McDonaldization of Further Education. In *A Lecturer's Guide to Further Education*, ed. D. Hayes, T. Marshall, and A. Turner. Maidenhead: Open University Press.

Clarke, John. 2010. After Neo-Liberalism? *Cultural Studies* 24 (3): 375–394. doi:10.1080/09502381003750310.

Clarke, J., and J. Newman. 1997. *The Managerial State: Power, Politics and Ideology in the Remaking of Social Welfare*. London: Sage.

Clarke, J., S. Gewirtz, and E. McLaughlin. 2000. *New Managerialism, New Welfare?* London: Sage.

Davies, W. 2014. *The Limits of Neoliberalism: Authority, Sovereignty and the Logic of Competition*. London: Sage.

Dean, Mitchell. 2014. Rethinking Neoliberalism. *Journal of Sociology* 50 (2): 13.

Deem, Rosemary. 1998. 'New Managerialism' and Higher Education: The Management of Performances and Cultures in Universities in the United Kingdom. *International Studies in Sociology of Education* 8 (1): 47–70. doi:10.1080/0962021980020014.

Deem, Rosemary, and Kevin J. Brehony. 2005. Management as Ideology: The Case of 'New Managerialism' in Higher Education. *Oxford Review of Education* 31 (2): 217–235. doi:10.1080/03054980500117827.

Department for Business, Innovation and Skills (DBIS). 2009. Higher Ambitions: The Future of Universities in a Knowledge Economy. http://www.bis.gov.uk/wp-content/uploads/publications/Higher-Ambitions.pdf

Dunleavy, P., and C. Hood. 1994. From Old Public Administration to New Public Management. *Public Money & Management* 14 (3): 9–16.

Finn, Mike. 2015. Education Beyond the Gove Legacy. In *The Gove Legacy*, ed. Mike Finn, 14. Basingstoke: Palgrave Macmillan.

Furedi, F. 2002. The Bureaucratization of the British University. In *The McDonaldization of Higher Education*, ed. D. Hayes and R. Wynyard. Westport, CT: Bergin & Garvey.

Gerth, H.H., and C. Wright-Mills. 1948. *From Max Weber: Essays in Sociology*. London: Routledge & Kegan Paul.

Gleeson, Denis. 2001. Style and Substance in Education Leadership: Further Education (FE) as a Case in Point. *Journal of Education Policy* 16 (3): 181–196. doi:10.1080/02680930110041015.

Habermas, J. 1984. *The Theory of Communicative Action, Vol. 1, Reason and the Rationalization of Society*. Trans. Thomas McCarthy. Cambridge: Polity.

Hargreaves, A. 2003. *Teaching in the Knowledge Society: Education in the Age of Insecurity*. New York: Teachers College Press.

Hayek, Frederik von. 2007/1960. *The Constitution of Liberty*. Abingdon: Routledge.

Hayek, Frederik von. 2013/1973, 1976, 1979. *Law, Legislation and Liberty.* Abingdon: Routledge.

Held, D. 2002. *Globalisation and Anti-Globalisation.* Oxford: Polity.

Held, D., and A. McGrew. 2000. *The Global Transformations Reader.* Cambridge: Polity.

Hood, C. 1991. A Public Administration for all Seasons? *Public Administration* 69 (Spring): 3–19.

———. 2000. Paradoxes of Public-Sector Managerialism, Old Public Management and Public Service Bargains. *International Public Management Journal* 3: 1–22.

Hughes, P. 2007. Learning about Learning, or Learning to Learn (L2L). In *Learning, Teaching and Assessing in Higher Education: Developing Reflective Practice*, ed. A. Campbell and L. Norton. Exeter: Learning Matters.

Humfrey, C. 2011. The Long and Winding Road: A Review of the Policy, Practice and Development of the Internationalisation of Higher Education in the UK. *Teachers and Teaching: Theory and practice* 17 (6): 12.

Hussey, Trevor, and Patrick Smith. 2010. *The Trouble with Higher Education.* Abingdon: Routledge.

Jenkins, Simon. 2006. *Thatcher & Sons: A Revolution in Three Acts.* London: Allen Lane.

Jiang, N., and V. Carpenter. 2013. Faculty-Specific Factors of Degree of HE Internationalization: An Evaluation of Four Faculties of a Post-1992 University in the United Kingdom. *International Journal of Educational Management* 27 (3): 17.

King, R. 2004. *The University in the Global Age.* Basingstoke: Palgrave Macmillan.

Le Grand, J., and W. Bartlett. 1993. *Quasi-Markets and Social Policy.* London: Macmillan.

Marginson, Simon. 2009. Hayekian Neo-Liberalism and Academic Freedom. *Contemporary Readings in Law and Social Justice* 1 (1): 86.

Maringe, F. 2009. Strategies and Challenges of Internationalisation in HE: An Exploratory Study of UK Universities. *International Journal of Educational Management* 23 (7): 10.

McGuigan, Jim. 2005. Neo-Liberalism, Culture and Policy. *International Journal of Cultural Policy* 11 (3): 229–241. doi:10.1080/10286630500411168.

Mirowski, P. 2014. The Political Movement that Dared Not Speak Its Own Name: The Neoliberal Thought Collective Under Erasure. https://www.ineteconomics.org/uploads/papers/WP23-Mirowski.pdf

Mirowski, P., and D. Plehwe. 2009. *The Road from Mont Pèlerin: The Making of the Neoliberal Thought Collective.* Cambridge, MA: Harvard University Press.

Olssen, Mark. 2016. Neoliberal Competition in Higher Education Today: Research, Accountability And Impact. *British Journal of Sociology of Education* 37 (1): 129–148.

Peck, J. 2010. *Constructions of Neoliberal Reason*. Oxford: Oxford University Press.

Peters, R.T. 2004. *In Search of the Good Life: The Ethics of Globalization*. London: Continuum.

Power, Michael. 2003. Evaluating the Audit Explosion. *Law & Policy* 25 (3): 185–202.

Ritzer, G. 2002. Enchanting McUniversity: Towards a Spectacularly Irrational University Quotidian. In *The McDonaldization of Higher Education*, ed. D. Hayes and R. Wynyard. Westport, CT: Bergin & Garvey.

———. 2011. *The McDonaldization of Society*. 6th ed. Los Angeles, CA: Pine Forge.

Robson, Sue. 2011. Internationalization: A Transformative Agenda for Higher Education? *Teachers and Teaching* 17 (6): 619–630. doi:10.1080/13540602. 2011.625116.

Singh, Mala. 2010. Quality Assurance in Higher Education: Which Pasts to Build on, What Futures to Contemplate? *Quality in Higher Education* 16 (2): 189–194. doi:10.1080/13538322.2010.485735.

Turner, R.S. 2011. *Neo-Liberal Ideology: History, Concepts and Policies*. Edinburgh: Edinburgh University Press.

Waters, Mick. 2015. The Gove Legacy. In *The Gove Legacy*, ed. Mike Finn, 12. Basingstoke: Palgrave Macmillan.

Wolf, M. 2005. *Why Globalization Works*. London: Yale Nota Bene.

CHAPTER 5

Where We Learn

5.1 Introduction

It has been suggested in previous chapters that there are systemic pressures which are brought to bear upon education. These have had the consequence of acting to make education tamer in accordance with the way in which the concept of tameness has been described in Chap. 2. However, what has also been indicated is that education is not homogenous. This is especially the case when it comes to the different levels of education in terms of how it is organised and provided for. This chapter considers some of these differences.

The developments which are being presented as leading to tameness have been established as resting upon an understanding of education as being a process which is tasked with achieving particular outcomes. This may be attractive to some educationalists and policymakers if we accept that tameness introduces a greater degree of certainty to this process. The epitome of tame education is, of course, rote learning. That said, it is easier to see a valid argument for the rote learning of literacy and numeracy than it is for the rote learning of certain, specified poems, something which Michael Gove recommended whilst Secretary of State for Education (Gopal 2012; Cambridge 2014). The danger in each of the examples referred to above though is that we produce the ability to repeat rather than to understand. This was referred to in Chap. 3 as the distinction between surface learning and deep learning.

© The Author(s) 2018
R. Creasy, *The Taming of Education*,
DOI 10.1007/978-3-319-62247-7_5

It is the case that we require children and young people to be educated to a certain level in relation to what are often referred to as key skills such as numeracy and literacy but I would argue that we also require them to understand these. At the same time, we also require pupils and students to understand a range of key concepts and issues which often form the basis of disciplines. Within Higher Education the subject benchmark statements published by the QAA are indicative of this but this does not support an argument in favour of rote learning. If we are to acknowledge the importance of developing creativity and originality, then it is important to establish educational approaches which develop understanding rather than those which promote tameness.

However, although I am not intending to give the impression that rote learning dominates within education in England, there is a strong tendency to focus upon the production of a "right answer". By the time that students enter Higher Education, the idea that there is an unambiguous or right answer often creates problems for students with respect to how they cope with the transition to what can be a very different style of education. This is because they will have had 14 or 15 years of schooling during which they have come to expect that there is a right answer to problems or questions, yet in education as a whole, this may not be the case. However, the focus on passing public examinations can be seen to have contributed to the idea that there is. This has had greater impact on compulsory and further education than is the case within Higher Education. It is accepted that there are some key concepts that students must learn, especially on courses with professional awards, but one thing which characterises Higher Education is a greater concern for what students can do with their learning rather than in the production of the right answer.

It would be wrong however to present a picture of Higher Education as populated by creative and flexible staff (wicked staff perhaps?), but who are faced with tame students. This is not the case. There are certainly tame staff within the Higher Education sector and developments within Higher Education which reflect tameness. Where teachers in schools and colleges may be accused of teaching to the test, there are also teachers in Higher Education who teach to the learning outcomes; there is little difference.

In particular, and in spite of his insistence on the need to adopt a holistic perspective with respect to assessment, the influence of the work of Biggs (2003, 2007, 2011) has done much to establish the role of learning outcomes. The role of Biggs in inadvertently establishing a somewhat rigid approach towards learning outcomes can be seen as being rooted in his principle of constructive alignment, the idea that teachers should align their teaching to focus on supporting the subsequent assessment of learning outcomes. In itself this idea seems perfectly sensible; if students are to be assessed against learning outcomes, then teachers should support them to ensure that they are prepared for such assessment.

However, consider the implications of teaching staff taking the idea of constructive alignment one (logical?) step further and dividing the time allocated to them according to each learning outcome for a module and focusing on the way in which each learning outcome can, and should, be met. For students this may mean a 2-hour class becomes four 30-minute sections with each section devoted to a learning outcome. Similarly, it would not be surprising to see teachers coaching students to explicitly address the learning outcomes within assignments and resisting any discussions which seem to move beyond them. Faced with this approach, it would not be surprising to see students submitting assignments within which the learning outcomes for a module are presented as subheadings within the work. In turn the analogy presented earlier, that education is a process, is reinforced by such a strategy. It should also be noted that this is not the intention of Biggs either. Biggs and Tang (2007, 54) make it very clear that the focus of constructive alignment is on intended learning outcomes "teaching and assessment should always allow for desirable unintended outcomes as these will always inevitably occur when students have freedom to construct their own knowledge". It seems that this element of what Biggs and Tang are saying is something which often gets overlooked.

Although I would consider that the utilitarian and mechanistic teaching approach detailed above is something to be avoided, it is also possible to recognise that from the perspective of a concern with auditing teachers work, or a concern with risk management, this approach has benefits. Rather than seeing this teaching strategy as impoverishing, and leading to a mechanistic educational experience, it could be promoted as a way of achieving managerial or administrative goals.

It might also be the case that such an approach would not necessarily be resisted by teachers. There are some Higher Education teachers who can be seen to readily adopt this type of process approach to their teaching. It is also the case that this is adopted by many when it comes to assessment. As such, there are staff who direct students to quite a significant degree as to what to write and how when it comes to assignments. Similarly, when it comes to marking, there are staff who direct their feedback to detailing the extent to which students have met, or not, learning outcomes. Not meeting a learning outcome can, and is, sometimes used as a reason to award a fail mark to a student's work. This is something which can only reinforce the utilitarian approach adopted by some students and it does little to promote creativity and originality. Approaches such as this, as reported in interviews with Higher Education teachers, will be explored further in Chap. 7.

It may be reasonable then to consider that those teachers who adopt these types of practices, that is to say, teaching and assessing to learning outcomes, would readily accept that education is a process and consider that their job is to get students through the process with favourable outcomes. Such staff may be less concerned with developing creativity and seeing originality in students' work if this moves beyond the boundaries of the stated learning outcomes, or where they know what will attract points in public examinations, and act to restrict what students do accordingly. Such an approach may increase the certainty of higher marks but at the same time, paradoxically, it may not be in the student's best interests. This type of situation seems quite disheartening and many would question why it is that some teachers appear to fall so readily into adopting a utilitarian, and tame, approach.

5.2   The Social and Economic Context of Education

It would be very easy to be critical of teachers who adopt tame approaches to their work on an individual level and to claim that it is some weakness or inability on the teacher's part which leads them to embrace tameness. The next step would be to juxtapose tame teachers with those teachers who demonstrate more wicked approaches to teaching, incorporating more creativity into their work, and see tame teachers as somehow lacking. Such an approach may sit easily with ideas about individualism, but can we reduce arguments to individual abilities? If we do we are more likely to fall into the trap of seeing good teachers as being born, not made, and undermining the value of both education and training. The fact is that individual teachers and educational providers do not exist in a vacuum. Education is not something that is immune from external or internal forces, as has been shown. How a society makes provision for education will always be subject to competing arguments regarding what is best and this will always be subject to social, political and cultural pressures. Therefore, as societies change it is inevitable that the provision of education will change but how it changes is always the consequence of human actions.

It was noted previously that the tripartite system as established by the 1944 Education Act within the UK served the nature of the economy at the time. The period following the Second World War was dominated by industrial work. The Grammar schools provided an education for those who were seen as being headed for non-manual work with technical schools providing an education to support skilled workers within the industry. There was no great need for most workers to have educational qualifications though, and for quite some time, the secondary modern schools simply provided a basic education with no exit awards. Chapter 2 introduced ideas about the knowledge economy and the knowledge society and, in doing so, demonstrated that the economy and society of the early twenty-first century is no longer as it was in the mid-twentieth century. At the same time, as the economy has changed so society has changed and UK society is no longer as rigid in terms of either class or gender so it is inevitable that how we provide for education has also been subject to change.

What can be seen then is that as ideas about the nature of society have changed so this has been reflected in other changes with respect to both politics and policy. Because of these changes, the ways in which we understand the purpose of education and how we conceptualise the ways in which it should be provided have also changed (Chitty 2014). Within my lifetime we have moved from ideas which argued for schooling for all, encapsulated by comprehensivisation being replaced by the idea of significant differentiation so as to satisfy demands for choice. As such education can be seen as a sector of policy which demonstrates very well how ideas can shape policy as will be discussed below. Inevitably, changes may do more, or less, to promote wickedity or impose tameness.

5.3   LEARNING LEVELS AND THE COMPULSORY SECTOR

The idea presented in Chap. 2, that education has come to be seen as increasing in importance, is not particularly new. The history of education in England is one of continual expansion with respect to provision and of change with respect to pedagogy across all sectors. What we have now is a situation whereby individuals are much more accepting of a view of employment as being competitive, and this is underpinned by an almost constant system of testing providing the basis for self-comparison. What this does is to emphasise the hierarchical nature of contemporary education. Such hierarchy can be seen in both the levels of education, as reflected in the designations of Early Years, Primary, Secondary, Further Education and Higher Education but also in the established use of positioning educational institutions and educational outcomes in the form of league tables. At the same time, the pressure on educational institutions to be successful in respect to the outcomes of pupils and students is seen by some as leading to grade inflation. The notion of success translates easily into achievement and there seems to be increasing pressure within the English system to continually demonstrate increased levels of achievement. This of course can cause problems if it just results in more awards being made in some upper band. Such a concern can be seen in respect to how changes have been made to the English national examinations at the General Certificate of Secondary Education (GCSE) level taken by pupils, traditionally, in their last year of compulsory schooling.

It is noticeable that the revised GCSE award scale that has been introduced in England from September 2015 (with the first awards being made in August 2017) inverts the manner in which the original GCSE awards were made. In the original GCSE award structure, the top grade was A, and awards were made from A to G. This was amended in 1994 with the introduction of the A*, an award established to identify and reward the best performing candidates at this level. In the new GCSE scale, the highest award that is expected to be made is 9 with 1 being the lowest. In comparison with the previous GCSE scale, a grade 9 is established at a higher level than the existing A* with grade 7 as corresponding to grade A (Ofqual n.d.). Of course, in this new grading system, it becomes far easier to extend the award scale in the future should that provide political capital; establishing a grade 10 as the highest grade will be less contrived than was the introduction of A*. Spinal Tap's customised amplifiers spring to mind. The changes to the ways in which GCSEs are awarded is pertinent because throughout the twenty-first century, it was the case that achievements, as reflected in the grades awarded, were rising each year, something which was only halted by other changes to the system affecting results in August 2016 (Adams and Weale 2016).

That said, even if grade 10 is introduced, it will still be a GCSE, and it still represents level 2 of the National Qualifications Framework (NQF). A hierarchical representation of education can be seen in the NQF. The NQF establishes the value of different academic and vocational qualifications in a system running from entry level to level 8. The standard school level qualification in England falls into levels 1 and 2 where level 1 reflects GCSE grades D–G and level 2 reflects GCSE grades A*–C (pre-2017) or level 1 equates to grades U–3, with level 2 being grades 4–9 from August 2017. Further Education is ostensibly positioned at level 3 (e.g. A levels; BTEC National Diplomas) but Further Education Colleges and Sixth Form Colleges are not restricted to the provision of level 3 courses. Both will generally offer courses below level 2 and many Further Education Colleges offer courses above level 3. Higher Education reflects levels 4–8 (e.g. Certificate of HE; BTEC Professional Diploma, Bachelor Degrees, Masters Degrees and higher awards). This aligns with the Framework for Higher Education Qualifications (QAA 2014; Moon 2002). In this way the NQF also acts to shape how we understand education by focusing upon the position of qualifications within a hierarchical model, albeit at a rather superficial level.

With respect to claims about the numbers achieving higher grades going up, it appears that pupils and students are getting cleverer, or more adept at passing assessments, or that markers and awarding bodies are lowering standards. However, such concerns can be seen as intrinsic to any particular award or course of study. What is not possible is for a performance to be so good that it merits the award of a higher level. In general, in English schools pupils are educated in year groups and although pupils may be entered for awards early, exceptional performance does not bring an award beyond that which has been entered for. Similarly in non-compulsory education, it seems that only the award that is entered for can be awarded. Even in universities, where the award is made by the institution, there is no tradition of rewarding exceptional performance with a higher award. In this way it seems that there are some real ceilings. Furthermore, it is obvious that in establishing the new GCSE award points, there has been a concern to make awards in similar patterns to the existing GCSE. Ofqual is clear in pointing out that although the awards may look different, "Broadly the same proportion of students will achieve a grade 4 and above as currently achieve a grade C and above. Broadly the same proportion of students will achieve a grade 7 and above as achieve an A and above" (Ofqual 2014, np).

This final point, regarding the proportion of candidates in a GCSE examination who will receive a particular grade, reveals an approach towards how we understand learning that creates some degree of tension and points to another aspect in respect of how education has been tamed: the role of the distribution curve. Although the distribution curve is a conceptual device for representing typical populations, within education it has often been used in a way which has some regulatory influence on imposing outcomes.

Up to 1987 the GCSE and A level public examinations were awarded based upon the principle of normative referencing. That is to say that the boundaries between grades could be moved so as to result in a regular proportion of awards being made at each grade band. This practice exerted pressure on cohorts in a way which suggested that they should reflect a normal distribution curve. In recent years examining bodies have been guided by Ofqual and now work on the basis of comparable outcomes (Beach 2015). The principle here is that exams are made fair on a year by year basis by setting grade boundaries which produce comparable outcomes. Beach explains this as such:

> All exam boards must have awarding processes that meet Ofqual's rules, which are set out in a code of practice. The basic principle is that if the group of students (the cohort) taking a qualification in one year is of similar ability to the cohort in the previous year then the overall results (outcomes) should be comparable. To do this, exam boards produce a reference matrix, based on the results of a previous cohort. This reference matrix, which compares Key Stage 2 attainment with the GCSE grades that this previous cohort achieved, is applied by each Exam Board to predict outcomes for the current cohort. For A levels, the starting position for predictions is the results achieved in GCSEs. (Beach 2015, np)

In adopting this approach, Ofqual effectively locates learning within the individual. Such an idea has a great deal of contemporary currency within society as a whole. There is an ease with which discussions about education come to be overlaid with ideas about ability and where ability is seen as in some ways fixed or immutable (Stobart 2014). There is some indication here which suggests that this can be seen as a form of biological determinism but where the focus is on the ability to learn and where any given population has a fixed ability to learn that can be summed up as the variance which is illustrated within a normal distribution curve. This sort of thinking fits easily with ideas about the provision of different types of education, whether that be for what would once have been referred to as remedial education or in relation to those pupils who are designated as gifted and talented (Sutherland 2012; Goodhew 2009). Of course the aim is to respond to accusations that exams have become easier in the face of rising examination results that happened after norm referencing was stopped. However, Warwick Mansell (2012, np) identifies an essential weakness in this system as it:

> … means that the quality of work produced by each cohort in each exam would appear to have little or no bearing on considerations as to whether more pupils should receive good grades in any particular year, or fewer. In fact, the only way for a year group to convince examiners that, collectively, they deserve higher grades in their GCSEs would be to have performed well not in those exams themselves, but in key stage 2 SATS five years earlier. Not only that, but any work that secondary schools do collectively with these pupils, over the five year period leading up to GCSEs, will not be able to have any impact on the overall national results picture, because of the way this system now works.

This is clearly a source of tension as England currently has an education system where the government demands year on year improvements, as measured by outcomes but this is in a system which effectively prevents an overall rise in awards. So, in spite of the many pressures upon teachers and schools to do better, and, in some cases, where better resources have been provided, it seems that the system itself cannot realistically produce what the government demands.

In effect Ofqual has established a system which could accommodate the awarding of higher grades, but only where results at key stage 2, at roughly age 11, were also higher than for previous cohorts, but the opposite is also true, awards may fall based upon key stage 2 SATs and in each case the boundary between grades can be, and is, subject to being changed.

The issue of the comparative quality of marks as raised above is complex and it does create concerns. In contrast to the compulsory education sector, at the level of Higher Education, the checks on the system are much less rigorous and it is also far easier to find that a cohort as a whole does very well or very poorly with a corresponding rise or fall in overall marks. This is because in general, marks are allocated by criteria. If a student meets the criteria, then the appropriate mark is awarded. Within the Higher Education sector, it appears that marks are purely awarded on merit, yet it is not at all uncommon to discuss the overall distribution of marks in any particular module in a way that suggests that a normal distribution curve should be evident with questions being raised when this is not the case.

This discussion of marks has been offered to give an indication of the way in which governments can act to change how education is provided for and/or experienced. Other examples will be offered when appropriate as it is obvious that education does not just happen, it must always be understood as taking place within a social context. In the case of the ways in which governments have acted to change approaches to public examinations and marking, it might be argued that this is for good reasons, especially if the focus is a concern that changes reinforce public trust in the awards that are made. The following section, detailing changes that have been made to the Further Education sector since the early 1990s, however, illustrates that sometimes changes are almost wholly rooted within ideological concerns and that, far from increasing trust in education, they may do significant damage.

5.4   FURTHER OR POST-COMPULSORY EDUCATION

If it is the case that proponents of the knowledge economy thesis are correct regarding the increasing importance of education to the economy, then it appears obvious that there needs to be some capacity to provide for this within the education system. This is also the case with respect to the sort of education that is applied to work roles and the needs of the economy, though that is not to say that training is the answer. Training is important within a modern economy but so is education. Historically, the development of the Further Education sector was associated with vocational courses acting to provide the skills and training required of industry and commerce, and, possibly because of this, it has often occupied a less obvious position with respect to its educational provision. Further Education as a sector is often referred to as the Cinderella sector and, since the early 1990s, has been subject to significant and widespread political interference (Hayes et al. 2007; Hyland and Merrill 2003; Cripps 2002), in a way which has resulted in an almost permanent state of crisis. This section will not only set out to illustrate the ambiguities of Further, or post-compulsory, Education, it will also illustrate how political and ideological forces have acted to refashion a key sector of educational provision within England on ideological grounds. As part of a consideration of these changes, this section will also illustrate how the changing context of Further Education Colleges in particular has accommodated a move towards tame education in a number of ways.

The compulsory education sector, schools, can be seen as establishing the base level of education required of individuals, but for those individuals to contribute to the economy more effectively, some continuing education is often required. In a simple sense, and with reference to the NQF as presented earlier, Further Education is the level of education which exists between compulsory education, as provided by schools, and Higher Education. Although it was referred to as Further Education for many years, in recent years the term post-compulsory education and training has often been used to refer to this sector although recent policy developments regarding the age at which young people leave education blur the distinction between education that is compulsory and that which is not. It is also pertinent to acknowledge that in recent decades many private providers of training have emerged in response to funding policies and that these also fit into the post-compulsory education and training sector. However, as my concerns are with the State sector, and with education rather than training, I will continue to use the term Further Education. In relation to the NQF, as described previously, Further Education is most accurately described as education which is at level 3. That may be where Further Education fits but is not a sufficient explanation to say what it is especially when it is evident that education at level 3 may be provided for by schools, Sixth Form Colleges and Further Education Colleges.

The distinction between compulsory education and Further Education is also complicated however by the recent introduction of a policy which asserts that all young people aged 16–18 should be engaged within one of four possible scenarios:

- Full-time education (e.g. at a school or college)
- An apprenticeship or traineeship
- Part-time education or training combined with one of the following: employment or self-employment for 20 hours or more a week
- Volunteering for 20 hours or more a week (DfE. 2015)

This policy blurs the distinction between schools, which were previously seen as compulsory, and Further Education which was previously optional, that is to say, post-compulsory. Since 2014, all young people leaving year 11 are now required to be in one of the four categories detailed above until they reach their 18th birthday. Alongside this the Further Education sector is further blurred by the long-standing policy of accommodating school pupils in school year's 10 and 11, those between 14–16 years of age, for the purpose of taking vocational courses (Lumby 2007), together with the long-standing provision of Higher Education courses in Further Education Colleges (Creasy 2013).

Hussey and Smith (2010) attempt to explain how Further Education differs from Higher Education by saying that it is concerned with practical and vocational training but, crucially, where this does not involve critical analysis. In relation to this, and in seeking to distinguish between Higher Education and Further Education, it is clear that Higher Education Institutions and Further Education Colleges generally take a very different approach to research and scholarly activity. The fact of this different approach regarding research and scholarly activity can be seen to act as a reliable marker of distinction between two sectors which sometimes appear to overlap.

In practice neither research nor scholarly activity can be said to be as important in the construction of the identity of the Further Education sector in the way that it is within Higher Education (2009). This is evident when the Chair of the Association of Colleges HE Group (Chris Morecroft) states "… I am not saying we are better than universities, but we are different and can give value for money through intensive teaching programmes without the need to be concerned about protecting costly research" (Nash 2010, np). Morecroft's sentiments may appear to undermine the activities of those Further Education College staff that are engaged in research, but in making this claim, he was in a strong position to influence both the activities of Further Education Colleges and the values that they hold. As such Morecroft can be seen as sending a clear message to the Further Education sector which negates the value and role of research.

Although the Further Education sector may often be characterised by practical and vocational training, it is certainly not restricted to it. Many Further Education Colleges have been engaged in the provision of what might be referred to as academic courses such as A levels and Access to Higher Education courses (courses aimed at providing an alternative route into Higher Education for mature students who do not possess the traditional entry requirements). Sixth Form Colleges, which are often focused on GCE A levels, should also be seen as residing within the Further Education sector, but there are significant differences between Sixth Form Colleges and General Further Education Colleges. Sixth Form Colleges have tended to be smaller than general Further Education Colleges with a much narrower range of courses being offered and which attract, on the whole, 16-year-old school leavers. The social context of educational provision can be seen in the fact that Sixth Form Colleges have traditionally been funded more generously than general Further Education Colleges. This is in spite of Further Education Colleges having a more challenging remit and suggests that Sixth Form Colleges have been valued more highly in recent decades. Further Education Colleges, then, can be distinguished from Sixth Form Colleges on the grounds that the ethos, provision and funding can be seen as having been quite different for each type of college.

5.5   FE Transformed

As a major provider of education and training, the Further Education sector can be said to play a vital role. It is also a sector that has been subject to significant structural and cultural change resulting from the introduction of policies which reflect neoliberal principles (Lucas and Crowther 2016). Although these changes are particular to the UK, the changes reflect the logic of neoliberalism and can be seen as relevant in a global sense in respect of the consequences of adopting market principles within education. These changes have done much to undermine the Further Education sector and can be seen to reflect the argument that education has been tamed.

Within the UK, the 1992 Further and Higher Education Act made both general Further Education Colleges and Sixth Form Colleges independent entities by removing them from local authority control. This is generally referred to as incorporation. Changes were inevitable because of this but it is not the fact that local authorities no longer controlled these colleges that change happened. Change happened because of the ways in which governments have acted upon them and the responses from staff working within the sector. In many ways change was more limited within the Sixth Form Colleges. Further Education Colleges however saw significant and far-reaching change. Some of these changes may have appeared to be quite superficial, resting upon changes to the language of Further Education as can be seen in the renaming of students as customers or the change to job titles. For example, in many Further Education Colleges, Principals came to rename themselves as Chief Executive. At the same time many posts within Further Education Colleges were renamed in ways that reflected business titles rather than educational titles. For example, many colleges sought to remove Senior Lecturer as a post and introduced titles such as Curriculum Area Manager or Director. Some Further Education Colleges sought to remove the title Lecturer all together as part of a move wherein job titles were changed in ways which seemed to privilege management and distance roles from education. For example, a review of FE posts on 3 March 2017 found Grimsby Institute offering positions for Learning Practitioners; across the sector as a whole, most posts were for tutors.

Although superficial in one respect, the changes do give some indication of how senior managers in position at the time of incorporation actively embraced the idea of colleges changing from providing a public service, to becoming a business, casting off those titles that were strongly associated with education and, instead, seeking credibility through imitating business titles.

The changes that followed from incorporation though were not just superficial. For staff in Further Education Colleges, the act of incorporation has led to significantly changed, and worsened, working conditions. For example, after incorporation, during the 1990s, teaching staff in Further Education Colleges experienced significant intensification of work, through increased teaching hours. This was as a consequence of the actions of senior management in Further Education Colleges who embraced the discourse of neoliberalism and sought to adopt more stringent approaches towards the operation of their organisations vis-à-vis the labour process (Mather et al. 2007; Mather et al. 2009; Nash et al. 2007). This saw management within many Further Education Colleges adopting hard-line approaches to push through new contracts for academic staff. Changes to the way that staff within Further Education Colleges are required to work however did not only see significant increases in teaching hours being accompanied by massive reductions in holiday entitlements, it was also accompanied by significant reductions in pay. This was achieved by colleges ceasing to pay in line with existing pay scales and offering lower salaries, often on fixed points rather than using incremental scales. In general existing teaching staff that resisted moving on to new contracts were denied cost of living pay rises until they did.

The outcome of this is that staffing within the Further Education sector has seen not only significant work intensification with increased teaching requirements but also increased levels of control together with worsening conditions of pay and service. For example, the Education and Training Foundation (2016) reports that for the period 2014–2015, the average pay for teachers in General Further Education Colleges was £29,600 and notes that this is much below the average pay of £37,400 received by school teachers. A consideration of trends in pay in the Further Education sector since incorporation in 1993 shows that where pay for teaching staff in Further Education Colleges used to be higher than that received by teachers in schools, this has now reversed. This has significantly impacted upon staffing. By 2002 significant problems with respect to the recruitment of appropriately qualified staff was being reported by the Association of Colleges (Tysome 2002). Although such changes were driven by management on the grounds of achieving business efficiencies, they were very often underpinned by government funding reductions. However, if salaries are reduced and working conditions worsened, this makes it more difficult to recruit staff of sufficient quality (Hartog and Maassen van den Brink 2007).

Over time this in turn impacts upon quality and standards within courses, as well as the student experience (Creasy 2013). An extreme example perhaps of what this means in practice is that in December 2009, a college in Yorkshire advertised for a Team Leader: Higher Education, Childcare. The person specification noted that candidates should hold a minimum qualification at level 3 but that level 4 should be achieved sometime in the future. This was to oversee a Foundation Degree. Foundation Degrees are awarded at level 5, yet this Further Education College was willing to appoint someone to oversee the quality and standards of a course that was positioned above the qualifications that they possessed. It seems very unlikely that this would not have an impact upon both the student experience and the quality of the course. Successive UK governments have expressed a desire to see more Higher Education courses being offered within Further Education Colleges; however, the recruitment problems within the Further Education sector suggest that this may end up being of a different quality compared to similar courses offered within the Higher Education sector. The issue of Higher Education within Further Education Colleges will be discussed in more detail later.

In considering the changes that have been evident as a consequence of the neoliberal reforms within Further Education, it can be argued that the view of education as a process has been firmly embedded within the sector (Cripps 2002). In this way the driving down of staff costs within Further Education gives the impression of management making efficiency savings so as to produce more for less. In a production line setting, this may appear attractive but only in so far as the outputs are able to maintain a consistent quality. The undermining of the quality of teaching staff within

Further Education, together with the intensification of work, will inevitably impact upon the quality of education being provided although if awards are achieved this may be overlooked. In the context of the Further Education sector, the pressure to recruit, retain and award is likely to contribute to the taming of education.

One suggestion for why the Further Education sector has been consistently undermined in recent decades is that alongside the fact that the neoliberal reforms were seemingly welcomed by Further Education managers (Nash et al. 2007), it has little political power compared to the schools sector or the Higher Education sector (Richardson 2007). In part, this may be a consequence of the impact of social class on education. Where Sixth Form Colleges tend to be seen as middle-class institutions providing routes into Higher Education, the vocational nature of Further Education Colleges, along with the ways in which the sector has traditionally provided a second chance for older students, sees it being identified with the working classes. Some ministers may dispute this analysis but the history of Further Education demonstrates that by the twenty-first century, the Further Education sector across the UK has been significantly undermined.

In spite of the policy changes which have led to the running down of Further Education, it is noticeable that this is rarely raised as a major concern. In some ways Further Education as a sector has been effectively depoliticised. For example, a consideration of books that are concerned with the practice of education within the Further Education sector reveals that the massive changes imposed upon both the sector and the staff teaching within it are rarely commented upon. Bryan and Hayes (2007) are a rare voice to reflect upon the negative aspects of how the Further Education sector has been changed by policies introduced since 1993 when Further Education Colleges were removed from local authority control.

5.6   HIGHER EDUCATION

Having considered the rather ambiguous status of Further Education, it is pertinent to consider Higher Education especially as I have already established that creativity and originality are intrinsic to the rhetoric, if not the reality, of this sector and the importance of this with respect to wickedity and tameness. For Hussey and Smith (2010, viii), Higher Education is "characterised by an emphasis upon the mastery of theories, technical and abstract concepts and general principles, together with skills of analysis and critical thinking". In offering this definition though, Hussey and Smith appear to overlook the role of research. This is in spite of its importance within the Higher Education sector. In one sense both the Research Excellence Framework and the Teaching Excellence Framework as applied to Higher Education reinforce why research is important with respect to establishing a definition of Higher Education. It may be more accurate then to assert that Higher Education is seen as being represented in the practices of an organisation where research is valued and where scholarly activity acts to support the maintenance of quality in respect of teaching. Implicit in this is that critical analysis is established as being a key value within Higher Education alongside other values such as an engagement with intellectual issues, autonomy and academic freedom.

The concern with creativity and originality owes much to the place of research within Higher Education. In the section above, it was noted that research is generally absent from the Further Education sector. Within the Higher Education sector though, research has been a key concern since the reform of the universities in the nineteenth century (Beard et al. 1968). The concern with research then can be seen as a core value and this acts to distinguish Higher Education, to some extent, from the compulsory and Further Education sectors. To some extent this also makes the issue of wickedity more relevant to Higher Education than it does to other sectors but that does not mean that it is not relevant for compulsory and Further Education.

We need to be careful though not to set up the Higher Education sector as having clear values along with a sense of identity and purpose and juxtapose this against the compulsory and Further Education sectors where this is presented as being lacking. This may not be as simple as it seems. As with Further Education, the Higher Education sector is not as unambiguous as the term suggests. The landscape of Higher Education is characterised by diversity with some institutions being seen as being of a higher quality, usually those providers who do the most to restrict entry to prospective students or where research appears to be positioned above teaching with respect to status. Because of this the nature of how Higher Education is both understood and provided for is seen as being quite different amongst providers. Consequently, it may be that arriving at a definition of what Higher Education is, is challenging, possibly because of differing experiences and expectations. So, when Stanton (2009) points to the term "academic culture" as representing what Higher Education is, this can be seen as being quite superficial. Academic culture would only be sufficient as a signifier of Higher Education if there was unambiguous agreement regarding what this means. This is not the case.

Additionally, in the same way that the Further Education sector has been impacted upon by government policies, so the Higher Education sector has also been subject to government policies which have changed its position or role. Neave (1996) notes that developments that took place during the 1990s led to the State repositioning itself so that it became a purchaser of Higher Education rather than as the provider of such education. Neave is correct to say that the ways in which the State sought to construct some semblance of a market within education as whole impacts upon Higher Education, and this may be seen as the beginning of changes to how Higher Education is understood. What has happened because of the way in which the State has changed its position is that Higher Education has come to be viewed as a private good rather than as a public good. This change fits with the argument presented earlier regarding the extent to which education has come to be seen as something for individuals to invest in. The consequence of this is that there is a sense in which education is reduced to being seen as a means to an end. That said, Goodlad (1976) illustrates that it would be naïve to suggest that historically students have entered Higher Education with a focus upon self-development rather than qualifications and that this only changed during the 1980s. The historical role of professions such as law and medicine is evidence that employability is something that is intrinsic to the work of the Higher Education sector. It is not something that is a novel development.

The consequences of policy developments as indicated above can be presented as the uncoupling of Higher Education from the State in a move that reflects a more utilitarian approach and where the focus is on the qualification as the key outcome (Taylor 1999). As such, the provider appears to become less important and this in turn facilitates the provision of Higher Education in Further Education Colleges, something which will be discussed further within the following section concerned, as it is, with credentialism.

In considering the idea that Higher Education has become an individualistic and utilitarian issue, in line with neoliberal thinking, it would be easy to consider that it is only the individual that should be concerned with the provider of them or, indeed, of their quality. Any qualification is presented as a proxy measure of an individual's skills and abilities. Because of this society as a whole must have confidence in a qualification as awarded.

One important aspect of change within the Higher Education sector can be seen to be associated with the expansion of numbers entering it. Whereas at one time Higher Education within England catered for a small minority, a number of developments have led to the establishment of a mass Higher Education sector with a much more diverse body of students than was once the case. Alongside this the administration and management of Higher Education has also changed with it increasingly becoming subject to bureaucratic regulation and with greater levels of managerial control. This has also been accompanied by other changes within the sector such as how the two-tier system which existed prior to the 1990s was swept away by the granting of university status to polytechnics (Ainley 1994).

However, this has not meant that the Higher Education sector has become homogenous as a consequence (Crozier et al. 2008) distinctions resting upon the role of research within Higher Education Institutions have increased in importance. For a number of years, there have been pressures on the Higher Education sector to break the link between teaching and research. Such views are seen in policies relating to funding and in developments surrounding doctoral training. The logical development of this is that a further division will open up within the Higher Education sector between Higher Education Institutions that are research intensive and Higher Education Institutions that become focused upon teaching only. It seems clear that currently Higher Education Institutions are not equal and developments which do split researching from teaching are likely to result in a widening of an existing gap within the Higher Education sector.

In sum then we can see how Higher Education as a sector is one which is characterised to a significant extent by the place of research. Taylor (1999) reiterates this by pointing to the values of diligence and of engagement with intellectual issues on an individual level. These coincide with more general values relating to autonomy and academic freedom. The NQF may act to establish where Higher Education sits in relation to the qualifications which it awards, but a Higher Education sector without research would not be in a position to achieve its remit of developing new knowledge. For this reason research must be seen as one of the integral features which define the Higher Education sector, along with the ability to make its own awards. However, no education sector is immune to developments within the society within which it resides and because of this

Higher Education as a sector, like other sectors of education, may be subject to change.

Goodlad (1976) considered the difficulty of defining the values of Higher Education as existing within a pluralist society quite some time ago. For him, societies that lack universal values tend to adopt an understanding of education as a means to an end rather than focusing upon educational values per se. Higher Education, then, may be seen as a system wherein some output is produced, such as graduates or research, or it may be seen as an educational process which acts upon individual students in a qualitative manner. This raises a debate regarding Higher Education as having a social function or Higher Education as having some intrinsic value for self-development. Notably, the latter approach figures less prominently in policies concerned with matters such as social justice or economic performance. The former is more easily recognisable though it is not without tensions. This dichotomy opens up the idea that Higher Education can be seen as a social good or as a private good, introducing a distinction that can be drawn between how Higher Education values itself and how it is valued by society. When the reason for education becomes the output in the form of the award though, we can see how, as was suggested above, the role of the provider is diminished.

5.7   CREDENTIALISM? HIGHER EDUCATION IN FURTHER EDUCATION COLLEGES

Parts of this chapter have sought to establish some conceptual understanding of the levels of education as they exist within England in the early twenty-first century. In some ways the compulsory nature of some levels of education acts to impose a dividing line. At the time of writing, Higher Education is not compulsory although in some ways it is becoming expected of many young people. For young people taking GCE A levels in particular, schools and colleges often tend to assume that this will lead into Higher Education. Alongside this, previous governments may be seen to have been seeking to increase the numbers of entrants to this type of education. That said, it is still on a voluntary basis.

As was demonstrated above though, Higher Education is not homogenous. In general, texts that are focused on Higher Education do so in a manner which locates Higher Education as the concern of universities. However, the provision of Higher Education in Further Education

Colleges demonstrates that universities do not have a monopoly on Higher Education. Higher Education courses are offered in over 200 Further Education Colleges within the UK (Hefce 2015), with the Association of Colleges (2016b) reporting around 159,000 people being enrolled on a Higher Education course in a Further Education College. The Association of Colleges, the body which represents Further Education Colleges, is very active in identifying a stronger future for Further Education Colleges with respect to Higher Education drawing attention to how parents and policymakers often have a "traditional and outdated understanding of higher education" (AoC 2016a, 3). In doing this they draw from government proposals to introduce more competition within Higher Education by facilitating more provision of Higher Education courses outside of universities (DBIS 2016).

In the section on the Further Education sector above though, it was noted how developments since incorporation in 1993 have had serious ramifications for the work of Further Education Colleges with major problems being reported in terms of staff recruitment. If the Further Education sector has such problems, and it is generally accepted that this is the case, then it seems a reasonable question to ask why Further Education Colleges would want to get involved in Higher Education.

One reasonable explanation for this is that for a long time the Further Education sector has been seen as providing opportunities to individuals who, for whatever reason, did not do quite so well at school. Because of this Higher Education in Further Education Colleges can act to fulfil calls for widening participation with respect to Higher Education. As was established above, some universities can be quite inaccessible when it comes to admitting applicants with low or non-existent qualifications, in which case Higher Education in Further Education Colleges provides a useful and laudable function. Most commentators on Higher Education in Further Education Colleges draw upon the discourse of widening participation to support this type of provision although it is apparent that those who study Higher Education within Further Education Colleges do not perform as well as those studying in the Higher Education sector in a number of areas such as pay and access to post-graduate study (Avis and Orr 2016). Such outcomes support the argument that the provision of Higher Education in Further Education Colleges diverts these students away from Higher Education in more prestigious institutions (Jary and Parker 1998).

In reality, few commentators consider the quality of Higher Education in Further Education Colleges in spite of obvious differences. Both Dhillon and Bentley (2016) and Feather (2016) draw on numerous studies which show that the academic culture experienced in Further Education Colleges differs from that in universities, something which must inevitably impact upon how students within Further Education Colleges come to understand Higher Education. Rapley (2014) offers a rare insight into the dissatisfaction felt by Higher Education students immersed within a Further Education culture.

I have commented elsewhere (Creasy 2013) on the weaker aspects of Higher Education within Further Education Colleges, and given the issues reported on above, it returns me to the question of why a Further Education College would want to get involved in the provision of Higher Education. There is no doubt that the imposition of neoliberal principles to the Further Education sector has changed the ethos of Further Education Colleges in a way that has encouraged Senior Leadership Teams to adopt competitive approaches which include seeking to extend their practice into aspects of education that were traditionally outside of their remit. One further reason though may be gleaned from the funding issues that were reported on previously. An important consequence of the introduction of neoliberal policies within Further Education is that the sector has been subject to significant funding cuts over many years. In spite of forcing the pay of teaching staff down and intensifying their work through reductions to course teaching hours in colleges, and requiring teachers to teach more hours, Further Education Colleges find themselves in very precarious financial positions with a number having merged. The ability to charge students' fees far in excess of those charged for typical Further Education courses means that Higher Education courses can become an important source of funding.

There is little to prevent a Further Education College diverting funding for Higher Education into the general budget of the college, and because of this, it could be considered that it is financial considerations that are the driving force behind the growth of Higher Education within Further Education Colleges. Higher Education within Further Education Colleges may be promoted on the grounds of widening participation and access, but it maybe does more to support the operation of the Further Education sector than it does to provide opportunities for students to access Higher Education of a high quality. For example, research is a necessary precondition for teaching in Higher Education (Barnett 2000). It is this which enables organisations, usually universities, to develop and advance, knowledge and understanding, and in doing so engage in a practice that is central to the activities of a knowledge society. From Barnett's position Higher Education involves embedding the value of challenging what is, and what can be, known. Students, he argues, have a right to expect their lecturers to be engaged in research. However, research activity is much less likely to be found in Further Education Colleges because of a combination of factors such as funding differences, values and capacity.

The provision of Higher Education in Further Education Colleges can be seen as a consequence of the emphasis being put on the award that a course of study leads to rather than the experiences that are intrinsic to that study. This returns us to the idea of education as a process with the idea that increasing the numbers of providers of Higher Education will increase access and so raise the numbers with higher qualifications. Such an argument clearly draws upon an acceptance of the knowledge economy thesis (DBIS 2016), but if staff within Further Education Colleges are less qualified, and if resources are poorer, then what is the real value of such provision? It leaves us with an important question regarding Higher Education in Further Education Colleges, is it fit for purpose or is it further evidence of the taming of education?

5.8   CONCLUSION

One reason for considering the ways in which education can be seen to be organised in levels, or sectors, is to illustrate diversity across the educational sector but in a manner that does not focus upon the differences between institutions within levels. In some ways the differences between institutions within levels can be taken as axiomatic. There will inevitably be differences between institutions because of factors such as differing staff, but by considering levels, we can see some of the ways in which the context of each level can be influenced by the social and political context in which they operate but also where the culture and values of each level acts to mediate external influence.

No sector has been able to resist the forces of the State and different governments have acted to change the context within which each sector operates. An example of how the State may change the context of education was illustrated firstly by considering how changes to the awarding of GCSEs impacts upon the schools sector. In respect of such changes, this can be seen to be following on from the points raised within Chap. 3

regarding increasing concerns over achievement. What was argued though was that achievement is very often associated with ideas about ability which are very often portrayed as being individual and relatively fixed. This is something which sits easily with ideas about ensuring that all children achieve their potential.

This idea of ability being an individual trait accommodates arguments for different types of schools very well, but there is also a contradiction with the idea that schools should be offered in ways which demonstrate differences and that attendance at these schools should rest upon parental choice. What this does demonstrate is that the provision of education often rests upon political considerations rather than educational ones. This was demonstrated by considering the role of the Further Education sector and the ways in which it has been transformed in line with political ideology. Such political concerns are not restricted to Further Education though and it can be seen how the logic of markets and competition draws all institutions in all sectors into being focused upon business interests. In this way schools, colleges and universities all come to be changed to some extent in ways that sees them being understood as economic entities rather than educational concerns.

Because of this the view of education as being a process is brought to the fore with concerns about outputs often taking centre stage. Institutions at whatever level that do not appear to perform with respect to the awards that their pupils and students leave with come to be viewed as failing institutions. This places significant pressure upon them to control the process by reducing or removing uncertainty. This pressure acts in ways which contribute to an approach that seeks increasing control over education and in exerting such control makes the taming of education more likely. However, it is the consideration of Higher Education within Further Education Colleges which maybe does the most to emphasise how outputs come to the fore whilst also indicating one of the ways in which the distinction between levels and sectors can be blurred.

The provision of Higher Education within the Further Education sector is often seen as a way of providing greater access to Higher Education in line with concerns for widening participation. However, parallels may be drawn with the US system of community colleges. These also provide access to Higher Education for groups who have traditionally been underrepresented, but there are also concerns that the awards made by community colleges, although being of the same level, do not carry the same value (Jary, Gatley and Broadbent 1998). One factor which may contribute to a lack of equity in terms of value is that, as has been shown, the Further Education sector has significant problems, some of which undermine the ability of this sector to perform. One of the consequences of the neoliberal reforms within Further Education was the way in which senior managers within Further Education have, from the 1990s, readily engaged in confrontation with teaching staff as a means of achieving control. This reflects more general concerns regarding control within education and it is control that is the focus of the next chapter.

REFERENCES

Adams, Richard, and Sally Weale. 2016. A*-C Grades in Dramatic Decline as GCSE Results are Published. *The Guardian*.

Ainley, P. 1994. *Degrees of Difference: Higher Education in the 1990s*. London: Lawrence & Wishart.

AoC (Association of Colleges). 2016a. College Higher Education. [Cited 2 July 2016]. https://www.aoc.co.uk/term/college-higher-education

———. 2016b. *Progress Through Practice: The Future of Higher Education*. London: Association of Colleges.

Avis, James, and Kevin Orr. 2016. HE in FE: Vocationalism, Class and Social Justice. *Research in Post-Compulsory Education* 21 (1–2): 49–65. doi:10.1080/13596748.2015.1125666.

Barnett, R. 2000. *Realizing the University in an Age of Supercomplexity*. Buckingham: SRHE/Open University Press.

Beach, P. 2015. GCSE Marking and Grading. *The Ofqual Blog*.

Beard, R.M., F.G. Healey, and P.J. Holloway. 1968. *Objectives in Higher Education*. London: Society for Research into Higher Education.

Biggs, J.B., and C. Tang. 2007. *Teaching for Quality Learning at University: What the Student Does*. Maidenhead: McGraw-Hill/Society for Research into Higher Education & Open University Press.

———. 2011. *Teaching for Quality Learning at University: What the Student Does*. Maidenhead: Society for Research into Higher Education & Open University Press.

Biggs, John B. 2003. *Teaching for Quality Learning at University*. 2nd ed. Maidenhead: Open University Press.

Bryan, J., and D. Hayes. 2007. The McDonaldization of Further Education. In *A Lecturer's Guide to Further Education*, ed. D. Hayes, T. Marshall, and A. Turner. Maidenhead: Open University Press.

Chitty, Clyde. 2014. *Education Policy in Britain*. 3rd ed. Basingstoke: Palgrave Macmillan.

Creasy, Rob. 2013. HE Lite: Exploring the Problematic Position of HE in FECs. *Journal of Further and Higher Education* 37 (1): 38–53. doi:10.1080/03098 77x.2011.644772.

Cripps, Sandy. 2002. *Further Education, Government's Discourse Policy and Practice: Killing a Paradigm Softly.* Aldershot: Ashgate.

Crozier, Gill., D. Reay, J. Clayton, L. Colliander, and J. Grinstead. 2008. Different Strokes for Different Folks: Diverse Students in Diverse Institutions— Experiences of Higher Education. *Research Papers in Education* 23: 167–177.

DBIS. 2016. *Success as a Knowledge Economy: Teaching Excellence, Social Mobility and Student Choice.* London: DBIS. Edited by Department of Business Innovation & Skills.

DFE. 2015. Policy Paper, 2010 to 2015 Government Policy: Young People [Online]. *HM Government.* https://www.gov.uk/government/publications/2010-to-2015-government-policy-young-people/2010-to-2015-government-policy-young-people. Accessed 3 Mar 2017.

Dhillon, Jaswinder K., and Jon Bentley. 2016. Governor and Course Leaders' Reflections on HE in FE: Strategic Ambition and Curriculum Practice in Two Large Colleges in England. *Research in Post-Compulsory Education* 21 (1–2): 137–150. doi:10.1080/13596748.2015.1125668.

Feather, Denis. 2016. Organisational Culture of Further Education Colleges Delivering Higher Education Business Programmes: Developing a Culture of 'HEness'—What Next? *Research in Post-Compulsory Education* 21 (1–2): 98–115. doi:10.1080/13596748.2015.1125669.

Goodhew, Gwen. 2009. *Meeting the Needs of Gifted and Talented Students.* London: Network Continuum.

Goodlad, S. 1976. *Conflict and Consensus in Higher Education.* London: Hodder and Stoughton.

Gopal, P. 2012. A New Kind of Class Warfare. *The Guardian* [Cited 28 June 2016]. https://www.theguardian.com/commentisfree/2012/apr/03/new-kind-of-class-warfare

Hartog, Joop, and Henriëtte Maassen van den Brink. 2007. Epilogue: Some Reflections on Educational Policies. In *Human Capital: Advances in Theory and Evidence*, ed. Joop Hartog and Henriëtte Maassen van den Brink, 233–235. Cambridge: Cambridge University Press.

Hayes, Dennis, Toby Marshall, and Alec Turner. 2007. *A Lecturer's Guide to Further Education.* Maidenhead: Open University Press.

HEFCE. 2015. Institutions that HEFCE Funds [Online]. Bristol: Higher Education Funding Coucil for England. http://www.hefce.ac.uk/workprovide/unicoll/. Accessed 9 Aug 2017.

Hussey, Trevor, and Patrick Smith. 2010. *The Trouble with Higher Education.* Abingdon: Routledge.

Hyland, Terry, and Barbara Merrill. 2003. *The Changing Face of Further Education: Lifelong Learning, Inclusion and Community Values in Further Education*. London: Routledge.

Jary, D., and M. Parker. 1998. *The New Higher Education: Issues and Directions for the Post-Dearing University*. Stoke-on-Trent: Staffordshire University Press.

Lucas, Norman, and Norman Crowther. 2016. The Logic of the Incorporation of Further Education Colleges in England 1993–2015: Towards an Understanding of Marketisation, Change and Instability. *Journal of Education Policy 31* (5): 583–597.

Lumby, Jacky. 2007. 14- to 16-year-olds in Further Education Colleges: Lessons for Learning and Leadership. *Journal of Vocational Education & Training* 59 (1): 1–18. doi:10.1080/13636820601143031.

Mansell, W. 2012. Ofqual's Apparent Use of Norm Referencing at GCSE [Online]. *NAHT*. http://www.naht.org.uk/welcome/news-and-media/key-topics/assessment/ofquals-apparent-use-of-normreferencing-at-gcse/. Accessed 28 June 2016.

Mather, K., L. Worrall, and R. Seifert. 2009. The Changing Locus of Workplace Control in the English Further Education Sector. *Employee Relations* 31: 139–157.

Mather, Kim, Les Worrall, and Roger Seifert. 2007. Reforming Further Education: The Changing Labour Process for College Lecturers. *Personnel Review* 36 (1): 109–127. doi:10.1108/00483480710716740.

Moon, Jenny. 2002. *The Module and Programme Development Handbook*. London: Kogan Page.

Nash, Ian. 2010. Widening Participation Will Be the First Victim of Funding Cuts: Funding Cuts Could Wipe Out Half of all the College Places That Are Linked with Universities. *The Guardian*.

Nash, Ian, Kathryn Eccleston, and Claire Fox. 2007. Symposium: The Future of Further Education. In *A Lecturers Guide to Further Education*, ed. Dennis Hayes, Toby Marshall, and Alec Turner. Maidenhead: Open University Press.

Neave, G. 1996. Higher Education in Transition: Twenty Five Years on. *Higher Education Management* 8 (1): 15–24.

Ofqual. 2014. Grading the New GCSEs in 2017 [Online]. *Ofqual*. https://www.gov.uk/government/uploads/system/uploads/attachment_data/file/377768/2014-09-12-grading-thenew-gcses-in.pdf. Accessed 28 June 2016.

Ofqual. n.d. *Grading New GCSEs from 2017* [Cited 18 October 2016]. https://www.gov.uk/government/uploads/system/uploads/attachment_data/file/537147/Postcard_-_Grading_New_GCSEs.pdf

QAA. 2014. *UK Quality Code for Higher Education. Part A: Setting and Maintaining Academic Standards*. Gloucester: QAA.

Rapley, Eve. 2014. Horses for Courses, or a Grumble in the Jungle? HE in FE Student Perceptions of the HE Experience in a Land-Based College. *Research in Post-Compulsory Education* 19 (2): 194–211. doi:10.1080/13596748.2014.897510.

Richardson, William. 2007. In Search of the Further Education of Young People in Post-War England. *Journal of Vocational Education & Training* 59 (3): 385–418. doi:10.1080/13636820701551943.

Stanton, G. 2009. A View from Within the English Further Education Sector on the Provision of Higher Education: Issues of Verticality and Agency. *Higher Education Quarterly* 63 (4): 419–433.

Stobart, Gordon. 2014. *The Expert Learner: Challenging the Myth of Ability.* Maidenhead: Open University Press.

Sutherland, Margaret B. 2012. *Gifted and Talented in the Early Years: Practical Activities for Children Aged 3 to 6.* 2nd ed. London: SAGE.

Taylor, P.G. 1999. *Making Sense of Academic Life: Academics, Universities and Change.* Buckingham: SHRE and Open University Press.

The Education and Training Foundation. 2016. *Further Education Workforce Data for England.* London: The Education and Training Foundation.

Tysome, Tony. 2002. FE Crisis Hampers HE Growth. *Times Higher Education Supplement* 1559: 9.

University of Cambridge. 2014. Project Seeks Nation's Most Memorised Poems to Investigate Power of Poetry 'by Heart' [Cited 28 June 2016]. http://www.cam.ac.uk/research/news/project-seeks-nations-most-memorised-poems-to-investigate-power-of-poetry-by-heart

CHAPTER 6

Education as a Process: Assessment, Outcomes and Achievement

6.1   INTRODUCTION

Chapter 1 introduced the idea that education can be seen as a process. This is because the ways in which we view education lend themselves to understanding it as effecting change on the individuals who enter education. Indeed, it would be frustrating to engage in education and not be changed. However, in an industrial process, it is obvious that there is an output in a way that is not clear with respect to education. In an industrial process, raw or primary materials enter the process, are in some way changed or transformed and exit the process in a finished state, relative to that process. However, if we do see education as a process, then we should also be able to recognise that there is no tangible output in the way that there is within industrial processes. The output of education may be a change in the individual being educated but this is certainly not tangible. Measurements of education then are always proxy measurements. In addition to measurement within education always being proxy measurements of change, they are always only partial measurements. Such measurements may be partial by virtue of being incomplete but they may also be partial because of bias with respect to what is being measured.

Seeing education as a process is not a new phenomenon and seeking to establish some measurement of the effectiveness of education also has a long history. As a consequence of this, it has become reasonable to see assessment as integral to education. As such teachers at all levels of educa-

© The Author(s) 2018
R. Creasy, *The Taming of Education*,
DOI 10.1007/978-3-319-62247-7_6

tion will be very familiar with discussions which focus on the results of assessment in a manner which treats such results as the product. Because of this the assessment of learning has become very important, and although this book is not focused on assessment per se, it can be seen that it plays a major part in relation to the taming of education. It is with respect to assessment that teachers often come to see themselves as engaged within a process by which their pupils or students are understood not as individuals, but in terms of the results that they are capable of or do receive. In the UK this can be seen within government calls for improved results and is reflected in claims which assert that some schools are "coasting" (Wiggins 2015; Philips 1999). The term coasting is used in this context to mean that if the school, or, in reality, the staff, were to work harder, then they could help their pupils or students to achieve higher results. It is reasonable to suggest also that in recent years the idea that better results could be achieved under certain circumstances fits very well with the idea that individuals are characterised by possessing individual potential. The concept of potential is often heard being used by government ministers, Ofsted, and by teachers themselves (Ofsted is a regulatory body charged with overseeing standards in schools, colleges and children's centres. Its full title is the Office for Standards in Education). This chapter will draw to a close by considering this further. It starts, however, by considering the idea that education is a process.

So, if education does come to be accepted as a process, as appears to often be the case, it is not surprising that attention becomes focused upon the ways in which uncertainty may be reduced or eliminated. Reducing uncertainty increases confidence that the process will achieve what is required of it. This appears reasonable in two ways. Firstly, if I was a parent, I would want to be confident that my child will receive a good education. In England a good education is generally taken to mean that the results that will be achieved will be high and a great deal of time and effort goes into establishing and publicising those educational providers which are good on this basis. At the same time, education within England is a system which accommodates the existence of selective and fee-paying schools. This has the consequence that a lot of money may also be spent by parents who consider themselves to be buying a good education for their child. Secondly, if I was a student, I would want to be confident that I will emerge from a course with a good qualification, especially when, in the case of Higher Education, I am likely to incur significant costs and/or debts as a consequence of engaging with education. Very often, this is linked to concerns held by students regarding employability, something that will also be considered later.

The problem in both cases is that education is not a process that is applied to a passive individual. Anyone being educated has to be active, they have to take part and engage with the process. What complicates the matter further is that pupils and students do not all come to education in the same state, and this state, sometimes referred to in Early Years education as readiness to learn, does not necessarily remain consistent throughout their educational experiences. This means that education is a complex business. It is something which is influenced by a range of factors beyond the control of the educators. In terms of managing a process then, this is not good and, as such, many strategies and practices have been introduced with the aim of increasing consistency within the educational systems that are in place. Chapter 2 introduced the concept of wicked and tame as something that can be used to make sense of this. What this chapter does is to focus upon issues related to assessment in particular to make the point that assessment can be seen as identifying, or creating, the product of education and that factors associated with assessment, especially the establishment of learning outcomes, contribute to the taming of education.

6.2   TEACHERS AND THE ASSESSMENT OF A STUDENT'S WORK

The assessment of pupils and students may be something that is carried out within an institution but it can also be a nationwide process such as in the case of public examinations. In England, at compulsory levels of education, public examinations tend to be taken at the ages of 16 with the sitting of the General Certificate of Secondary Education (GCSE) and at 18 with the General Certificate of Education Advanced Level (GCE A level). In these public examinations, teaching staff are often not involved in assessing pupils' work in a manner that leads to an award. At the same time, there have been parts of awards, which may involve teacher assessment. However, although this has happened previously to a much greater extent, recent developments surrounding coursework which contributes to a final grade are such that it has generally been removed from the GCSE and GCE A level awards that are typically studied for in English schools and colleges. Because of this teaching staff may be seen as preparing pupils for assessment but are not involved in the assessing of their own pupils themselves. This situation starts to differ in post-compulsory education with a distinction being drawn, for example, between A levels which are examined externally and, for example, Business and Technology Education Council (BTEC) awards which are assessed internally but awarded by an external body. Once again, the teacher of A levels may now be seen as removed from the assessment of their own students, although they may be employed by awarding bodies to mark papers. With respect to awards made by BTEC, teachers are engaged in assessing their own students, though not in determining how the assessment will be carried out.

By the time a student enters Higher Education, however, it is expected that assessments are internal and that teaching staff carry out the assessment. Typically it may be assumed that the award being studied for, especially at undergraduate level, is awarded by the institution at which the student is studying, but the existence of Higher Education courses that are taught within Further Education Colleges means that this may not always be the case. Teachers of Higher Education within Further Education Colleges will be expected to assess a student's work but they will generally have much less input into how work is assessed when compared to teachers within Higher Education Institutions.

At each level, however, it can be seen that the practice of conferring awards means that some form of assessment of a student's work has to be carried out. It is noticeable though that at the level of compulsory education although the English system is seemingly riddled with assessment, these assessments have little bearing on pupils' progress; pupils are not held back in a year group if assessment is not passed in the school system. Once a student enters Further Education, this may change and it definitely changes at the level of Higher Education. Within Further and Higher Education in England although students may, and often do, opt out of some of the teaching that is provided for them by simply not attending, they are unable to opt out of assessment if they are to continue with their studies and achieve.

The issue of assessment is essentially the concern to assure ourselves as teachers, and to assure others, that a student has been changed by the educational process. Assessment makes a judgement about the extent to which a student has learnt something that was intended. As Knight and Page (2007) argue, however, some types of learning, which they assert as being attributes that are valued within Higher Education, such as creativity and critical thinking, are difficult to define and are constantly changing. Knight and Page (2007) refer to such attributes as wicked competencies. This reflects more recent approaches to identify graduate attributes as being an indication of what it means to be a graduate in addition to what might have been learnt as part of studying any particular discipline (Hill et al. 2016; Kalfa and Taksa 2015).

Assessment also has consequences for Higher Education Institutions in a number of other ways, ranging from integrity concerning its practices, to the need to respond to national agendas. Yorke (2008) makes the point that because assessment is carried out for different purposes tensions inevitably arise, which may lead to compromises being arrived at. Some of these tensions may be understood as arising in part from what Barnett (2011) refers to when describing the university as being both bureaucratic and engaged in surveillance. Within Higher Education bureaucracy and surveillance are very often linked to concerns relating to accountability. Assessment may rest upon teaching and learning but it takes on greater significance when understood within agendas of accountability. As such, assessment is not something that simply takes place after a period of teaching and/or learning. Assessment is taken into consideration from the planning stage of a module or programme and is pertinent throughout the lifetime of a module or programme. Typically, Higher Education courses within England are built up out of modules of varying sizes, each of which carries a particular value with respect to the award overall. This is something that was discussed previously when considering how standardisation impacts upon the student experience of learning within Higher Education.

Assessment within the Higher Education sector is normally carried out by teaching staff but the responsibility for assessment is not theirs entirely. This is because they will invariably be working within a particular organisational and national framework. Such frameworks become manifest as the assessment policies which govern what teaching staff can, or are able to, do.

Teachers may be constrained, and frustrated at times, by an assessment policy which appears too rigid or which places undue emphasis upon particular forms of assessment. They may find that the bureaucratic processes referred to by Barnett (2011) with respect to Higher Education mean that assessment becomes a pragmatic task which appears to serve the administration of the institution or awarding body rather than to assess learning. This may reflect the concerns of staff who recognise the complexity of the learning process and who desire an approach to assessment that is able to capture the extent of this. It is the complexity of learning and development which moves us towards an appreciation of the value of the concept of wickedity if we consider that assessing something that is complex, especially where this involves creativity and originality, is rarely straightforward.

For some teaching staff, however, the complexity of learning may pose an essential problem with regard to how they are able to make judgements when assessing students. The teacher who sees complexity as challenging may be relieved if the organisation's policy removes, to a significant extent, the need for them to engage with what is a wicked problem. In one sense, however, this does not remove the problem; it only serves to construct the illusion that the problem has been dealt with. In addition to this, it may restrict assessment so that only particular aspects of learning are considered, as will be shown. This is unlikely to be in the student's best interest.

The wicked nature of the problems faced by teaching staff in assessing student's abilities can be seen in calls from governments that concepts such as employability should be assessed as part of Higher Education courses. In considering the relationship between assessment and employability, it can be seen that what happens is that a judgement that is made about a student's achievements is translated from a consideration of what they have done, to a judgement of what they are capable of doing (Knight and Yorke 2003). This rests upon assumptions being made about future situations being extrapolated from existing assessment practices. As assessment tasks are rarely carried out in real work situations with real problems, there must be some question mark over the ability of teaching staff to assess future capabilities based only on hypothetical or simulated situations. This may be seen as raising issues relating to the fairness of such a requirement. It may also reflect a general belief that such abilities can be assessed by adopting certain procedures which simplify the task. Such an approach represents an aspect of the taming of assessment.

The issue of fairness is important when it comes to considering how assessment is carried out. This holds true for students and for employers. Employers, who use achievements for the purpose of sifting applicants for jobs, and use these to determine who is appropriate, will be concerned that standards are valid. Similarly, assessment must be seen to be fair so as to maintain the trust of students (Flint and Johnson 2011). In pointing to a concern for procedural justice, Flint and Johnson recognise how assessment practices may involve a guessing game which students are drawn into. It is also the case that the complexity of learning at Higher Education level militates against the provision of overly detailed assessment briefs, but this is something that resonates at all levels of education. If students are coached with respect to passing assessments, then we may doubt the extent to which the result is accurate. Whilst students should clearly know how they will be assessed and on what they will be assessed, the assessment process should be a measure of their ability rather than their ability to follow clear guidelines. Institutions and awarding bodies need to employ assessment tasks which provide fair and equitable opportunities for all students to demonstrate what they are able to achieve and be marked accordingly. That said, the extent to which we can fully know what a student has learnt or is capable of may always be contested, especially once we move beyond issues which can, and which it is appropriate to, be rote learnt.

In sum then assessment practices purport to reveal the extent to which a student has learnt something about the issues being studied. However, learning is a complex matter. The complexity of learning and the fact that it always refers to the development of knowledge and understanding that are in the mind of the individual raises questions as to how it is that assessors are able to know the extent to which it has taken place. I argue that we cannot directly know the extent to which a student has learnt something. The quality of the claims that we make in respect of what a student has learnt rests upon the quality and suitability of our assessment practices. As such, how we understand assessment practices and the possibilities for assessment in general is important. It will always be the case that teaching staff who carry out assessment will operate within organisational structures and that these structures may determine how assessment is carried out, but this does not mean that such practices should not be subject to critical evaluation.

6.3   ASSESSMENT AS TAMING A WICKED PROBLEM

The argument that is being put forward within this book is that education in England is being impoverished because it is being tamed. A major factor within this taming of education is the fact that education is increasingly being seen as a process. However, as the process of education is intangible, there is pressure to construct a proxy output; this is achieved through assessment and certification. However, in setting out to assess students' learning, we are faced with a wicked problem. The challenge of revealing what any student has learnt is significant given the extent and complexity of learning especially as we progress upwards through the levels of education.

As has already been noted, the complexity of education poses a challenge when it comes to establishing valid means of assessment. This can be particularly true for the type of soft skills that employers value in graduates, such as critical and original thinking (Knight and Page 2007). So, with respect to the suggestion that the practice of assessment may be seen as a mechanism which serves to tame the wicked problem of assessing the nature of the learning that has taken place, what this leads to is a situation whereby we focus our assessment on those things that are valued but where we then come to value that which we assess (Edwards 2000). In other words, it may not be the extent of learning and development that is being assessed at all, only that which is feasible, or seen as possible, to assess.

In taming the wicked problem of being able to make a judgement about the outcome of learning, we face the risk that we simplify the process by which we do this and, in doing so, downplay the extent and complexity of learning. There can be some value, then, in being aware of the potential of wickedity within assessment. By this I mean assessment that can accommodate and reward creativity and originality. This is because it can serve to remind us that there are benefits to be gained from an assessment strategy and/or practices which are able to preserve the challenge of education and which reflects the richness of the learning experience. As such, there are benefits to be gained from assessment that is wicked rather than tame. The need to recognise wickedity in assessing learning requires a consideration of how it may be possible to capture and represent the richness and complexity of education and learning. In this way, to approach education from the perspective of wicked problems can be seen as legitimate given the interplay between education, its goals and its practices.

The aim of assessment is to reveal the nature of the learning that has taken place. Put like this, the idea of assessment is a simple one. It is tame. Implicitly though it reflects a process which seeks to reveal what another individual both knows and understands, to generate empirical evidence about the individual. There is an ontological aspect to this in that it rests upon an assumption that a change in knowledge and understanding, intrinsic to an individual, can be directly known. This often leads to the mistaken idea that higher levels of cognitive and interpersonal abilities, qualities that are intrinsic to learning, can be accurately measured. Within education as a whole, this approach is bound up with the idea that the operationalisation of abstract understanding to enable measurement to take place is possible. What starts off as a simple idea then becomes the complex task of establishing a process to measure the development of knowledge and understanding, something which only ever exists in an intangible form. As such, rather than the tame problem that appears to underpin assessment, the problem is best understood as being wicked.

As such it is pertinent to consider how certain approaches, adopted in relation to assessment, and which reflect the idea that education is a process, may give rise to the taming of assessment. One particular approach that has become endemic within education at all levels is the establishment, and subsequent assessment, of learning outcomes (Stoller 2015). The value of considering learning outcomes in this discussion is that within contemporary practice, it is usually the learning outcomes that are being assessed. However, as Hussey and Smith (2010, 2008) point out, learning outcomes reflect a misunderstanding in respect of what can be known about the learning and development of students as will be considered.

6.4   How Learning Outcomes Tame Assessment Within Higher Education

Hussey and Smith (2010, 2008) do not deny that establishing the intended learning outcomes of a module or programme has some use to educators as part of the planning process. Indeed, it would be somewhat inconceivable to think that teachers, or others charged with planning an educational programme, do not consider what it is that they expect and want students to learn when they write both programmes and modules. Hussey and Smith accept also that establishing the intended learning outcomes can be used by educators as a tool in enhancing educational practices.

In practice though, although learning outcomes are familiar to most teachers, it can be seen that they are not approached in the same way across all levels. There is a greater sense of them acting as part of the planning process for teaching within the compulsory and Further Education sectors compared to how they are used within Higher Education, though they are not limited to this. For example, the awarding body the Assessment and Qualifications Alliance (AQA) refers to assessment objectives, whilst the awarding body, Oxford, Cambridge and Royal Society for Arts (OCR), refers to assessable learning outcomes. This term suggests what may be assessed but provides some leeway whereby not all assessable learning outcomes will be assessed. Alongside this an OCR A level paper specifies assessment objectives. These assessment objectives are more general themes such as knowledge and understanding and application of knowledge and understanding.

However, in Higher Education in the UK, the actions of the Quality Assurance Agency (QAA) for Higher Education, in particular, have seen Higher Education teachers come to have a much more explicit relationship to learning outcomes with respect to their work. This is because within Higher Education, and to an extent within Further Education, it is teachers who are engaged in assessing the students that they have taught. Furthermore, within Higher Education in particular, it is teachers who write learning outcomes as part of the process by which new programmes and modules are developed and validated. This is not the case for a teacher of GCSE or A levels. The teacher of GCSEs or A levels is not involved in establishing learning outcomes in the same way as the Higher Education teacher often is.

At a basic level then, learning outcomes can be seen as perfectly reasonable aids that are used within the planning of educational courses and which may be used to guide teaching. In this way we could see that their use can contribute to enhancing educational practice. In addition to this though, learning outcomes may be transformed into a mechanism or strategy that is used for the purposes of managing the educational process through the establishment of learning outcomes as thresholds which must be achieved. This is a very different position compared to when we see learning outcomes as existing for the purpose of enhancing educational practice. This is particularly pertinent for the way in which learning outcomes come to be used as a way of managing assessment within Higher Education.

In demonstrating their argument, Hussey and Smith (2010, 2008) point to the role of the QAA in establishing the place of learning outcomes within UK Higher Education. This argument is echoed by Daugherty et al. (2008) who argue that the QAA has been driven by an instrumentalist view of accountability, and in particular, by political concerns, rather than any concern for pedagogical issues. What Hussey and Smith (2010, 2008) argue is that learning outcomes are used to achieve and demonstrate very specific outcomes. A fuller consideration of the factors that have shaped both the landscape and the practices of education over recent decades was offered in Chap. 4; as such this discussion will be limited to considering particular aspects of this scenario.

In considering learning outcomes, we can once again consider that what, on the face of it, appears simple or straightforward is less so in practice. The use of learning outcomes can be confused to an extent by the ways in which varying stakeholders all manage to exert some influence over them for differing purposes (Daugherty et al. 2008). Learning outcomes may appear to be focused upon the consequences of learning but considerations relating to what it is that is valued impact upon how they are selected and established. This reflects the different ways in which learning outcomes are understood and the different uses to which they may be put. This distinction is identified by Prøitz (2010, 123), who argues that learning outcomes come to be used for two different purposes depending upon the conceptual understanding and objectives that are held: "learning outcomes are either perceived as a tool for educational and instructional planning, and curriculum development, or as a tool for measuring effectiveness and accountability". In associating effectiveness with accountability, however, it may be argued that Prøitz is accepting a managerialist discourse. Similarly, Prøitz suggests that this is an either/or situation, failing to recognise that it may be possible to accept them in tandem. These may both be ways of using assessment but there are significant differences. It does mean however that learning outcomes are a contested concept. In turn this tension between the differing ways in which learning outcomes may be used can be seen as influencing the forms of assessment that are adopted which, in turn, reflects the learning outcomes that are specified.

6.5   TYPES AND LEVELS OF LEARNING

Further to the ways with which learning outcomes can be understood though is the nature of education, as was considered earlier. Learning outcomes may be relatively straightforward where the subject matter or skill is similarly straightforward, such as the learning of multiplication tables, but this becomes less clear when we engage with more complex forms of learning such as is often found as individuals move through the different levels of education (Bahous and Nabhani 2011). It becomes even more complicated when the aim is to reflect creativity and originality rather than being focused on the acquisition of some ability or the demonstration of particular knowledge.

In considering the complexity of learning, Biggs and Collis (1982) point to the actual outcomes of learning and argue that a distinction can be made between surface learning and deep learning. It is important to note that I am not seeking to suggest that the terms employed by Biggs and Collis, surface and deep, are synonymous with the terms wicked and tame, but it can be seen that there is some correspondence with respect to what each signifies. The distinction lays in respect of how wicked and tame are being used to refer to how education is being organised. Surface and deep refer to how students respond to education with respect to how they orient themselves towards learning.

The outcomes of learning are then seen as being related to the student's orientation to their studies with two different approaches towards work being identified and similarly characterised as "deep" or "surface" approaches (Biggs 2003; Ramsden 2003; Light and Cox 2001). Surface learning and surface approaches to assessment are generally accepted as being preoccupied with rote learning and repeating information rather than with the development of knowledge and understanding. As such, it is knowledge and understanding that reflects "deep" learning and which is generally accepted as the type of learning that is desirable (Hargreaves and Fink 2006; Biggs and Collis 1982).

Biggs (1999) argues that the nature of assessment practices contributes to the student's orientation to learning and is credited with developing this into an approach to planning learning which he calls constructive alignment. For Biggs, constructive alignment is concerned with how teaching and assessment take heed of what is explicitly stated within the intended learning outcomes of any module or programme. In practice the guiding principle is more likely to focus on whether or not assessment allows a student to demonstrate that the learning outcomes have been met. This makes the writing of intended learning outcomes very important. Hussey and Smith (2008) point to two aspects of this which give them cause for concern. Both relate to the argument that assessment is a practice which has the potential consequence of taming assessment.

The first point made is that learning outcomes establish a threshold approach and that this can lead to a situation where the quality of a response is overlooked. Knight and Page (2007) raise a similar concern. In respect of practical learning outcomes, this may be considered in terms of how well or how effectively an outcome has been demonstrated, though Knight and Page's concerns with wicked competencies demonstrates that this is not as straightforward as it may first appear. In respect of abstract learning outcomes, however, we are returned to a point made above in that assessment rests upon knowing what another person understands about any particular issue. We may be able to recognise that there is a laudable case for developing deep understanding but this approach may be undermined if we treat learning outcomes as being unproblematic as will be demonstrated below.

The second concern raised by Hussey and Smith, however, is that learning outcomes inevitably carry with them a certain degree of reductionism. The consequence of this is that the establishment of learning outcomes can therefore act to constrain learning. This may serve to undermine approaches towards education which seek to develop creativity and originality. As these attributes are seen as intrinsically bound up with Higher Education, it can be argued that the use of learning outcomes within the Higher Education sector may not be achieving the outcomes that are sought. They may be counterproductive.

In developing this point, Hussey and Smith (2010) argue that alongside intended learning outcomes, that is to say, those outcomes that have been predetermined or defined, there are also a range of other learning outcomes which they define as: contiguous, related, incidental and emergent. These are those learning outcomes that are less predictable or even unpredictable and which are rooted in the student's own engagement with the process of education. These may be more accurately described as being the actual learning outcomes (Cowan and Cherry 2012), a term that is also used by Biggs and Collis (1982), albeit in a somewhat different way. For Cowan and Cherry, actual learning outcomes may go beyond what was intended. Although there are predictable and intended learning outcomes which may guide the work of teachers, it is the existence of other learning outcomes which distinguishes education from training. It is these other outcomes of learning that are at the heart of education. Graham (2008) points to this distinction as being rooted in the origins of universities and distinguishes between learning for a practical end and learning for its own sake, though he recognises that these two concepts may overlap.

For example, Brown (2007) reports on how cultural heritage institutions have adopted the use of generic learning outcomes as a proxy measure of what visitors to museums gain from the experience. This is based upon the idea that it can be known what will be learnt and that this can be identified. For Brown, however, it is not predetermined learning outcomes that are being identified, it is emergent learning outcomes that are revealed. This is because it is not possible to predetermine how visitors to a cultural heritage institution, such as museum exhibitions, for example, will engage with the environment.

What should also be evident then is that there are, to all intents and purposes, implicit learning outcomes. These are those learning outcomes which are not made explicit. These implicit learning outcomes are rarely made explicit by contemporary practices of assessment that are driven by a learning outcomes approach. Indeed, a student who submits work which is not focused on the stated, intended, learning outcomes may very well demonstrate what he or she has learnt but could end up "failing" because they have not demonstrated that they have achieved the stated learning outcomes. It is the possibility of this which underpins my concern that tame assessment can impoverish education. Wicked assessment would be able to accommodate the contiguous, related, incidental and emergent learning outcomes which are the consequence of the student's engagement with education. I would argue however that in practice it is easier to find approaches to assessment that are tame than it is to find those that could be characterised as wicked.

In establishing practices that are tame then, I contend that we are impoverishing education. The contemporary approach, which sees education as a process and which pursues outcomes based upon credentials, is one which results in the potential of learning being constrained even whilst educationalists and politicians talk of ensuring that we provide for all children to achieve their full potential. This is certainly a laudable claim, but is it what we are really doing within the contemporary education systems that we provide?

6.6   THE LIMITS TO ACHIEVING OUR POTENTIAL

It is quite common in education circles to hear demands that we must ensure that children are able to reach their full potential. If we place this call within the context of seeing education as a process, then we can see that it is a call which suggests that there are barriers to this within the process itself. However, although much of the argument within this section is concerned with children, it is important to note that with respect to educational opportunities, adults may also find that there are barriers although as will be seen, the barriers may be with respect to entering the process in the first place.

Although schools and colleges are part of the expected growing up process for young people, there are many older individuals who seek to return to education beyond the expected ages that are typical within education. Although many colleges and universities will be able to point to adults achieving very high results from a very low base, there are also many who restrict entry to adults without formal qualifications on the basis of the risk that they pose with respect to non-completion. Maybe I should declare my own position here as someone who entered Higher Education as an undergraduate on the basis of passing a GCE O level at the age of 25 (still the only O level that I have; Sociology, grade B). At the time of writing, I know that the university which employs me on a full-time basis would not admit my 25-year-old self.

Given that so-called mature students are often very committed to their education, the struggles that some face when seeking entry to Higher Education can be seen as a potential waste of talent. However, it is not just the admissions policies of Higher Education institutions which can provide obstacles to such students. In the UK in the early 1960s, a concern that the tripartite educational system was responsible for wasting the abilities and talents of many children led to the introduction of comprehensive schooling. The tripartite system was clearly based upon segregation within education and reflected the economy of the post-war era. In this way comprehensivisation might be seen as recognising the changes that were to come within the economy. By the twenty-first century, the idea of a job for life has been firmly consigned to the dustbin of history yet it is clear that policies do not always reflect this.

During the summer of 2016, the UK government reignited debates regarding selection in schooling, appearing to suggest that England will return to some extent, to the system that comprehensivisation replaced. The rationale behind the calls to return to such a system tends to be promoted as Grammar schools existing as mechanisms for social mobility. This is not a well-evidenced argument but the existing educational arrangements within England make it difficult to assess. It is more accurate to say that Grammar schools as a whole appear to do better by creaming off the most able pupils from a geographical area and that poorer children are not well served by them (Andrews et al. 2016; Coe et al. 2008). There is no strong evidence to indicate that they are educationally or socially beneficial. They do provide some benefits to those pupils who attend them but these will always be in the minority. It is almost unheard of for supporters of the Grammar school system to argue in favour of denying opportunities to most children even though in reality that is what the system does. There are often calls for the return of Grammar schools, far fewer for the return of secondary modern schools, those schools generally populated by the children that were denied entry to Grammar schools under the tripartite system.

Further obstacles or barriers to education can be established through funding systems. Although the phrase "lifelong learning" is often bandied about access to education this very often rests upon funding mechanisms being in place to facilitate this. The introduction of funding restrictions for students seeking to change career paths and take courses leading to qualifications at a level for which they already have seems to deny the economic realities that individuals are faced with (House of Commons 2008).

In considering the obstacles to individuals entering the different levels of the education system, we can see that education does not exist within a vacuum. Education always exists within a socio-political context wherein policies at a range of levels not only influence how education is provided for, they influence who enters education and how it is experienced. The pressures that schools, colleges and universities are under to achieve results mean that it becomes very risky for teachers to take risks and to try out new approaches. Although this is not to imply that change does not happen, for it is obvious that it does, it can be argued that such pressure does exert a conservative influence across education and that this may slow down changes.

At the same time, institutions and teachers are distracted by such pressures in a way which means that individuals come to be viewed by their potential to achieve results for the institution rather than for themselves. There is a dehumanising effect evident here that is masked to some extent by calls to ensure that institutions ensure that all individuals, but children in particular, are able to achieve their full potential. This is one of those phrases which is very powerful in that it is hard to present a counterargument. It is also very seductive. Teachers would, in general, want their pupils and students to do well. They would want them to achieve. In this way it becomes almost inconceivable for a teacher to resist the call that they enable those that they teach to achieve their full potential. There are however three problems with this.

Firstly, arguments based upon achieving potential adopt a positivist position in an ontological sense in how they assert that each individual does indeed have some limit to their potential, some point at which they cannot learn or develop any further. If this represents an ontological position regarding the knowable and finite capabilities of any individual to learn and develop, it follows that some epistemological solution applies which will enable teachers to assure themselves of their role in assisting the individual to achieve that. This then reinforces and legitimises the need for testing.

Secondly, it has the effect, as indicated above of dehumanising the teaching relationship by effectively reinforcing the understanding of it as a process whereby achievement towards potential is only made valid through certification. Because of this potential comes to be seen only as the ability to achieve a level of certification.

Thirdly, it ignores the socio-political context of education as it applies to contemporary education within England. This reflects a neoliberal position in respect of how education has come to be governed by the logic of competition at the level of both the individual and the institution but where structural factors in relation to performance are overlooked in favour of individualist explanations. In adopting such a position, teachers are faced with the cruel optimism of working to increase aspirations and achieve educational success with pupils and students but in ways which effectively ignore the significant disadvantages which arise from social inequalities and which are faced by many (Moore and Clarke 2016).

In this way we can see how the demand to ensure that every pupil or student be enabled to reach their full potential is a rhetorical device. There is no real meaning behind it. One reason for claiming that there is no meaning behind it is, with respect to the idea that is intrinsic to the claim, that we can know the extent of any individuals' potential and that this is fixed. There are shades of predestination within claims about achieving full potential, and although contemporary debates about education may have moved beyond seeing potential as associated with social categories such as class, gender, ethnicity or disability, as was the case in such as the 1944 Education Act, there is still a degree of explanatory potential within these categories which may be called upon to explain or legitimise social inequalities.

In contemporary UK society, there is a strong and readily accepted discourse of choice which may be seen as relevant to this discussion of potential and which demonstrates the complexities of any education system. In turn this also resonates with the idea of legitimising social inequalities and rests quite heavily on the idea of a meritocratic system. It side-steps concerns about social categories such as class, gender, and ethnicity in particular and assumes a degree of individual mobility which also enables it to undermine concerns about regional inequalities. It is the idea that the social formations that are evident within society, and which may be seen as manifest within social inequalities, are the outcomes of individual choices throughout a lifetime. In can be argued that this fits with a neoliberal view of society, though, at the same time, it is an argument which clearly predates neoliberalism.

In UK education the pertinence of choice can be seen very clearly in the Aimhigher project. Aimhigher ran from 2004 to 2010 and was intended to increase the number of young people classed as coming from low-income families entering Higher Education. Again, it would be hard to find teachers arguing against the aims of this programme. The idea of widening participation is valid, but the message encapsulated within the language adopted by the Aimhigher programme is revealing of a particular understanding of society in that the key to improving the numbers of young people from poorer backgrounds entering Higher Education rests within each individual. The solution that was intrinsic to Aimhigher is to raise the aspiration of these young people. As such, raising the aspiration of young people from poorer backgrounds can be seen as establishing within them some motivation for action which in turn is expected to see them choosing to apply for and enter Higher Education.

This has consequences in respect of the social landscape. It clearly locates social inequalities as being the outcome of choices made by individuals. In doing so, it avoids questions about structural conditions which may advantage or disadvantage some, as is explained by the concept of life chances, and, instead, locates achievement within a narrative of personal endeavour. Although the implications for educational achievements may be well documented with respect to how class, gender and ethnicity impact upon it (Reay et al. 2005, 2001; Gillborn and Youdell 1999), these are all reduced to the interplay between families and schools especially where this interplay is seen as supporting, or not, the individual child. This then may be seen as legitimising social inequalities as being a feature of individual character rather than as a consequence of structural features within society. This is particularly the case where educational qualifications come to be cast as the consequence of not only individual effort and ability but also as being a consequence of individual motivation and, to an extent, making the "right" choices. Choosing not to enter Higher Education, or choosing to opt out of education, is presented as an individual failing rather than any weakness within the system. Similarly, parents are required to make the right choice in respect of choosing the best school for their child but it is inconceivable to think that all parents can choose the best school. At the same time, it seems inconceivable for UK governments to think that they may establish a system whereby choice is not necessary.

What can also be seen here is that this creates a potential problem for schools and colleges in that schools and colleges are being judged on their ability to produce more, or higher, achievements in terms of qualifications but where the work which ultimately counts is carried out by pupils and students. This reflects the sports team manager dilemma. The manager of a sports team is charged with achieving good results in the same way that the head teacher of a school, or the principal of a college is, but those results are the result of the performance of each player. In such a situation it is highly unlikely that threats will work, there has to be some degree of coercion or motivation. However, where the sports team player may be motivated by financial rewards in the form of win bonuses, this is an option that is not feasible in a school. One way of enhancing results is in institutions choosing the strongest applicants. In both the schools sector and the Higher Education sector, those institutions which set the highest entry tariffs, which seem to do the most to be exclusive, then appear to gain the advantage of being seen as having the highest standards. In schools which are not selective, one strategy to improve results may be by gaming the system (Ofsted and Spielman 2017). In England this is evident by the possibility of entering pupils for qualifications which offer an alternative to the standard GCSE or A level but which are seen as easier or which provide more certain results.

The number of schools in the UK offering courses such as the European Computer Driving License can be seen as being engaged in gaming in that this is a course that may be taught in a matter of days but which was seen by the Department for Education as being equivalent to a GCSE. As Adams (2016) notes, there are pressures upon head teachers to engage in such strategies which results from schools being cast into a situation whereby they compete with others on the basis of course results. In this way, head teachers are drawn into adopting the sorts of strategies employed by other schools lest they come to be seen as less effective. Even where schools resist the pressures upon them to offer alternative qualifications, there is much to suggest that their approaches towards existing qualifications are being driven by accountability (Finn 2015; Coffield and Williamson 2011; Stobart 2008). As such, the consequence for head teachers in schools that do not do well is likely to be the loss of their job.

In such a pressured situation, there is increased pressure on pupils to rote learn key concepts or buzz words if this means that results are not threatened. What pupils learn in such a system is that there is a right answer. The teacher knows it and the pupil has to learn it. The overall consequence of this is that the analogy of education as a process is reinforced. It is also the case though that the agency which rests with pupils and students, as evidenced by arguments and approaches which rest upon choice and aspiration, creates potential problems for the school in that they introduce variables to the process. As such, the school comes under pressure to exert control over the process so as to reduce the uncertainty that is introduced by those who are expected to be educated. In other words there is pressure upon the school to make the process tame.

In seeking to tame education though, there is the real possibility that enjoyment is removed, and that education becomes a chore, something which can only create counterproductive forces relating to achievement and retention. This is not just with respect to how pupils and students experience education but also how teaching staff experience their work role. This is unsurprising really in that just as those individuals who are being educated bring complexity and uncertainty to the process, that is, pupils and students, so do those individuals who are tasked with teaching. As has been suggested earlier, if there is pressure to achieve a certain level of results, then it is understandable that some roles within educational institutions will turn their attention to reducing the scope for uncertainty, not only in terms of those being educated but also those who are the educators. It will not be surprising then to find that teaching staff are subject to pressures which may be seen as taming them. Though teachers may start out with, or seek to maintain, a pedagogical approach which is focused on pupils or students, this can be distorted by the demands of an educational system which is concerned with the production of credentials.

6.7   CONCLUSION

The aim of this chapter has been to explore the relevance of the concept of wicked and tame in understanding how it applies to aspects of education such as assessment practices and to consider also some of the ideas that surround the notion of achievement. In particular it offers further discussion of the idea that education is a process and considers what this means for education. Assessment is important to those who see education as a process because of the way that the award, or credential, comes to be cast as the output. In turn this supports the arguments which call for all children to achieve their potential, notwithstanding the fact that such potential can never be known, nor can any unambiguous method for measuring it be arrived at. It is also the case that there are characteristics of the system which impact upon the ability of children and adults to achieve and which rest upon issues related to admissions. In sum, this chapter has presented an argument that the complexity and richness of learning makes assessment of it a wicked problem but that this is often overlooked. In this way assessment practices may be seen as taming the wicked problem of assessing learning by focusing upon intended learning outcomes. The concern is that tame education is counterproductive to the potential of education at all levels.

What is required is an assessment strategy which is able to preserve the potential wickedity of learning. This will help to ensure that assessment is a system for evaluating learning rather than a system for ensuring accountability. To achieve this it is necessary to consider what our assessment practices do and why they do it.

When planning assessment there is a need to ensure that the methods and criteria that are adopted are compatible with outcomes which will be valued. This should not however be restricted to the intended learning outcomes but should accommodate contiguous, related, incidental and emergent learning outcomes also as these will reflect the actual learning outcomes. An assessment task which is able to demonstrate and reward these types of learning outcome will be more able to accommodate the complexity and richness of learning. Achieving this may mean that there is a need for a reorientation of the approach towards assessment.

For teachers who are engaged in the practice of assessing their students for the purposes of making an award, the benefits of such an approach are that assessment practices will draw upon the exercising of professional judgement and may contribute to their own learning as contiguous, related, incidental and emergent learning outcomes are revealed. For the student the benefits are that the full range of their learning can contribute to their assessment and ultimately to their awards. Alongside this it is more likely that wicked assessment will provide a better student experience by being able to accommodate their interests to a much greater extent. But there are also benefits to be gained for society in that modern economies rely increasingly upon intellectual capital and this rests upon creativity and originality. What is ironic is that in spite of government policies which ostensibly promote the benefits of creativity and originality in terms of their rationale, the space for achieving these is squeezed out within a neo-liberal system that ultimately privileges efficiency. That said, there are political benefits to be gained from establishing an education system which appears to be effective. For politicians the outcomes of education may be held up as the success of their policies or derided as the failures of the policies introduced by others, and so reinforce arguments for change, but such arguments often rest upon a superficial consideration of statistics only. The quality of the awards which constitute the statistics being used tends to be taken for granted. The measure of success is apparently not the quality of the output, it is the quantity. If that is the case, then it can be seen why it is that politicians, and some educators also, may be drawn to the taming of education if it is that tame education guarantees outputs in a way that wicked education cannot.

REFERENCES

Adams, R. 2016. Schools Under Scrutiny on Crackdown on League Table 'Gaming'. *The Guardian*.

Andrews, Jon, Jo Hutchinson, and Rebecca Johnes. 2016. *Grammar Schools and Social Mobility*. London: Education Policy Institute.

Bahous, R., and N. Nabhani. 2011. Assessing Education Programme Learning Outcomes. *Educational Assessment, Evaluation and Accountability* 23 (1): 21–39.

Barnett, R. 2011. *Being a University*. Abingdon: Routledge.

Biggs, John B. 1999. *Teaching for Quality Learning in University*. Buckingham: Society for Research in Higher Education and Open University Press.

———. 2003. *Teaching for Quality Learning at University*. 2nd ed. Maidenhead: Open University Press.

Biggs, John B., and K.F. Collis. 1982. *Evaluating the Quality of Learning*. New York: Academic Press.

Brown, S. 2007. A Critique of Generic Learning Outcomes. *Journal of Learning Design* 2 (2): 8.

Coe, Robert, Karen Jones, Jeff Searle, Dimitra Kokotsaki, Azlina Mohd Kosnin, and Paul Skinner. 2008. *Evidence on the Effects of Selective Educational Systems*. Durham, NC: CEM Centre, Durham University.

Coffield, Frank, and Bill Williamson. 2011. *From Exam Factories to Communities of Discovery: The Democratic Route*. In *Bedford Way Papers*. London: Institute of Education.

Cowan, John, and Diane Cherry. 2012. The learner's Role in Assessing Higher Level Abilities. *Practitioner Research in Higher Education* 6 (1): 12–22.

Daugherty, Richard, Paul Black, Kathryn Ecclestone, Mary James, and Paul Newton. 2008. Alternative Perspectives on Learning Outcomes: Challenges for Assessment. *Curriculum Journal* 19 (4): 243–254. doi:10.1080/09585170802509831.

Edwards, C. 2000. Assessing What We Value and Valuing What We Assess? Constraints and Opportunities for Promoting Lifelong Learning with Postgraduate Professionals. *Studies in Continuing Education* 22 (2): 201–217.

Finn, Mike. 2015. The Gove Legacy and the Politics of Education After 2015 (2). In *The Gove Legacy*, ed. Mike Finn, 10. Basingstoke: Palgrave Macmillan.

Flint, Nerilee Ra, and Bruce Johnson. 2011. *Towards Fairer University Assessment: Recognizing the Concerns of Students*. Abingdon: Routledge.

Gillborn, D., and Deborah Youdell. 1999. *Rationing Education: Policy, Practice, Reform and Equity*. Buckingham: Open University Press.

Graham, G. 2008. *Universities: The Recovery of an Idea*. Exeter: Imprint Academic.

Hargreaves, Andy, and Dean Fink. 2006. *Sustainable Leadership*. San Francisco, CA: Jossey-Bass/Wiley.

Hill, Jennifer, Helen Walkington, and Derek France. 2016. Graduate Attributes: Implications for Higher Education Practice and Policy. *Journal of Geography in Higher Education* 40 (2): 155–163.

House of Commons, Innovation, Universities Science and Skills Committee. 2008. *Withdrawal of Funding for Equivalent or Lower Level Qualifications (ELQs)*. London: The Staionary Office.

Hussey, Trevor, and Patrick Smith. 2008. Learning Outcomes: A Conceptual Analysis. *Teaching in Higher Education* 13(1):107–115.doi:10.1080/13562510701794159.

———. 2010. *The Trouble with Higher Education*. Abingdon: Routledge.

Kalfa, Senia, and Lucy Taksa. 2015. Cultural Capital in Business Higher Education: Reconsidering the Graduate Attributes Movement and the Focus on Employability. *Studies in Higher Education* 40 (4): 580–595.

Knight, Peter, and C. Anna Page. 2007. *The Assessment of 'Wicked' Competences*. Milton Keynes: Open University Practice-Based Professional Learning Centre.

Knight, P.T., and M. Yorke. 2003. *Assessment, Learning and Employability*. Maidenhead: SRHE/Open University Press.

Light, G., and R. Cox. 2001. *Learning and Teaching in Higher Education: The Reflective Professional*. London: Sage.

Moore, Alex, and Matthew Clarke. 2016. 'Cruel Optimism': Teacher Attachment to Professionalism in an Era of Performativity. *Journal of Education Policy* 31 (5): 666–677. doi:10.1080/02680939.2016.1160293.

Ofsted, and A. Spielman. 2017. Amanda Spielman's Speech at the ASCL Annual Conference. HM Govt [Cited 24 March 2017]. https://www.gov.uk/government/speeches/amanda-spielmans-speech-at-the-ascl-annual-conference

Philips, Jane. 1999. Not Learning, But Coasting. *Checklist for School Governors in Great Britain* 4309: 30–30.

Prøitz, Tine S. 2010. Learning Outcomes: What Are They? Who Defines Them? When and Where are They Defined? *Educational Assessment, Evaluation and Accountability* 22 (2): 119–137. doi:10.1007/s11092-010-9097-8.

Ramsden, P. 2003. *Learning to Teach in Higher Education*. 2nd ed. Abingdon: RoutledgeFalmer.

Reay, D., M. David, and S. Ball. 2005. *Degrees of Choice: Social Class, Race and Gender in Higher Education*. Stoke-on-Trent: Trentham Books.

Reay, Diane, Jacqueline Davies, Miriam David, and Stephen J. Ball. 2001. Choices of Degree or Degrees of Choice? Class, 'Race' and the Higher Education Choice Process. *Sociology* 35 (4): 855–874. doi:10.1177/0038038501035004004.

Stobart, Gordon. 2008. *Testing Times: The Uses and Abuses of Assessment*. Abingdon: Routledge.

Stoller, Aaron. 2015. Taylorism and the Logic of Learning Outcomes. *Journal of Curriculum Studies* 47 (3): 317–333.

Wiggins, K. 2015. 'Good' Schools May Be 'Coasting', Too. Times Educational Supplement. Times Supplements Ltd.

Yorke, Mantze. 2008. *Grading Student Achievement in Higher Education: Signals and Shortcomings*. Abingdon: Routledge.

CHAPTER 7

Taming Assessment in Higher Education

7.1 INTRODUCTION

By now it should be apparent that my aim in writing this book is to make sense of the ways in which education has developed over the last few decades but that this endeavour has not been taken from a neutral standpoint. I am approaching this from a critical position. This does not imply that I favour some anarchic approach to education wherein the education that pupils and students receive is wholly at the whim of whoever is teaching them at the time. That is not the case. There are benefits to be gained from having a structured and ordered approach to the provision of education, and I am not so naïve to believe that students would take their education more seriously should we do away with the assessments that lead to formally recognised qualifications. My criticism however stems from a growing concern that contemporary approaches towards education are becoming so rigid that it is becoming counterproductive. This sees education becoming increasingly tame.

The previous chapters have put forward an argument which illustrates how a range of factors act to shape the practice and provision of education in England. Such factors should not be seen as unique to England though and will be familiar in other parts of the world. These factors intersect and overlap. It is not that one is more important than any other but rather that they combine in ways that shape how education is organised, practised and experienced. As such, it can be seen that education is subject to complex

R. Creasy, *The Taming of Education*,
DOI 10.1007/978-3-319-62247-7_7

and diverse forces and because of this it can sometimes be difficult to resist particular developments. What has been argued though is that recent developments have had the consequence of taming education, of reducing it to a process within which particular actions lead to particular outcomes and where those outcomes are generally seen as qualifications rather than abilities or in terms of self-development. I have approached this from the position that this is not good, that this impoverishes education in respect of how it becomes focused upon achieving awards and how pupils and students come to understand assessment tasks as having a right answer.

One major problem with this is that a belief that there is a right answer guides activities into searching for the answer rather than opening up learning. This is why the concept of wickedity has value, especially when understood as part of a continuum with tameness. Within education wickedity can be seen as accommodating unexpected outcomes. Wickedity accommodates new ways of thinking which are unlikely to be accommodated in tame systems. This chapter explores the extent to which wickedity and tameness are evident within one sector of education, Higher Education, by exploring how some staff understand assessment.

As was outlined earlier, the concept of wicked and tame emerged in the discipline of town planning and refers to the way in which the complexity of some situations means that what works in one situation may not necessarily work in another. Although this resonates with education at all levels, it can be seen to have particular relevance when considering the work of Higher Education Institutions. This is because in seeking to establish the distinction between Higher Education and other levels of education, it is commonplace to hear the concern that Higher Education endeavours to nurture originality and creativity with respect to what it seeks from students. Higher Education is concerned with generating new knowledge and new understandings. As such it can be argued that the modes of assessment within Higher Education are important in achieving this aim. Because of this, education that is tame is impoverished as a consequence of limiting the horizons of students.

A consideration of assessment within Higher Education shows that it can be seen to have been subject to forms of standardisation, as has been illustrated earlier, and as a consequence of this, it may be failing to capture originality or creativity. This is because assessment practices have increasingly been tamed through the introduction of various techniques such as the use of learning outcomes when what is really required are assessment practices which reflect what we can see as wickedity.

So, having considered some of the reasons why education is becoming tame through a consideration of the context of education and the forces which shape it, this chapter introduces empirical findings so as to demonstrate the validity of the concept of wickedity. It does this by applying it to assessment practices within one Higher Education Institution. In sum then this chapter offers an illustration of the practical use value of the concept of wickedity.

The importance of assessment to contemporary educational practices should be apparent by now. If we view education as a process, it has been demonstrated that the outcome of that process is not the learning that takes place per se, but rather the outcomes of the forms of assessment that are adopted at any level and which act as a proxy measure of learning. However, although it can be seen that applying the concept of wickedity to any level of education is legitimate, there is a significant difference between Higher Education and those levels below it. This is because matters relating to quality and standards at the level of Higher Education have traditionally been seen as the responsibility of the Higher Education sector rather than of external bodies such as examination boards. Because of this, each Higher Education Institution has been seen as responsible for establishing its own standards in a way that is very different from other levels of education.

So, whereas pupils in the compulsory education sector, as well as students within the Further Education sector, take national, public examinations, students within Higher Education are assessed, in general, by the institution at which they are studying. There is some variation here with respect to those students taking Higher Education courses in Further Education Colleges where these awards are overseen and made by a separate Higher Education Institute, or where a Higher Education Institution lacks degree awarding powers, but in general assessment with Higher Education is a matter for each institution rather than for national examination boards.

7.2   Warrantable Claims

The aim of this chapter then is to give an indication of the value of wickedity as a concept and to illustrate how it can be used in an evaluative sense, as a counter to forces which I am arguing are undermining education. It does this through a consideration of empirical findings that were generated by applying it to assessment within Higher Education and assessing the different ways in which assessment was understood by two different stakeholder groups: teaching staff and Quality Officers. In focusing upon assessment, I was aware that it is this part of education which supports the argument that education can be seen and understood as a process. Although I am not arguing that education is tamed only as a consequence of the ways in which it is being assessed, assessment has come to be seen as a key part of education, and I would argue that a particular understanding of assessment has contributed to the increasing tameness of education.

Over time, teaching staff within Higher Education have established assessment practices which they consider to be able to demonstrate learning. However, it would be wrong simply to consider the position of teaching staff in any evaluation of assessment within Higher Education. Teaching staff do not have free rein to determine how their students are assessed. The Higher Education sector in England has seen a significant rise in the number of staff employed with a responsibility towards what is generally understood, or referred to, as quality. For that reason the views of staff that can be identified as Quality Officers because of their role were also included in this research regarding assessment practices. This was on the grounds that Quality Officers have significant input into how assessment is carried out.

In determining these two groups, the issue of semantics is evident as each designation carries with it particular meanings. It might be assumed that a clear distinction can be drawn between teaching staff and Quality Officers but this is not as straight forward as it seems. For this research teaching staff were designated as such to distinguish them in terms of their role in relation to assessment. It also distinguishes them from academic staff who may not teach. It is possible, within universities, for academic staff to be focused on research or to engage in management and not to carry out any teaching. Similarly it is possible for staff with significant quality assurance responsibilities to have started as academics. The individuals designated as teaching staff within this research were primarily involved in undergraduate teaching. The individuals designated as Quality Officers were either wholly focused on matters relating to quality, for example, being employed within a registry position rather than holding an academic post, or held a senior position within the institution wherein much of their work is concerned with quality matters.

In summary then, this chapter illustrates the extent to which wickedity and tameness are evident within the epistemological positions held by two different stakeholder groups regarding assessment practices employed within Higher Education. Assessment is a central part of educational practice and it can be argued that there is a reality, to an extent, in respect of learning. However, it is more accurate to consider this reality as being a transitive reality (Plowright 2011); it does not exist independently of the mind. The process of studying and/or learning will lead to some change but this is mind-dependant. Indeed, it may be argued that it is learning which makes changes in meanings as held by individuals possible. In arguing this I am defining learning as both a reordering of existing knowledge and understanding together with the development of new forms of knowledge and understanding. This fits with a constructivist view of reality (Plowright 2011).

The approach that was taken within this research however was not concerned with assessing this learning per se but rather with assessment practices within an organisation and their relationship, or fit, with the epistemological position evident within two stakeholder groups. As practices these are social in nature. Assessment practices within Higher Education can be seen to rest upon positivist ideas regarding the reality of development but they constitute a social practice.

The research was undertaken as a small-scale study, aimed at evaluating the usefulness of the concept of wickedity. It reflects a qualitative approach in that it was an attempt to understand assessment from the perspective of teaching staff and Quality Officers so as to evaluate the extent to which their understanding of assessment facilitated tameness. In doing this the aim was to establish warrantable claims (Plowright 2011). I recognise that no claim to objective replicability can be established within this research but that was not the aim. My approach reflects the argument that the validity of this type of study within educational research rests upon the development of what has been called "fuzzy" generalisations (Bassey 2001, 1999). This means that different situations, which deal with the same general concerns, are likely to reflect similar issues. As such, "fuzzy" generalisations can contribute to cumulative knowledge because they reflect general experiences. Assessment in different Higher Education Institutions may differ in some ways but the general approaches will be recognisable across the sector. Because of this the particulars are not the salient features of assessment. The aim is to explore general themes which fit with the argument that has been established regarding wickedity and tameness. This chapter will explore this by focusing upon two key aspects of assessment within Higher Education: the purpose of it and the use of learning outcomes.

7.3   THE PURPOSE OF ASSESSMENT

In the world of education, no one would be surprised to find that an assessment of a student's work is carried out. This refers to staff and students, who encounter assessment directly, but it also refers to outside agencies and other bodies such as parents, employers and governments. As such we may consider that the term, assessment, is mundane but this does not mean that how we understand assessment is shared. Because of this subjects within the research study were asked "what is assessment for?"

The response from one Quality Officer (T11) illustrated the idea of education as a process quite starkly:

> We use assessment to judge or assess whether the students have met the module learning outcomes.

In this response the learning outcomes take precedence. This is a response that is echoed, but is given more meaning, by another of the Quality Officers (T1):

> It will check if the students know or understand something or actually can do something to demonstrate it as well.

In providing this response, T1 merges three different possible outcomes: knowing, understanding and being able to do something. In turn, a consideration of which of these is to be assessed, or which is privileged, will shape the assessment practice used. T1 (QO) expanded on their comment, stating that:

> I see assessment as being as having two purposes. Firstly as part of the learning process and then secondly going to some form of calculation that comes up with whether a student has passed and how well they have done and then that comes back to the first part.

It may be considered that T1 reflects tameness within their response and in doing so also supports my concerns regarding developments in education. Not all respondents offered such basic responses. Consider what one member of teaching staff (T5) said:

> You tend to end up with a taxonomy of reasons for assessment and that's at the heart of it really. You've got assessment for discrimination between students, you've got right to practice, you've got indicators to members of staff

to what has been learnt and therefore what needs to be compensated for, it's for the formal recognition of qualifications, you know there is a long list of reasons for assessment.

This teacher appears to be drawing upon Bloom's taxonomy, a ranking of intellectual or academic activities which range from knowledge to evaluation. When ranked they reflect how we may want students at different levels to be able to perform. So, gaining knowledge of a subject can be seen as a basic activity, whereas being able to evaluate represents a higher-level ability.

For teaching staff the idea of summative and formative assessment is a major feature of how assessment is used and what it is for. This was evident in what T2 (TS) says when s/he also raises the concept of summative and formative purposes:

… that's the summative aspect of it if you like, we are making a judgement, we are summing up where they are, what they have done and then the second point about it is the formative aspect which is where we're sort of showing them how to improve the things they need to do to make it better, to improve their learning if you like.

A more nuanced understanding of the purpose of assessment is put forward by T3 (TS) who begins by stating that:

Assessment can be for a lot of things. I think we can, at a rather mechanistic level, assess students in terms of competencies, whether they are demonstrating certain competencies if we are working within an environment which has certain skills which students need to demonstrate, and by skills I'm really thinking of the more competency end of things.

Again we see an understanding of the different abilities which students develop, as is reflected with Bloom's taxonomy, underpinning these comments, but this teacher is moving beyond the tame approach of just measuring learning outcomes. This is further evidenced as T3 goes on to say that:

I might be assessing to see whether or not a student is able to demonstrate an ability to evaluate, to analyse, to synthesise, and that might be to evaluate two different perspectives on a given philosophical argument, it might be about synthesising a number of different theoretical frameworks and bringing them together and applying them to a given problem so there I feel I am moving beyond just the testing of knowledge, of understanding a given concept but then being able to apply my understanding of that knowledge perhaps to a new context.

This comment raises the idea that as part of the educational process, we seek to develop new skills or refine existing skills. In doing so there is a recognition that within Higher Education there is often an understanding that we will go beyond just providing students with opportunities to acquire new knowledge but that in addition we will be seeking to develop their abilities to do things with that knowledge. This point is pertinent to the argument regarding the need for education that can accommodate wickedity because the developing of the ability to do something with knowledge reflects the student's creativity. This is particularly important because once students have this ability they become capable of generating insights into things in ways that cannot be predetermined or predicted.

It could be considered that this opens a range of possibilities in respect of what pupils and students do as a consequence of their education and suggests that if we are to foster such skills, there must be the conditions in place within which they are able to explore their developing abilities in an environment where failures do not carry sanctions. This returns us to the concept of formative assessment that was briefly introduced previously. Typically, assessment, at all levels of education, has been dominated by summative assessment. Recent decades however have seen a significant growth in the use of formative assessment, often referred to as assessment for learning.

Such a concern has become important within Higher Education and was considered briefly by at least two of the teachers interviewed, who noted that:

The formative aspect which is where we're sort of showing them how to improve the things they need to do to make it better, to improve their learning if you like. T2

Although I recognise assessment as a summative activity for me as a practitioner it is a very formative process and I use formative assessment a lot in my practice. T7

Although there is evidence to suggest that assessment is seen as having different purposes, there is also a subtle shift in some responses in that when asked "what is assessment for", a comment upon who assessment is for was often given. The concern that assessment is for teaching staff in that it provides them with guidance with respect to the progress of their students is encapsulated within the comments about formative assessment. This may not necessarily be explicit but a familiarity with the concept of formative assessment will be bound up with an understanding of how teaching staff can or should use this, and an emphasis upon using formative assessment has been a feature of Higher Education for quite a few years.

What some respondents also commented upon though was an understanding of how parties that are external to the university, to a lesser or greater degree, have concerns with what happens within Higher Education. This moves away from the role that assessment plays in respect of driving, or contributing to learning, and does more to rest upon the process whereby assessment leads to a judgement being made. This approach is evident where assessment is summative and where the assessment process provides a mark that is formally recorded by the university. This was elaborated upon by T4 (teaching staff) who explored the use that employers make of the outcomes of summative assessment to some depth and contrasted the importance of the outcomes of summative assessment, the mark or classification, with a concern within academia with formative assessment:

> It seems to me that there is an element of conflict in thinking regarding assessment in HE. We are all mindful that assessment has a purpose to play in the minds of students and their parents and in terms of employers in terms of assessment for a job.

As such T4 recognises that what is done within Higher Education does not take place within a vacuum and echoes the discussions regarding what shapes education made in earlier chapters. Contemporary concerns such as the concept of employability do have an impact upon what is done and how students experience Higher Education. For one teacher, T4:

> We have a problem with it because in the background is all this business of the mark is what counts and as we know it's the first thing that the student looks for and they don't often bother with the formative feedback that we give them.

Whilst not necessarily accepting his/her comments regarding the argument that many students do not look at feedback, the importance of the mark is something that most teaching staff, and students, would recognise. Recent developments within undergraduate Higher Education in particular may be seen as contributing to this. If students are effectively investing in their own education, as a consequence of the introduction of fees that at the time of writing are £9000 each year alongside maintenance loans, it may not be surprising that the concept of returns enters considerations about the value of Higher Education. Indeed the White Paper on Higher Education (DBIS 2016) reinforces this view with respect to the imminent introduction of a Teaching Excellence Framework which sees future employment as a proxy measure of teaching quality and which is intended to be used to prevent fee increases in those institutions that are deemed to be unsatisfactory.

However, to suggest that students have only recently considered where a degree will get them in respect of the labour market is somewhat misleading. It has long been seen that getting a degree enhances the possibility of securing a "good" job, and so it can be argued that Higher Education has always operated as a mechanism for enhancing employability and in some ways for facilitating social mobility. In considering the demands required of a knowledge economy though, it can be seen that the current educational practices within England are unlikely to produce innovative, original and creative employers. A knowledge economy may require workers who are creative but our educational practices are more likely to stifle this through the provision of tame education.

7.4   TAMENESS IN EDUCATION

Evidence of tameness was revealed when talking to teaching staff about their experiences. What was apparent though is that there was a sense that students were entering Higher Education having already been tamed in certain ways. At least one member of teaching staff referred to changes that had taken place within other educational institutions, schools and Further Education Colleges, that are experienced prior to Higher Education suggesting that the experience of students before entering Higher Education has reified an approach whereby acquiring the means to pass forms of assessment has come to dominate the student experience of education as a whole. This then becomes manifest as the belief that there is a right answer and that success is bound up with providing the right answer. Such an idea is evident within comments provided by one member of teaching staff as thus (T2):

T2:   You are getting students who come through a culture of feed me ...... just tell me what I need to put

This reflects anecdotal evidence that many teachers in Higher Education will be familiar with and is something that I recognise personally. But there is little that is surprising here. What happens prior to entering Higher Education can be seen as shaping the ways in which students have come to understand education. The Education Reform Act, 1988, did much to establish a culture within schools that emphasises the meeting of targets with respect to the qualifications that are achieved. The policy changes within Further Education Colleges which did much to create Further Education as a market-based sector, in line with neoliberal thinking, reinforced a focus on qualifications in that student withdrawal or failure can result in a reduction in funding. In both cases this can be said to have contributed to an educational system which privileges achievement as measured by successful completion of programmes or awards rather than in terms of educational development. The consequence of this is a student body in Higher Education now wherein individual students have had around 15 years' experience within educational establishments where the focus has been upon arriving at the correct answers.

One member of teaching staff (T4), however, introduced the idea that the use of learning outcomes, as will be discussed further below, intersects with issues of accountability in stating that:

T4:   we shoot ourselves in the foot in terms of having learning outcomes
RC: Why? How do you mean we shoot ourselves in the foot?
T4:   Well we set ourselves up to be asked well if you've said there is a learning outcome then it's your job (it's my job) to make sure I understand how and know what I have to do to achieve that learning outcome therefore have I got it right

This teacher was talking in general about a perception that students tend to adopt a rather utilitarian and/or positivist view towards assessment tasks. It is not unusual for teaching staff to see students as perceiving that there is a perfect answer or response corresponding to any assignment task. This is something that many teachers will have encountered as students seek to ascertain the extent to which their assessed work represents the correct thing to do and is something that indicates how previous experiences of education have moulded students into adopting a particular approach to their studies.

It may not be surprising then that when such students enter Higher Education, they may find it difficult to be told that they have some flexibility and that it may not be that there is a right answer per se. As such asking students to take ownership of their work can be daunting for some of them.

What should be apparent then is that when considering how the State impacts upon Higher Education, it is pertinent to consider that it may do directly by imposing regulatory bodies such as the Quality Assurance Agency for Higher Education or changing funding mechanisms; but it can also do so indirectly by changing the institutions which feed into Higher Education. One teacher, T2, said a lot about how the State had changed the ways in which schools work arguing:

> So the State, you have State defined teachers and you have State defined knowledge so if you think about it teachers are trained within a certain rhetoric a certain rubric, they have to meet standards, standards that are defined by the State, the State defines what it is they will learn and how they will learn it. So all of that is a, you know a pre-determined teacher, I can't remember the phrase they use but they are set like that, you then have pre-determined knowledge because the State defines what it is you are going to learn.

Another teacher (T6) discussed such developments with respect to what they saw as a decreased level of trust in academic staff:

> I think its accountability and I think its surveillance, I think its people who use what I would call the pseudo-science of quality assurance who want to produce everything into uniformed boxes.

What is evident within these comments is that there are significant tensions that exist between the State and Higher Education. The issue of accountability fits with this and may be seen to drive tameness in the way in which a concern to ensure that accountability is always explicit leads to the establishment of a system which can provide for this. In turn this is something that fits very easily with the concept of New Public Management although with the proviso that this is not, in itself, an uncontested concept and that it is not a consistent or unitary approach or strategy. New Public

Management, then, incorporates a range of approaches and strategies which have the aim of exerting levels of control over individuals who work within public services. One of the most obvious aspects of assessment though is the way in which the use of learning outcomes has become widespread.

7.5   STANDARDISATION: LEARNING OUTCOMES

Learning outcomes appear to be ubiquitous within education as a whole and are certainly in common use within Higher Education. As has been discussed previously, the use of learning outcomes has some bearing upon ideas relating to assessment when we approach it through the lens of wicked and tame. For those who work within Higher Education, it may be hard to remember a time before learning outcomes or to be able to pin a date upon the time when they were first introduced. Their origins have a long history, but by the beginning of the twenty-first century, they were in common use within the UK. Their use can be seen to have been consolidated by the Bologna agreement within Europe, which aimed to ease the movement of European students across borders through the standardisation of different national approaches to Higher Education (Kennedy 2008; Adam 2004). From the perspective of the Bologna agreement, learning outcomes have value if they contribute to the movement of students across national borders. This aim, however, inevitably impacts upon teaching within Higher Education and, as has been argued, has an impact upon assessment practices.

As with responses to questions about the purposes of assessment, questions about learning outcomes reveal that they are not seen in a uniform manner. As such, it can be suggested that there are two basic understandings of learning outcomes, a soft understanding, wherein they are seen as guiding practice and development, and a hard understanding, where they are seen as constraining and possibly counterproductive. The latter view reflects the arguments put forward within the work of Hussey and Smith (2008, 2010) who express concerns about the ways in which learning outcomes impact upon academic work and learning. The soft view, the idea that learning outcomes exist as a guide, is reflected within the two stakeholder groups included within this investigation. As one Quality Officer (T11) said:

> Learning outcomes presumably give them a framework within, a kind of a basic idea of what they are being asked to demonstrate .....

T2, a member of teaching staff, is much more explicit in respect of how s/he uses learning outcomes and illustrates how they can be used in a soft way:

> When I'm marking I use them as guides

Such an approach though can be seen to be being reinforced in terms of how some teachers approach the provision of feedback to students. One of the teachers interviewed, T5, talked about how some members of staff use them to provide an explicit framework when they are marking. As such s/he referred to another member of staff who s/he presents as:

> Very good when s/he is marking, I don't know whether you have seen the way s/he marks but; learning outcome 1 was very well met because, learning outcome 2 wasn't because …

Indeed, it might be very hard to argue against learning outcomes if they did ensure that what was happening within teaching was effective. In the example just provided, giving feedback that specifically refers to how a student has met or addressed each learning outcome provides a framework for their performance overall and could be seen as a way in which both summative and formative functions, as have been discussed above, are provided for. However, T5 also recognises that such an approach may be less effective than it first seems:

> There now seems to be a counter argument that atomising the learning into learning outcomes even if you have only got 3 or 4 actually militates against long term development in learning and actually has negative consequences.

In discussing whether or not this illustrated that this approach becomes too precise and that the consequence is that the process becomes reductionist, his/her response was to offer an example taken from a module that s/he had taught jointly with another member of staff where they:

> Failed about 10 people, 5 people because they hadn't met one of the learning outcomes. One of the learning outcomes was about marketization and globalization, it wasn't about they had done globalization and marketization very well but well it was about …… satisfactorily meeting the outcomes. If they had missed that bit out they failed, which I don't have a problem with but you could see what I'm saying.

In response to this example I suggested that in actuality the students who had failed could have done a very good assignment, and have demonstrated learning, but had been failed for omitting to cover a particular aspect of the task:

> Yes and one or two of them did actually, one or two of them wrote pretty well but they just missed that bit off, but it was a learning outcome.

In this discussion T5 makes it clear that because the module that is being assessed has specific learning outcomes that are to be assessed, the absence of a response to any learning outcome is grounds for failing, even when the assignment as a whole could be very good in all other respects. The possibility that a student can fail an assignment which is, in all other respects good, can be presented as a major failing with how learning outcomes are used and supports the proposal that we can see educational practice, in this case with respect to assessment, as tame. This occurs when they are used in a way that determines what must be learnt in a very specific way rather than guiding learning and where the learning outcomes are unable to accommodate creativity. This situation reflects the uncritical adoption of a device that can be seen to be advantageous in the planning stage but which can have real consequences for students learning.

This is not to say that all teachers adopt this apparently harsh, if somewhat logical or inevitable, approach. The failing of students who had not demonstrated meeting a particular learning outcome was not a universally accepted practice amongst the teachers involved in this research. Other teaching staff were well aware of the limitations of learning outcomes with most making comments that could be seen as critical of either how they are used or what they do:

> They narrow and restrict if you slavishly follow them and if you put them at the forefront of everything then they restrict by their very nature. As my history teacher used to say the more you define something the more you restrict it so by keeping it very narrow and assuming those particular things are what you are looking for by its very nature you are going to guide the students into some sort of common type thing and it doesn't allow them to move outside of that, T2 (TS).

> Learning outcomes can be very restrictive, T3 (TS).

> They are reductionist, they serve to be reductionist, T4 (TS).

> I think for a teacher it's quite constraining, when you are constructing your lessons and you are making sure you are meeting the learning outcomes how you are measuring them .... learning outcomes in a sense undermine creativity and in validations I think people are focused on learning outcomes rather than the content of modules ..... they are reductionist, T6 (TS).

The consequence for students of not meeting one of the learning outcomes is a key area wherein individual approaches can provide different responses. Where T5 (TS) is very clear that not demonstrating that any particular learning outcome has been met is grounds for failure, T2 (TS) takes a different approach:

> I'm quite happy if someone produces something which is a really good piece of work which shows criticality, originality and all that and if they haven't managed to meet one of the learning outcomes personally that wouldn't bother me too much.

It may be, as T2 claims, that s/he is not bothered when a student produces a good assignment but fails to demonstrate that all learning outcomes being assessed are met, but the extent to which s/he is able to accommodate such a sentiment within the constraints of what s/he has said is a quite constraining system is questionable. As quality assurance systems such as moderation and consideration of work by the external examiner are in place, the extent to which T2 can overlook a learning outcome not being met and justify the mark that they have awarded is limited. A further question may then be what does this teacher do if two learning outcomes have not been met? At what point do they consider not meeting outcomes to be unsatisfactory?

Not meeting one or more learning outcomes clearly poses problems within a system where they are used in a hard way. It is not the only problematic issue related to them. The extent to which learning outcomes are equally weighted can be seen to reflect the problem that arises when not meeting one learning outcome out of a range is evident. Should all learning outcomes be met equally by the student and do all learning outcomes carry equal weight? This is clearly something that some members of staff have given some consideration to with one teacher commenting upon concerns that s/he has that learning outcomes may not be equal with respect to the opportunities for achieving high marks:

Obviously I am alert to what they need to know and what they need to be able to do but I don't like the idea of being; will they be able to be score highly on learning outcome 1 or learning outcome 2.

This teacher demonstrates that how we plan assessment tasks is important because this can result in either a fragmented assessment experience or, on the contrary, a holistic and coherent experience:

I think some of the best tasks anyway combine the learning outcomes.

The comments reproduced above point to two things which are relevant to this argument. Firstly, that it is possible for a student to produce a piece of work that is intrinsically good but which is awarded a fail mark on the grounds of not meeting a learning outcome; secondly, that the use of learning outcomes may produce a fragmented assessment experience. A further issue is also pertinent; that the use of learning outcomes can act against the development, or at least of the reward, of creativity or originality. This is evident in responses from two Quality Officers. For example, T9 comments:

I think setting out intended learning outcomes themselves tend to militate against assessing originality and creativity because one of the obvious ways of being original and creative is to go outside the remit of the intended learning outcomes or indeed the very intentions of the teacher or lecturer. So it's, intended learning outcomes in particular can, don't have to, but can militate against creativity.

This Quality Officer appeared to be wrestling with the concept of learning outcomes. His/her responses clearly saw them being supportive of the use of learning outcomes whilst recognising that this approach may have some unintended, negative, consequences. S/he went on to comment:

I like intended learning outcomes for many reasons, but in terms of assessment it can be harder if you are judging entirely by that and if your comments are entirely restricted to comments on the meeting of intended learning outcomes.

In saying this they reflected the concerns voiced by others that although learning outcomes can have value, they can also undermine the intentions of Higher Education. In establishing that creativity can be measured whilst also supporting systems such as assessing to learning outcomes, there is a tension that arises because of the idea that assessment can be tamed. This is not to say that this is done on purpose, but it does reflect the manner in which recent developments, such as the introduction of learning outcomes, can have unintended consequences.

Another Quality Officer demonstrated the tensions that the use of learning outcomes can generate. T10 also acknowledged that the situation can and does arise whereby a student submits a piece of work that is strong in many ways but which does not meet a learning outcome, but in being questioned regarding the consequences of that, s/he never adequately answered the question. Instead they referred to what they felt would have happened in another university and in a different time:

T10: we've had that before where somebody has done a stunning piece of work which should have been an 80 but they haven't addressed the question, haven't addressed the learning outcome
RC: What do we do? What do we want to do?
T10: If you were at Cambridge in 1980 some tutor would have gone oh that was really interesting, what did you think about this?

The value of this response is that this Quality Officer recognises that alternative actions are possible. They recognise that we can have a system whereby not meeting a learning outcome is permissible but then referred to why we are unlikely to adopt this approach because of the numbers involved and the fact that the student to staff ratios within the university where this research was carried out can be high. At no point does this Quality Officer state that not meeting a learning outcome will mean that the student fails. Instead, this is left unspoken but in a way that is accepted as something that will happen.

7.6   RECOGNISING THE WIDER FORCES

Amongst teaching staff there was a clear sense that Higher Education operates within a particular context, a context that is increasingly being understood in economic terms but where this also generates taming forces. For example, one teacher T2 drew upon wider forces when considering the ways in which Higher Education has developed and how it may develop in the future with explicit comments about consumerism and economisation.

T2: that's the external pressure that we are under and I think as students they feel they are paying for their degree and this is one of the problems. I think they are not paying for their degree they are paying for access but they feel they are paying for their degree

RC: And that's being promoted?

T2: Yes because it's a consumerism perspective its part of the marketization we are going through

More than one teacher raised concerns about the consequences of increased consumerism within Higher Education, pointing to how it changes the relationship between teachers and students in a way that creates pressure for staff. What that pressure is, was not voiced but there was an inference that it relates to the judgements that are made about students' work. Making judgements about students' work has been a long-standing part of assessment within Higher Education and is closely tied to the outcomes that students leave with in that this becomes a classification of their performance during their time studying. As such, the awarding of a mark, often in the form of a number, is not at all unusual. What marketisation does though is to elevate the role of such judgements as measures of quality which have currency within the labour market. Consider how T6 (TS) reflects upon the way in which universities themselves contribute to this:

> It's about corporatisation of and I think it's about marketization and league tables and all of that, that in a sense the message we give out from day one on the website are statistics and numbers, x numbers get graduate jobs, x numbers get 2:1s, the NSS says this, in a sense we socialise them into an expectation of looking for a number.

Drawing from experience, T6 reflected upon how this has shaped the student's approach or understanding of their Higher Education experience and referred to the ways in which, for students, the marks take precedence with learning and development being seen as:

> A by-product in a sense for me. If you ask them what they have learnt I think they often say 'well if I remember this module I got 58', and what does that mean?

T6 was obviously disheartened by this sort of response from students, but it may be a consequence of staff and students approaching and understanding Higher Education differently.

When a preoccupation with the mark is taken alongside the idea that students are buying a degree, it comes as little surprise that students want the highest number, the best outcome: the best return from their investment. As the final classification is the outcome of all other marks achieved, it puts pressure on students which in turn can be transferred to staff. T2 (TS) sums this up when noting that:

> Students are saying 'but I need to get this' so we've got this pressure coming through.

Here, the student need is for staff to award a particular mark. What students often appear to assume though is that the mark is something which is gifted by the staff marking their work rather than a judgement based upon the quality of what they have done. That outcome is always the consequence of the assessment process wherein the student is judged as performing at a particular level. For T2 this becomes problematic when the responsibility for that outcome is either seen as resting with the university or becomes appropriated by it:

> … with the lifting of the cap [the limit on student numbers previously set by the Government but which was lifted during 2015] you are really going to see bargain basement stuff come to us; we will guarantee you a degree, no one will leave without one; you know you can start to see, you are going to get the marketing rhetoric is going to come through and I just wonder how much longer we are going to hold onto this romantic liberal view of self-development.

T2's reference to a romantic liberal view of self-development may already have faded into the background. Most teaching staff are likely to have some understanding that the work of universities, and staff relationships with students, has changed over the previous few decades.

7.7   WICKEDITY

The interviews that were undertaken as part of this research did not ask, explicitly, about wickedity. The aim was to explore how assessment was carried out as an example of the usefulness of the concept as an evaluative tool. In considering the idea of wickedity and tameness within assessment though, some comments can be seen to fit with the concept as it was explained in Chap. 2.

For example, one Quality Officer (T11) commented upon the fact that students are not passive participants within the educational process and that there is a need to elicit, in his/her words, the information that we want from them so as to be able to make a judgement. S/he also demonstrated some understanding of wickedity when commenting upon students being safe within how they are assessed:

> Sometimes it's encouraging as well for students to fail on some things, if they are making an artefact or doing something and that process fails but then they are reflecting on why that has failed, learning on how it fails in itself is demonstrating some form of learning isn't it? You don't always want students to be safe in what they do, you want them to be, to experiment and take risks.

In expressing these thoughts, T11 not only revealed a good understanding of the learning process, s/he also recognised the challenging nature of learning. In stating that "you don't always want students to be safe in what they do, you want them to be, to experiment and take risks" s/he demonstrates that s/he is not necessarily uncomfortable with the ideas which underpin wickedity.

In one sense though, T11's comments point to a distinction between learning and assessment. Students do not enter Higher Education to be assessed. For teaching staff there may be a somewhat idealistic idea that students enter Higher Education to learn and develop; for students, however, the purpose of Higher Education is varied. Students may enter Higher Education with the aim of getting a job or to get what they see as a better job. Some may see Higher Education as a challenge and use it to see what they are capable of. However, once in Higher Education, the need to get the award for which they are studying for will be central to many. This is important because to get an award students have to engage with assessment and successful achievement will only happen where students have learnt and developed. Maybe a more pragmatic approach would be to recognise this; to recognise that students are there to gain an award, whatever level that award is and as such, they are compelled to engage with some form of assessment. This also means that the university must establish some system whereby a judgement can be made.

For teaching staff the concepts of wicked and tame are evident but, as with Quality Officers and students, they are not voiced in this language. For example, one teacher comments that:

> At the minute assessment has a very functional role and I don't think it necessarily has to, I think assessment can be part of learning it doesn't have to be the measure of learning.

This comment from T8 (TS) relates to other comments that were made regarding a distinction that can be drawn between assessment of learning and assessment for learning, an issue that was discussed at the beginning of this chapter. T2 also reiterates points that were made earlier regarding why we are working within a particular way with a comment which suggests that Higher Education is not unusual in its approach:

> I just think we work within very restricted perceptions of what we are meant to be doing but that's not just HE, the whole system is set up like that.

This reflects the comments that were made earlier regarding the ways in which standardised approaches as per Weber's concerns regarding rationalisation permeate society. This is echoed to some extent by T6 (TS) who suggests that there is a tameness to assessment whilst pointing towards recognition of the possibility of a more wicked approach with respect to learning outcomes:

> I do have some sympathy with the view that ….. you might not have them because in a true learning experience you might not know what the outcome is.

This comment in particular shows an understanding of the complexity of the learning experience, something which sits well with the concept of wickedity. However, s/he went on to make a comment which draws upon an understanding of different educational levels and which sheds some light on the forces which shape how educational systems are run:

> For me that was part of the HE-ness, you know lower down you have your exams, you have your learning outcomes, HE-ness had that fluidity, however, it relies on a higher degree of professionalism and has very little accountability that makes it hard to monitor.

T2 (TS) provides some insight into the possibility of wickedity when s/he makes the comment:

You could have a form of assessment which is totally formative that you don't need to come to some judgement, is it a 60, 80 or a 35 whatever, you could talk about it you could engage with the students about it.

In saying this T2 is recognising that assessment itself is generally predicated upon the making of a judgement which sees the student's work being awarded a mark. A system such as T2 suggests could be seen as being more wicked because the focus would be on encouraging development rather than working towards a mark. S/he develops this idea further in a manner which recognises that in some ways there are forces upon assessment practices which tame the process and said a lot about issues which fall in to the conceptual scope of wicked and tame problems. S/he was particularly critical about the way in which Higher Education has become tame, albeit not using that particular word:

What we get at the moment is we've got prescribed learning. We as lecturers determine what they are going to learn. We decide how it's going to be put across. You know, basically, we are in total control yet we talk about the rhetoric of independent creativity, criticality, where even the criticality is within limited bands of what we determine as criticality.

For T2 this control feeds into the way we assess so that, in general, the student's output is rarely original or surprising:

So the way we work at the moment I have got a pretty good idea of what a good one will look like at the end and some students surprise you by showing you a different version of what a good one will look like but basically you've got an image in your head of what a good piece of assessed work will look like so all the way down the line we are working within certain tram lines you know.

T2 does, however, offer an understanding that this is not in itself inevitable by ending his/her discussion of this matter as follows:
It doesn't have to be that way.

7.8   CONCLUSION

This chapter set out to demonstrate how the concepts of wicked and tame might be used as an evaluative tool within education. It did this by reporting on research carried out with two stakeholder groups within Higher

Education focusing upon one aspect of education within Higher Education, assessment. The research sought to evaluate the epistemological position adopted by each group with respect to assessment. In each group there was evidence to support the claim that assessment can either embrace wickedity or lead to tameness.

With respect to the problems that they saw, Quality Officers tended to locate issues with assessment in the students rather than the system. That one Quality Officer (T10) commented that "we can only assess what students choose to share with us" illustrates this. It was revealing in locating assessment performance within the students rather than seeing it as bound up with the approaches that are adopted. Quality Officers did reveal an understanding of wicked issues within assessment, but it did not appear as strongly in their responses when compared to teaching staff and there appeared to be a general acceptance of existing practices in spite of some misgivings.

For teaching staff, similarly, there was an appreciation that how we assess students can tame the process albeit not being articulated through the use of this terminology. Teaching staff were more pessimistic regarding assessment and were more likely to see Higher Education being tamed but their comments were generally focused on concerns with existing practice rather than a consideration of how this may be countered. It is also important to reiterate that responses from teaching staff were not homogenous.

Overall there was little sense of wickedity demonstrated by either of these two groups but that may not be unexpected if we consider the factors which constitute the context within which each group works. For example, a concern for equity provided a strong driver for standardisation. Chapter 4 argued that standardisation can be seen as a broad social force in its own right. In that sense the concern for equity simply has the effect of giving credence to standardisation and reducing the possibility of resistance to it.

This example illustrates the ways in which different factors overlap with each other and demonstrate why this, itself, is a wicked problem and why there can be no silver bullet which solves the problem of tameness within education. As such there is a need to appreciate that multiple factors influence all levels of education and that there is no one overriding factor which lies at the heart of any problem.

The research did suggest that to achieve and accommodate wickedity, there is a need for assessment practices to be revised and amended but alongside this is a need to change how assessment and assessment practices are understood by different groups. This, then, raises the question of how this might be achieved. As such, the question becomes that of establishing how we can achieve a situation whereby wickedity is accommodated.

I would argue that the use of wicked and tame as concepts with which to evaluate education are useful in that they establish a guiding principle. An analogy may be drawn here with children's services during the last decade or so where a guiding principle was established by which policies and practices were assessed against a simple requirement; what provides the best outcomes for the child? Returning to education as a whole, the aim should be, ideally, that any practices which are adopted are able to accommodate wickedity and, in doing so, avoid being tame. What will be valuable in achieving this is to establish an understanding that a key purpose of education is to promote creativity and originality rather than just the mastery of what is already known. As such, the concept of wickedity may be drawn upon in a way that reminds us that we cannot foresee what students will learn or what they will contribute and that we need to find a way to reward them for being creative. If this is the case, then we need to establish how we can achieve not only wicked assessment, as was the focus of this study, but wicked education as a whole on the grounds that providing education that is tame, at whatever level, will impoverish education.

REFERENCES

Adam, S. 2004. Using Learning Outcomes: A Consideration of the Nature, Role, Application and Implications for European Education of Employing Ëlearning Outcomesí at the Local, National and International Levels. In *UK Bolgna Seminar*. Edinburgh: Heriot-Watt University.

Bassey, Michael. 1999. *Case Study Research in Educational Settings*. Maidenhead: Open University Press.

———. 2001. A Solution to the Problem of Generalisation in Educational Research: Fuzzy Prediction. *Oxford Review of Education* 27 (1): 5–22. doi:10.1080/3054980020030574.

Department for Business, Innovation & Skills. 2016. *Success as a Knowledge Economy: Teaching Excellence, Social Mobility and Student Choice*. London: HMSO.

Hussey, Trevor, and Patrick Smith. 2008. Learning Outcomes: A Conceptual Analysis. *Teaching in Higher Education* 13 (1): 107–115. doi:10.1080/13562510701794159.

———. 2010. *The Trouble with Higher Education*. Abingdon: Routledge.

Kennedy, Declan. 2008. Linking Learning Outcomes and Assessment of Learning of Student Science Teachers. *Science Education International* 19 (4): 387–397.

Plowright, David. 2011. *Using Mixed Methods: Frameworks for an Integrated Methodology*. London: Sage.

CHAPTER 8

Where Are We Now?

8.1 INTRODUCTION

Much of this book has been given over to considering what the contemporary landscape of education within England looks like in circa 2017. In doing so it has argued that for a number of reasons, education has come to be seen as a process. Understanding education as a process, with both inputs and outputs, has implications for those who are being educated, as well as for those who seek to employ individuals who have been educated and those who work within education. The argument as presented has generally taken a critical approach and has done much to argue that education in twenty-first-century England has been subject to a number of diverse forces which have contributed to it become increasingly tame. The aim throughout has been to present the argument that tameness impoverishes education and that this is not in anyone's interests.

Chapter 2 developed the concept of wickedity that is implicit in the idea of wicked problems as first used by Rittel and Webber (1973). The idea of wicked problems has gained a great deal of currency since 1973 and is often invoked across a range of disciplines with respect to problems that might be characterised by their complexity. These are problems where what works in one situation does not work, or certainly does not work as well, in another similar situation. This applies very well within the field of education. There will be few teachers who are not able to tell of a tried and tested strategy or approach to their teaching which suddenly appears to not work or which works with all groups bar one.

© The Author(s) 2018
R. Creasy, *The Taming of Education*,
DOI 10.1007/978-3-319-62247-7_8

In establishing just what I mean when I refer to wicked problems, and, in offering a development of the concept, Chap. 2 presented an approach whereby the concept of wickedity and tameness could be used as an evaluative tool with which it is possible to assess the extent to which approaches to education are becoming tame. The use of this was demonstrated above, in Chap. 7, wherein assessment practices within one university were explored to consider the extent to which they were either wicked or tame. It was not suggested that all universities adopt the same assessment practices; rather that assessment within this university was not all that dissimilar to assessment within others.

Having argued strongly that education is becoming tame, with the corollary that this is not a welcome development, this chapter seeks to explore contemporary aspects of education with a view to how this may contribute towards increasing tameness. The value of considering what the contemporary landscape of education is now is so that we may begin to establish what is required if we are to move away from tame education and towards wicked education. What will be evident is that there is no silver bullet available by which the move towards tame education can be halted. We cannot just agree that education is becoming tame and then, in recognition of the way in which this impoverishes education, change our ways. There are powerful groups within education, allied to it or who are associated with it. These groups will often hold entrenched positions and will not be inclined to give them up easily whatever the evidence that is provided. There will also be many staff who are themselves quite accepting of tame education and who might see wickedity as challenging. However, unlike Margaret Thatcher, I do not agree that when it comes to the direction of policy, there is no alternative. I think that there is always an alternative; history demonstrates that there are no policy approaches which cannot be changed. Paradoxically, in spite of her mantra that there is no alternative, Thatcher is credited with doing the most to change the direction of social and public policies within the UK in recent decades. Maybe what Thatcher meant, and what subsequent politicians actually mean when they say that there is no alternative, is "I won't consider an alternative to my intentions". To my mind, adopting such a position may signify power or control but it most certainly does not demonstrate leadership. However, this position is not confined to politicians. It can be seen that many leaders of educational institutions at all levels have either embraced the developments which lead to tameness or have simply accepted them as inevitable. In many ways then educational leaders have contributed to the taming of education.

We can see also how educational leaders have increased managerial control, as discussed earlier, and consider how this has reinforced the idea of education as being a process by shifting the focus away from the practice of teaching and towards the idea of learning, on the grounds that learning represents the outcome of education. When considered alongside concerns about the student experience, it can be seen how the practice of teaching is often no longer the focus for those concerned with education. Teaching may be an integral part of education but other aspects of it have appeared to have taken precedence in recent years, and as a consequence of this, it is reasonable to say that a concern for teaching, as a key aspect of education, has declined. This chapter explores the idea that a range of concerns have arisen and become established within education in a way that has meant that teaching, possibly the most important aspect of education, has declined in importance.

8.2   THE PATH TO TAMENESS

Although I have presented a number of factors which have shaped the nature of education over recent decades, we should recognise that for the most part there is an abstract quality to these factors. They rest upon ideas and concepts. What happens though is that these ideas and concepts move from abstraction as they come to shape policies, which in turn shape practice. That said it can also be seen that policies operate at different levels. They can be seen in national policies and legislation. They can also be seen in organisational policies. One aspect of the ongoing changes within education which offers some explanation as to why this has been possible is that education policy has been subject to a process of depoliticalisation (Clarke and Phelan 2017; Clarke 2012; Fischman 2008). This depoliticalisation has led to critical voices being negated or muted. In recent decades this has resulted in an instrumentalist approach towards education being taken for granted within a marketised context which is itself being accepted as normal (Ball 2016). Within this perspective the idea of education as being a process is supported as the focus of education shifts towards viewing results as outputs.

Talk to teachers, at any level within education, and it is not difficult to gain a sense of education as being understood as a process. Much of this book has put forward the idea that viewing education as a process is not at all a good thing and that viewing education as a process lays the foundations for the adoption of practices wherein outputs, in the form of results, come to take precedence. This leads to a dehumanising system whereby on the one hand the measure of an individual becomes the certificate that applies to them and on the other hand where the value or worth of individual pupils and students becomes reduced to the value that they can add to the results or status of any institution. Consider, for example, how the schools and universities which have the highest status within the UK tend to be the institutions which do the most to restrict admission.

Such a situation did not just happen. The policies which have been applied to schools, colleges and universities are underpinned by values and ideas, such as the valuing of market-based forms of organisation, as has been argued. For example, within the UK the 1988 Education Reform Act introduced the idea of parental choice with respect to school admissions. This effectively negated the system of catchment areas, whereby all children living in a defined area would normally be allocated to a particular school, though this did not necessarily mean that children would attend the closest school to their home. This did not apply to all schools however as some areas of England persist in having Grammar schools with a selective intake, and the existence of private, fee-paying schools similarly illustrates that entry to education may not have been an experience shared by all children. Nevertheless, in general, prior to the Education Reform Act 1988, children were allocated to schools based upon where they lived.

The introduction of the concept of choice to state education implied that parents would, as with any market transaction, be able to select a school for their child (West 2001). Implicit in this notion of choice is that parents would choose the best school. It also reinforces arguments against a comprehensive education system arguing that educational standards would improve because of the introduction of marketisation (Regan 2008). The origins of this policy reflect the neoconservative tendency towards a belief in differential ability requiring differential provision. The idea that parents would choose the "best" school was then underpinned by the introduction of "league tables" purporting to illustrate which schools were better and which were poorer. Such league tables are now also constructed out of aspects of university performance and even national performance. From a neoliberal perspective, this is necessary as in any market there is the idea that consumers make rational choices based upon market knowledge. It also rests upon the idea that quality will vary but where quality rests in the organisation, such as the school.

The 1988 Education Reform Act can also be seen as having paved the way for the development of specialism in schools and the idea that diversity is preferable to the comprehensive system that was in place. Later, this approach was developed further with the introduction of the Technology Colleges Programme in 1993 (Gorard and Taylor 2001), these colleges being schools, and in the White Paper "Schools Achieving Success" (DfES 2001), with more emphasis being placed upon types of schools. The move towards establishing specialist types of schools was ushered in as a policy whereby schools would specialise in certain discipline areas such as technology or arts (Gorard and Taylor 2001). This development can be seen as being underpinned by a combination of ideas resting upon pupil difference and parental choice (SSAT, 2007). This led to the situation in England whereby schools ostensibly became centres of excellence in particular academic disciplines and was often accompanied with changes to names wherein schools rebranded themselves as colleges and with Head Teachers being recast as Principals. It is maybe ironic that Head Teachers were seeking to be designated Principal at around the same time that College Principals were seeking to be retitled as Chief Executives, both groups seemingly being seduced by a title which appeared to give greater status than that which had traditionally been applied to their position.

However, when it comes to schools, what appears to have happened is that by the twenty-first century, the choice that parents were intended to have had been usurped by the schools themselves, though the initial proposal was always for parents to be able to state a preference rather than providing them with real choice. Rather than parents choosing a school, we now have a system whereby it is often more accurate to state that it is the schools which choose their pupils. So, within a system wherein the educational performance of pupils can be so important to the operation of the school, those pupils who may not do as well as others may find themselves in less demand irrespective of the claim that funding should follow pupils. An extreme version of what this may lead to emerged in early 2016 when an academy trust made the decision to move children with special educational needs and disabilities from the school that they were expecting to go to, to another school six miles away (Perraudin 2016). No consultation with parents had been entered into regarding the change of school.

In one sense though, this action, like many actions within the education sector, is a response to the policy context in place at the time. As such we can argue that an appreciation of existing policies is always the starting point for change. So, if the aim is to move towards wickedity within education, it is important to assess the extent to which existing policies are either able to accommodate this or if they are obstacles to it. Alongside this it is also important that teachers acknowledge that they themselves might be adopting the sort of approaches to their work which may demotivate students or not prepare them for moving on, whether that is to the next level of education or to work, but that this may be because of the forces which shape education. It is only when teachers recognise this that they may be able to offer resistance to it (Ball 2016; Preston and Aslett 2014; Ball and Olmedo 2013). In the study reported on in Chap. 7, teaching staff appeared to be critical of how students behave but a consideration of how some teaching staff approach learning outcomes illustrates that many of them inevitably encourage what students do. As such, it may not be surprising to see that where staff act in a manner that accommodates tameness, their students develop mechanisms with which to cope with the system.

Alongside this though is also a growing concern with the educational experience of pupils and students. This is particularly important within Higher Education where students have significant freedom to choose where they will study and particularly affects those institutions who are concerned with recruitment rather than selection. As such, the ways in which students experience their studies become important with respect to how unhappy students may provide negative reviews of an institution which has a detrimental impact upon subsequent recruitment.

8.3   THE STUDENT EXPERIENCE

An understanding of the concern with the student experience may be seen as a consequence of more widespread changes with respect to how different stakeholder groups are seen within education as a whole. Chapter 5 provided an extensive discussion of how the neoliberal project within Further Education has led to increased workloads, significant reductions in real pay for teachers and a generally demoralised teaching staff. Some aspects of the changes that were brought about within the Further Education sector are being echoed in Higher Education. Within Higher Education in the UK, income differentials between academics and senior management have widened dramatically, and this has also been accompanied by widespread casualisation of academic staff, often on the grounds that this is a necessary business model (Chakrabortty 2016; Chakrabortty and Weale 2016). The changes that teaching staff have experienced within both the Further and Higher Education sectors can be seen as indicative of a general disregard for such staff. In some ways they are understood simply as part of the process whereby outputs are produced. Alongside this change though is another change, one where the pupil or student comes to be seen differently also.

The impact of neoliberalism upon teaching staff in England is hard to refute. There is a further consequence though that can be seen as being shaped by the acceptance of market principles as being valid within education and this may also contribute to taming. It also has an impact upon the work of teachers and is particularly relevant to Further and Higher Education. Students who fail to pass the courses that they have enrolled on tend to be unhappy students, and unhappy students are likely to see the cause of their failure as being rooted within the teaching that they have received rather than as being bound up with their own abilities or efforts. This introduces a concern with what is generally being referred to as the student experience.

Within the Higher Education sector, in particular there is an increasing move towards recognising, and enhancing, the student experience. This is important for in an environment where the student experience is becoming ever more prominent, it is wickedity that is required. This might seem counterintuitive as wickedity can be seen to be more challenging in some ways. Tameness, however, is unlikely to generate either motivation or creativity. The focus on the student experience can be understood in relation to the marketisation of education and with the recasting of students as consumers. Because of this, their experience of education comes to the fore irrespective of the value of this. It is a reflection of the maxim that the customer is always right, that the customer knows what is best for them. But do they? It seems strange that we are promoting a system whereby the disciplinary and professional knowledge and expertise of education staff are seen as less important than the idea of ensuring a good student experience. As a consequence of this though, the student experience is being privileged over the academic experience and this is where the student experience is increasingly a "safe" experience (Hayes 2015). For safe substitutes tame.

This can be seen as creating a dilemma for teachers, even those who might go along with the idea of education as a process which affects change. Consider the dilemma faced by a teacher who is convinced, because of their disciplinary and professional knowledge and expertise, that a particular activity will be in the students best interest in the long term, but that he or she is well aware that it is not an activity that students express enjoyment of, based upon previous experience. Ex-students have reported that the activity is very worthwhile but that they only realise this after a period in work. Does the teacher use the activity?

This is a real dilemma in a system whereby student feedback is seen as an accurate reflection of the quality of teaching that they have received. In Higher Education the annual National Student Satisfaction survey is taken seriously in most Higher Education Institutions and the hypothetical activity referred to above might lead to students reporting dissatisfaction. Indeed, students may express dissatisfaction with being challenged as part of their studies yet challenge is necessary if students are to develop academically. A student may not enjoy the experience that comes from an academic challenge but a student who is not challenged is unlikely to develop. As was reported in Chap. 7, Higher Education teachers do encounter students who expect the teacher to tell them, the student, what to write in assignments or provide detailed plans. At the same time there are a growing number of students expecting to be able to resubmit work that has been assessed so as to secure higher grades on the grounds that this is what they had been able to do whilst in Further Education. But, if we consider the use of model answers, the provision of detailed plans, and the ability to resubmit work as being characteristics of the Further Education sector, this may not be surprising. The teaching strategies that are adopted in one sector of education, adopted for good reason when retention and results have become so important, will inevitably impact upon how students will experience a subsequent sector. The problem is that for some students the previous experience may have become cast as the right approach and where such students are loathe to adapt to new practices.

Because of this there is a need to recognise that although we may want pupils and students to enjoy their education on the grounds that this is likely to generate greater engagement on their part, we should not fall into the trap of allowing the beauty contest, that is, student feedback, to pressure us into removing what is difficult or to reduce the challenge of education. This is not to suggest that feedback has no part to play, it does. The type of feedback generated in class, for example, from Brookfield's (1995) approach, can contribute to showing us what works well and what works less well. Brookfield provides us with a quick and easy, informal approach to gathering feedback which has the added attraction of demonstrating to pupils and students that they have a voice as a matter of course rather than just at the end of an educational programme, but teachers must also recognise that their professional judgement has validity.

Educational organisations which overlook the value of teacher professionalism are very likely to be the sort of organisation which adopts a deterministic approach regarding what a good lesson looks like and establishes systems to ensure that all teachers follow the same format irrespective of the subject, the level or the characteristics of the teacher. In this way a justifiable concern with the pupil or student experience becomes buried under a standardised approach and the concept of teaching becomes cast as a procedure to follow to obtain a particular result.

8.4   The Decline of Teaching

Education systems are dynamic. It is without doubt that the education system in place at any given time will differ from what it has looked like before. There may be some features which give the illusion of continuity but these often only mask the changes that take place. Some changes may be minor but some may be more profound. For anyone working within education throughout the twenty-first century, one of the most significant changes has been the way in which the focus on learning has come to dominate what happens within institutions at each level and in terms of how education is understood. By 2017, debates about education are very often bound up with concerns about learning rather than teaching. This does not imply that contemporary approaches to education provide the basis for learning in a broad sense. It should be obvious by now that this is not the case. In reality learning is valued because, in a system where the output is the key concern, learning reduces uncertainty.

It is evident that learning has come to shape education when we consider the discourse that accompanies it. This is very often associated with the idea of learning outcomes as have been discussed extensively already, and learning styles, which will be discussed in more depth below. Many teachers will, no doubt, be familiar with the changed lexicon of education which has seen pupils and students being recast as learners with each learner having a particular learning style that must be catered for.

In some ways it is difficult to make a case which appears to be critical of the focus on learning. This is because the vast majority of teachers are deeply committed to seeing their pupils and students learn. Evidence of learning is used by most teachers to demonstrate the value of their work. However, the focus on learning has led to a neglect of teaching and this may be problematic (Biesta 2013, 2012). By neglecting the role of teaching within education, we reinforce the idea that education is a process which rests upon procedures and techniques. It contributes to the way in which education has been dehumanised and acts to tame it.

In making such a claim then, I am leading up to staking a claim for this to be rebalanced. I say this because I reject the idea that we can see education as a process in the way that manufacturing processes operate. It is the case that education results in change and this lends itself to being seen as analogous to a process, but the fact that it is a process whereby some individuals act to change other individuals means that we cannot reduce it to the same level of process as that involving human action on inanimate materials.

As with many new ideas, the shift to learning can be seen as seductive. It has a common-sense value that is hard to deny. If I, as a teacher, am concerned about doing the best that I can for my students, then I need to shift my focus away from me, towards them. In considering them, they are in my class to learn so it makes sense to refocus my activities, even the activities of the institution that I work for, on their learning because that is the reason that they are here. What may be recognisable to teachers in many institutions is that as a consequence, this has seen a major change in the discourse of teaching, a change that diminishes the role of teaching.

Such a development is another aspect of the marketisation of education in terms of how discourse conveys a message regarding what the institution can provide for the student. Within this model of student as learner, the pupil or student, or their parents, is effectively cast as consumer, with the ability to choose the institution that can most effectively meet his or her learning needs whilst providing the type of student experience that is most appealing.

At the same time, it represents the move towards seeing teaching as part of the process of education in that it shifts attention away from what teachers do, in so far as this reflects teacher expertise. Instead it effectively acts as a critical turn towards a consideration of the outcomes of what teachers achieve. Given that teachers have been subject to sustained criticism over recent decades, it can be seen how this criticism provides a seedbed for a focus on learning. In some ways this can be seen as part of the process of the depoliticalisation of teaching that was referred to earlier (Clarke 2012), in that debates about the contextual matters of education come to be cast as being of no importance by a focus upon the outcomes of education. Concerns regarding who enters education, the worsened working conditions that teachers experience or time allocated to teaching, for example, are all arguments that are silenced to some extent as a consequence of a focus upon the extent to which learning can be evidenced.

A word of caution is important here. Although, for Clarke, education is depoliticised as part of the neoliberal project, this should not be accepted uncritically. The depoliticalisation of education only extends so far. It operates at a superficial level only, for decisions regarding how any society provides for education can never really be removed from a political process. The practices within educational systems are always the outcomes of understandings and concerns and these are rarely likely to be homogenous within diverse societies such as the UK. Because of this we must recognise that the depoliticalisation of education really only extends as far as being a project to silence critical voices regarding education in a manner that is, essentially, anti-democratic.

With respect to the emergence of a concern with learning, however, it is the case that some commentators such as Biesta (2013, 2012, 2010) have drawn attention to the extent to which debates and concerns regarding education have become dominated by a focus on learning to the detriment of concerns with teaching, even going so far as to suggest that teachers should not be concerned with learning. From the perspective of the UK, in 2017 this is a very radical claim. Biesta (2013) makes much of the idea that education has been changed by a process which he refers to as *learnification* (italics in the original). In doing so he also refers to how the discourse of education has changed offering examples of how titles and names have changed to incorporate learning, such as libraries becoming learning centres and teachers becoming learning facilitators. Such developments have even led some schools to drop the title school. For example, although many schools have changed their names, usually to college or academy, possibly the most extreme example is in the North East of England where Cramlington Community High School changed its name to Cramlington Learning Village! Along with pupils and students being referred to as learners, as detailed above, this effectively demonstrates that we can see how the notion of learning has come to dominate what happens within educational systems.

Biesta adopts a critical approach to these developments and draws a distinction between learning from a teacher and being taught by a teacher. As part of this argument, he makes a strong case for education as being purposeful. Across a range of children's services, there has a been a growing concern with respect to children and young people's learning as part of their development, but this often misses the point that children and young people will learn and they will develop, irrespective of what is provided for them. The real issue is with respect to what they learn and how they develop. Education is a focus on learning something quite specific.

Alongside the concerns about learning though is an increased concern with the context of learning. This has particular resonance for concerns about the idea of emotional readiness to learn. Such concerns can be seen to have influenced policy and practice within educational institutions in a number of ways, which can be seen as the moves towards an obligation to both reveal and confess (Macfarlane 2017), as is evident in a focus on reflection, and in respect of the development of a therapeutic culture within education.

The therapeutic turn in education can be seen in a positive light as an approach which seeks to develop social and emotional skills, alongside promoting educational institutions as welcoming and safe places (Irisdotter Aldenmyr and Olson 2016; Wright 2014), though it can also be seen as unwelcome (Ecclestone and Hayes 2009). It is associated with what might also be seen as the rise of a counselling culture that has developed within education (Hayes 2003). Such a perspective can be seen to support a range of programmes within schools such as circle time. It can also be seen within Further Education Colleges and Higher Education Institutions in the proliferation of counselling and wellbeing services, services which may well be necessary for some students. However, a more pessimistic perspective on the therapeutic turn sees it as casting children and young people as struggling to cope with modern life and being lacking in resilience (Ecclestone and Hayes 2009). More worryingly, Leach and Lewis (2013) suggest that the pressure that can be brought to bear on children to share sensitive matters, as is often the case within therapeutic approaches, may actually contribute to the problems that such children face. This is indicative of how the focus of education has moved away from teaching and towards the idea of meeting needs.

In some ways the therapeutic turn can be seen as a broader concern with inclusivity in that it responds to issues which may contribute to pupils and students becoming excluded from participation. It is hard to argue that such an approach should not be supported, but there is a need to ensure that strategies act to overcome obstacles to participation and do not tame education to the extent that pupils and students are unable to cope with the next stage of their development. There is the potential within therapeutic education to foster reliance upon support rather than strengthen resilience and to provide a justification for reducing the challenge that education provides. It might be argued that one consequence of seeing education as a process is that pupils and students expect to progress within the system and that, as a consequence of this, they do not welcome being challenged. Challenges come to be viewed as an affront to their ability rather than as the inevitable consequences of education. Where challenges come to be viewed as disrupting the system though, there is the potential for finding ways to reduce this which some teachers may refer to as "dumbing down".

In considering the idea of the therapeutic turn within education, it can be seen to contribute to the decline of teaching in the way in which it moves the focus towards the experience of pupils and students in a manner which has the potential to see challenge as both uncomfortable and undesirable. This reflects a further aspect of taming in terms of how it increases the potential for ensuring certainty. However, an approach which may be seen as originating within a concern for inclusivity, something which is not being argued against here, becomes distorted as an approach which seems to place more value upon emotions than it does upon educational development. There is some merit in both the focus upon learning and the concern to be inclusive, but there is also a need to ensure that the practice of education does not become bogged down within concerns for individual wellbeing if this means that we seek to remove the challenge from education.

8.5   LEARNING STYLES

In one sense the decline of teaching corresponds with concerns about the student experience and with the move to meet pupil or student needs. Alongside the growing concern to ensure that pupils and students have a good experience though is the idea that this experience will be enhanced if teachers are able to meet the learning style of each "learner". The idea of learning styles can be seen to fit well with concerns about the provision of education which is inclusive as well as with the idea that ability rests on particular intrinsic qualities or characteristics.

The idea of learning styles, when considered alongside aspirations to be inclusive, is something that is very seductive but is a concept that has little to support it. I must, at this point, make it clear that I am not advocating exclusive teaching or exclusive education but I am concerned that ideas about how to be inclusive often rest upon a mistaken understanding of the concept of learning styles (Pashler et al. 2008). What was originally put forward as preferences for teaching styles has become endemic within education circles at all levels irrespective of the lack of evidence to support it (Busch 2016; Coffield 2008; Stobart 2008). What it means in practice is that teachers are often required to demonstrate that they are able to accommodate both inclusion and differentiation within their practice by producing lesson plans which illustrate how they meet the differing learning styles of all "learners" within their class. Of course, where this falls down, even if we accept, for arguments sake, that each "learner" will have different learning styles is that whilst the teacher is meeting the needs of the visual learners within their class by tailoring a part of the class to these "learners", the audio and kinaesthetic "learners" are effectively excluded, at least until the teacher changes his or her approach to a mode of teaching which suits those "learners". It should be evident then that any approach adopted by the teacher can only be meeting the needs of any one particular style at any time which means that inclusion within a class can only ever be episodic. In spite of this, however, learning styles, as a concept, has become quite firmly embedded within education.

Where the idea of learning styles becomes even more problematic though is when it becomes an obstacle to learning itself. Teachers within the Further Education and Higher Education sectors will probably have experienced the "learners" who proclaim, early on in their course, that they are one sort of learner or the other and this is why they cannot be expected to understand what you are teaching them at any particular time. That said, I don't wish to imply that such an attitude is established in "learners" minds before they enter Further or Higher Education. It is not that the individual "learner" is a product of their own self-knowledge. Rather, it is a case that they come to know themselves by the actions of others who act to shape self-knowledge. Many colleges and universities promote the concept of learning styles as part of courses or approaches that are aimed at developing effective study skills, and whilst effective study skills will do much to aid "learners" in their studies, the practice of encouraging them to see themselves as being one type of learner or another is in reality counterproductive.

The value of considering learning styles in an argument that is promoting wicked education is that they may be seen as one aspect of the way in which education is tamed. Instead of acknowledging the complexity of learning, the adoption of learning styles draws attention to the student in terms of how they are able to learn and narrows this in the process. The learning style approach acts to tame education. Learning styles contribute to the taming of education by providing an explanation to the "learner" which illuminates the reason for them finding something difficult but which seemingly ignores the fact that some issues are, indeed, difficult. The problem is that it does this in a way that effectively shuts down the efforts of the "learner". Instead of recognising that some things may be difficult to learn, and as such, seeing this as contributing to the challenge that they are faced with, the danger is that some "learners" shift the onus back to the teacher who is now charged with presenting the material that is causing the problem in a manner which suits their learning style.

This creates a situation whereby not learning is a consequence of not being presented with material in an appropriate manner and returns us to the argument that teaching is basically something which relies upon the mastery of certain techniques. In one sense though, there is an assumption that because each "learner" is endowed with a particular learning style, meeting that learning style will enable them to learn anything. I don't profess to having a learning style but I do know that I enjoy a good lecture or presentation, just like I enjoy a clearly written book. But that might be because my current work and interests concern abstract ideas. Such ideas are intangible. However, before embarking on an academic career, I was an electrician in heavy industry. I left school at the age of 16 and started an apprenticeship. One of the first things that I learnt was how to join different types of electrical cable. I was shown how to do this and I then practised doing it in the company of other apprentices. I am not at all convinced that I would have learnt how to join a cable as a consequence of having a lecture. Similarly, when it came to learning about electrical impedance, I am certain that I could not have learnt what it is by kinaesthetic means. I now teach students abstract concepts such as discourse or social constructionism, I rarely find kinaesthetic approaches work well.

What I take from this is that in actuality, rather than promoting the understanding that we each learn in particular ways, we would be better off recognising that certain practices can be more useful than others in certain situations. Something that can be summed up in the phrase "horses for courses". To achieve this though, we need to get our pupils and students to recognise that learning, and what we learn about, is not simple, it is complex. If we seek to tame learning, we are in danger of restricting it and of preventing our students from taking responsibility for the part that they have to play in learning. I do accept that the teacher who has a limited repertoire of approaches to teaching is likely to be less successful but this does not mean that they will never be successful. Similarly, I ascribe to the idea that adopting a variety of teaching styles is beneficial but not because this means that I am able to meet the varying learning needs of my students. There is no convincing evidence for the existence of learning styles. This means that when teachers are encouraged to adapt their teaching so as to meet these mythical styles, something else is at work.

8.6   PUPILS, STUDENTS OR CONSUMERS?

A recent advertising campaign for a popular, and extensive, network of burger outlets ran under the strapline "Have it your way". Similarly, a major mobile phone company has recently adopted the strapline "power to you". These are just two examples of a range of marketing and advertising campaigns which draw upon a strong discourse which asserts the idea of individual difference and choice, alongside the primacy of the consumer. This has some resonance with the concept of learning styles. We, as teachers, have contributed to the development of an approach which reinforces a degree of individualism into teaching and which reflects the consumerist culture within which we live. As we have developed an understanding of ourselves as individuals with different needs, needs that the market can satisfy, so the idea of learning styles falls into line with this. We find it easy to accept the concept of learning styles as real. This means that as teachers we find it difficult to resist the call to meet the needs of our pupils and students.

   In this sense pupils and students, as "learners", are the consumers of the services that we provide. Different parts of the education system as a whole may respond to this in different ways but the idea of choice and of meeting consumer needs is not something that is an alien concept within education within the twenty-first century. It is something that has shaped education for some time. So, in hindsight it may not be surprising then that after the incorporation of Further Education Colleges in 1993 in the UK, many colleges, as part of their embracing of marketisation, started to refer to students as customers and renamed Student Services departments as Customer Services (Cripps 2002). Of course, we also know that "the customer is always right" so it falls upon us to provide our services in the way that the "learner" wants. Such an idea also underpins the focus on choice that has become entwined with the English school system wherein it is expected that parents will want to choose the best school for children. Such a claim is currently being utilised as part of proposals to reintroduce selective Grammar schools. The reintroduction of Grammar schools was raised by the UK government in September 2016, not because of any compelling evidence that the Grammar school system is beneficial but, ostensibly, because it will offer more choice. Of course we are unlikely to see Grammar schools being supported on the grounds that a school of inferior quality is now a choice.

If we take the idea of meeting customer needs further, many Higher Education teachers will recognise the student who states that they need a 2:1. This need may be asserted either before or after submission of their work. It might be seen, then, that the acceptance of learning styles fits comfortably with an overall view that teachers are there to provide for students, who, in post-compulsory education, may well be paying a significant amount to be on the course. Of course, I have previously argued that it is erroneous to equate students with customers per se but it must also be accepted that this does not mean that some students do not see themselves as customers. Because of this, for many, what the student wants with respect to the outcome of their education takes precedence over their engagement with their studies.

So, in Higher Education in the twenty-first century in England, it is not unusual for students to be provided with class notes and selected readings via the eponymous Virtual Learning Environments that are in general use. Alongside this contemporary ICT systems provide access to e-books in a manner that means that the library can actually stock sufficient core texts for every student and enable them to be able to search for and access statistical evidence and journal articles in a way that was unthinkable only 20 years ago. Yet in spite of the massive advances in how students are now provided for, many still seem to overlook their own role in the achieving of awards.

8.7   CONCLUSION

What can be seen within the landscape of contemporary education then is a number of developments which are not directly focused on education itself, but which exist to serve interests or concerns which may be seen as affecting education. We can see this in the rise of a therapeutic culture that is aimed at meeting the needs of pupils and students with a view to assisting them to fit in with education. As focus has turned towards the needs of pupils and students though, we can also see how it has been accompanied by a change of focus, away from teaching and towards learning. There is a common-sense aspect to this turn towards learning though as we would all accept that we want learning to take place. What has been suggested though is that such developments also contribute to the taming of education and to the view of education as being a process.

In many ways then the contemporary context of education is one in which much time and effort has gone into removing the uncertainty from education. Education has come to reflect a process, at least in the minds of many who are involved in it, be they policymakers, education staff or pupils and students. It has become a process that exists within a culture of consumerism though and this exerts some influence over how education is provided for and experienced. That does not mean though that education has been improved because of this. In many ways, what we have become left with is an approach that is so bound up with meeting consumer need, or meeting externally imposed targets, that it has been tamed. It is as though all parties have come to know what to expect from education because this is bound up with particular ways of organising and providing education. The primary concerns of organisations are to get the consumers of education in, to keep them in and then to see them leave with qualifications that are deemed to be valid. In schools it may be 5 GCSEs at grades A–C, soon to be 6–9; in Higher Education it tends to be 2:1 and above. In all cases the concern is to remove uncertainty, to make it more certain that pupils and students will leave with the right awards, to remove all risk. It is such concerns though that emphasise the student experience in a way that can reduce the challenge to students so as to make outcomes more certain, to not trying new approaches because that adds an element of risk and to give so much effort over to meeting student needs. In other words, in the contemporary landscape of education, it is a concern with issues such as these that also contribute to the taming of education.

REFERENCES

Ball, Stephen J. 2015. Education, Governance and the Tyranny of Numbers. *Journal of Education Policy* 30 (3): 299–301. doi:10.1080/02680939.2015.1013271.
———. 2016. Neoliberal Education? Confronting the Slouching Beast. *Policy Futures in Education* 14 (8): 13.

Ball, Stephen J., and Antonio Olmedo. 2013. Care of the Self, Resistance and Subjectivity Under Neoliberal Governmentalities. *Critical Studies in Education* 54 (1): 85–96.

Biesta, Gert. 2010. Learner, Student, Speaker: Why It Matters How We Call Those We Teach. *Educational Philosophy & Theory* 42 (5–6): 540–552. doi:10.1111/j.1469-5812.2010.00684.x.

———. 2012. Giving Teaching Back to Education: Responding to the Disappearance of the Teacher. *Phenomenology & Practice* 6 (2): 14.

———. 2013. *The Beautiful Risk of Education*. Boulder, CO: Paradigm Publishers.

Brookfield, S. 1995. *Becoming a Critically Reflective Teacher*. San Francisco, CA: Jossey-Bass.

Busch, B. 2016. Four Neuromyths that are still Prevalent in Schools – Debunked. *The Guardian*.

Chakrabortty, A. 2016. Think Only Low–Paid Workers Get the Sports Direct treatment? You're Wrong. *The Guardian*.

Chakrabortty, A., and S. Weale. 2016. Universities Accused of 'Importing Sports Direct Model' for Lecturers' Pay. *The Guardian*.

Clarke, Matthew. 2012. The (Absent) Politics of Neo-Liberal Education Policy. *Critical Studies in Education* 53 (3): 297–310. doi:10.1080/17508487.2012 .703139.

Clarke, M., and A. Phelan. 2017. *Teacher Education and the Political: The Power of Negative Thinking*. London: Routledge.

Coffield, Frank. 2008. *Just Suppose Teaching and Learning Became the First Priority*. London: Learning and Skills Network. Edited by Learning and Skills Network.

Cripps, Sandy. 2002. *Further Education, Government's Discourse Policy and Practice: Killing a Paradigm Softly*. Aldershot: Ashgate.

DfES. 2001. *Schools Achieving Success*. Annesley: DfES. Edited by Dept for Education and Skills.

Ecclestone, K., and D. Hayes. 2009. *The Dangerous Rise of Therapeutic Education*. London: Routledge.

Fischman, Gustavo. 2008. Introduction. In *Contesting Neoliberal Education: Public Resistance and Collective Advance*, ed. Dave Hill. Abingdon: Routledge.

Gorard, Stephen, and Chris Taylor. 2001. The Composition of Specialist Schools in England: Track Record and Future Prospect. *School Leadership & Management* 21 (4): 365–381. doi:10.1080/13632430120108916.

Hayek, Frederik von. 2013/1973, 1976, 1979. *Law, Legislation and Liberty*. Abingdon: Routledge.

Hayes, D. 2003. Managerialism and Professionalism in Post-Compulsory Education. In *Working in Post-Compulsory Education*, ed. J. Lea, D. Hayes, A. Armitage, L. Lomas, and S. Markless. Maidenhead: Open University Press.

————. 2015. As They Compete to Lay on the Best Student Experience, Universities Mustn't Forget the Academic One Too. http://theconversation.com/as-they-compete-to-lay-on-the-best-student-experience-universities-mustnt-forget-the-academic-one-too-45197

Irisdotter Aldenmyr, Sara, and Maria Olson. 2016. The Inward Turn in Therapeutic Education—An Individual Enterprise Promoted in the Name of the Common Good. *Pedagogy, Culture and Society* 24 (3): 387–400.

Leach, Tony, and Ellie Lewis. 2013. Children's Experiences During Circle-Time: A Call for Research-Informed Debate. *Pastoral Care in Education* 31 (1): 43–52. doi:10.1080/02643944.2012.702781.

Macfarlane, B. 2017. *Freedom to Learn: The Threat to Student Academic Freedom and Why It Needs to Be Reclaimed*. Abingdon: Routledge.

Pashler, H., M. McDaniel, D. Rohrer, and R. Bjork. 2008. Learning Styles: Concepts and Evidence. *Psychological Science in the Public Interest*. 9 (3): 15.

Perraudin, F. 2016. Academy Trust Accused of Discriminating Against Disabled Pupils. *The Guardian*.

Preston, Susan, and Jordan Aslett. 2014. Resisting Neoliberalism from Within the Academy: Subversion Through an Activist Pedagogy. *Social Work Education 33* (4): 502–518.

Regan, Bernard. 2008. Campaigning Against Neoliberal Education in Britain. In *Contesting neoliberal Education: Public Resistance and Collective Advance*, ed. Dave Hill. Abingdon: Routledge.

SSAT. 2007. By Schools for Schools: The Origins, History and Influence of the Specialist Schools and Academies Trust, 1987–2007. Specialist Schools and Academies Trust.

Stobart, Gordon. 2008. *Testing Times: The Uses and Abuses of Assessment*. Abingdon: Routledge.

West, Anne. 2001. Choice and Diversity: The Case for Small Specialist Schools. *New Economy* 8 (4): 208.

Wright, Katie. 2014. Student Wellbeing and the Therapeutic Turn in Education. *The Educational and Developmental Psychologist* 31 (2): 141–152. doi:10.1017/edp.2014.14.

CHAPTER 9

Towards Wicked Education

9.1 Introduction: The Need for Risk

Although it is inevitable that this final chapter will do more to make a case for wicked education, it may be fruitful to start with emphasising something which has previously been implicit rather than explicit, that there are benefits to be gained from being challenged and taking risks (Biesta 2013). Education is risky but that risk should not be equated with being problematic or troublesome. Risk is necessary for development and development may be seen as integral to education. In making such a claim though, this can be seen as offering a rather different approach towards the idea of risk compared to the safety-first approach that appears to have become endemic within social and public services.

Understanding risk can be seen as pertinent to the argument that education has become tame. In the move towards an understanding of education as a process, it has been shown that much effort has gone into removing uncertainty. Uncertainty is not something that is welcome in contemporary society. As a consequence the role of teachers comes to be pulled back from engaging in activities which are new because within newness there is uncertainty. Because of this teachers, at all levels, are much more likely to be risk averse. In part this is because the sorts of techno-rational, bureaucratic systems that have been constructed within education make innovation more difficult, but also because a constant focus upon results makes innovation risky. When coupled with a culture of performativity, taking risks with teaching becomes a risky business.

© The Author(s) 2018
R. Creasy, *The Taming of Education*,
DOI 10.1007/978-3-319-62247-7_9

The idea of risk as shaping social life can be seen as having been documented by Beck (1992). For Beck, late modernity has seen the concept of risk becoming a major concern with respect to social life. This is especially true for those charged with the provision of social and public services. However, although on the face of it risk can be seen as being associated with events and practices which may lead to harm, it can also be seen that it is associated more accurately with a concern about outcomes, especially unwanted outcomes.

As a concept the idea of risk is relevant to wickedity and tameness because of the way in which a concern with risk has come to be manifest as underpinning risk-averse practices. In turn this reflects some of the arguments put forward earlier with respect to how control over processes has sought to remove uncertainty. In terms of risk, sensitivity to the potential negative consequences of risk can be seen to have led to restrictions on social practices as certainty has come to be viewed as preferable to uncertainty. As was argued earlier, certainty is made more possible by tame practices. Wickedity is much less certain and is therefore associated with risk.

We also need to consider a broader picture of risk though. It is easy to argue that an aversion to risk that originates within a target-driven culture, where results and accountability dominate, leads to teachers being reluctant to try new approaches. It is also worthwhile to consider the ways in which educational leadership promotes risk aversion and consider how that also impacts upon pupils and students. So, when Spielman, speaking as the head of Ofsted, criticises schools for gaming the system, we can also see how risk aversion may come to limit the opportunities afforded to some pupils on the grounds that these pupils pose a risk to the school (Ofsted and Spielman 2017; Bloom 2017). In this situation a focus on the process coincides with a form of governmentality which is focused primarily upon organisational image in a manner that effectively denies education to some.

We can provide a justification for ensuring that risk is preserved within education then on the grounds of the benefits for learning and development that it can provide (Biesta 2013), but this should be seen not only in terms of what teachers do within the classroom, it should also be in terms of what institutions do in terms of admission and provision. The call to take risks however may create tensions where politicians and managers seek certainty with respect to outcomes. Because of this we might understand how it is that teaching has become subject to increased levels of control and how standardisation and performativity have become endemic.

Where this has relevance for teachers is with respect to how tried and tested methods become established as good practice in a way that discourages innovative approaches. Innovation inevitably introduces uncertainty. It is a risk. This is not to say that nothing can, or will, change, but it does point to the way that change may be avoided by some and how tame approaches, approaches which are more likely to secure positive results, become privileged. What follows from a combination of following good practice and being risk averse is a situation whereby standardisation becomes more possible, where resistance to standardisation is reduced.

9.2   STANDARDISATION: EQUITY AND ACCOUNTABILITY

Standardisation was shown to be important previously. The importance of considering standardisation as one of the forces which shape education was established as being because it can be seen as very influential in the taming of education. Standardisation does not sit easily with creativity and originality. This is because creativity and originality make outcomes uncertain. In fact creativity and originality are intrinsically uncertain. However, as argued previously, promoting and nurturing creativity and originality is a significant part of what we should be wanting of an education system. In many ways it is creativity and originality that should be seen as the most desirable outcome of education. Because of this, we should not be satisfied that creativity and originality have come to be seen as the preserve of just one sector within education, Higher Education. The importance of originality and creativity means that it is something that we should seek to develop and nurture throughout all levels of education. It seems perverse to establish an education system whereby students need to persevere through around 13 years of mundane education before being given the scope to be creative. Of course, the real danger is that even the Higher Education sector becomes tame. As has been argued throughout this book, a number of developments, as typified by those related to standardisation, are quite likely to lead to pupils and students at all levels being taught to be tame, by tame teachers. As such we need to establish that there are benefits to be gained from an approach which promotes wickedity but that a wicked education may resist standardisation. Our pupils and students are not standardised, they are not uniform, and neither should their education be also.

Developments that have led to increasing standardisation were established in Chap. 4 and concerns about standardisation were evident within the interviews referred to in Chap. 7. Indeed, there is a strong case for standardisation as it can be promoted on the grounds of equity. It can also be seen in discussions regarding accountability. If accountability is established as a goal, then standardisation can be recognised as a way of achieving that. Accountability and standardisation, however, fit more easily with processes that are tame than they do with processes, such as teaching and learning, which can be better understood as wicked. This reiterates a concern for all parties engaged in education though. The question may be asked regarding what education is for and whether or not accountability and standardisation should be privileged over the development of creativity and originality. There is a sense wherein it appears as though that is precisely the situation that has been arrived at.

Currently it appears that education can be seen as being squeezed, to an extent, between two external forces which share similar concerns. On the one hand, the position of regulatory bodies such as Ofsted or the QAA for Higher Education acts as a force which pushes for increasing standardisation on the grounds of accountability; on the other hand, pupils and students have a strong claim to be treated in an equitable manner. There is some degree of synergy in these two forces because standardisation can be seen to give the illusion of equity but each may act to tame education. For example, with regard to assessment, as was considered in Chap. 7, a more wicked approach to assessment could appear to undermine standardisation if this means that some degree of choice regarding assessment is developed. This could be seen as inequitable if not presented clearly. Because of this, the issue of equity might be something that can be seen as problematic within a wicked approach to assessment that incorporates different approaches. Any calls for wickedity within education then must be able to incorporate the range of benefits that it may afford.

Consider the way in which, in the UK, coursework, to be completed outside of school, was introduced to national examinations such as the GCSE and A level, but which has been subsequently reduced or removed because of concerns regarding authenticity. This illustrates the argument about accountability but it can be argued that that are good reasons for not privileging accountability if the outcome is a system that stifles creativity, a tame outcome (Hurst 2013).

As part of the research reported in Chap. 7, it was noted that one teacher defended the use of learning outcomes because such a standardised approach affords a degree of protection to students by restricting the activities of academics. The argument being offered was that in previous decades teachers in Higher Education had free rein to focus all of their teaching on their own, often esoteric, interests and that this was not in the student's best interests. In this way reducing the power of academics who teach was presented as a positive development but this was not for academic reasons, it was for bureaucratic reasons. If, by reducing the power of academics who teach, their power to motivate and stimulate students is also reduced, it might be argued that this has the consequence of impoverishing the potential of education.

This is not an argument that is restricted to Higher Education. If, because of a desire to standardise education across all levels or sectors, we transform teachers from professionals to technicians, we build in the potential to distance teachers from their subject (Bottery 2008). By shifting the focus of teachers to the outcomes of their work, that is to say, the results achieved by their students, we run the risk of removing the joy, the fun, from teaching and end up with teachers who just go through the motions. The processes which impose measurements of quality onto teachers work, and which foster the growth of performativity (Macfarlane 2017; Ball 2015, 2013), may be seen as doing just this. They have been able to become established within education because of the move towards seeing it as a process and where the focus is on the measurement of results. The school, the college and the university then become just another form of factory (Coffield and Williamson 2011). There will be some who may respond to this comment by claiming that such work is not meant to be fun but talk to pupils and students though and take note of how often they rate teachers who they perceive to be taking enjoyment from their discipline as better teachers. The converse of this holds true; those teachers who are seen as going through the motions are rarely seen as good teachers.

This is not to suggest that academics should have no restrictions per se but it does provide support for research-informed teaching. It also provides an argument for a system of quality assurance which evaluates the outcomes of programmes of study in a way that can accommodate the demonstration by students of creativity and originality rather than determining what will count as a valid outcome to begin with. Such a system will not be one which emphasises the types of performativity that are currently fostered by a focus upon accountability and the types of performance which rest upon an understanding of teaching as technique. In achieving this there is a need to recognise that it is teachers who have expert knowledge.

So, if we are aiming towards establishing wickedity within education, there is a need to be clear as to what standardisation achieves. I am not advocating educational systems wherein chaos reigns over order but I am arguing that standardisation should not be a goal in itself or that standardisation should be established solely for the purposes of accountability. This is particularly pertinent where standardisation is used to determine the perfect lesson. Such a view is often embedded within processes of quality audits of teaching. I am minded of an observation of my own teaching. The class was a seminar, something that I took to mean an opportunity for students to discuss the content of a lecture that they had previously attended.

After being observed within the one hour of the seminar, my observer reported that it had been an excellent class but that she was unable to award me the highest grade that was available because I had not employed ICT within the class. My response was that this was because the class was a seminar; it was a space for discussion. The problem for the observer, however, was that the pro forma being used dictated that an excellent class would not only demonstrate differentiation, something it was agreed that I had clearly demonstrated through my questioning and challenging of students, but that it would employ ICT also. This was no doubt influenced by the fact that the college had invested heavily in Smart boards and wanted to see them used. My observer was in agreement that students had been engaged and that they had clearly had a good learning experience, but the pro forma determined that without the use of technology, no matter how irrelevant, this could not be recorded as excellent. The standardised system that was in place was what was important.

Where standardisation comes to dominate within any educational organisation, we are more likely to see teachers become akin to automatons, following scripts or routines within their classes, presenting to pupils and students who know exactly what to expect and who themselves are stripped of their humanity and individualisation. The standardised classroom or school is the classroom where pupils and students become disengaged and who join the teacher in going through the motions.

For me, the standardised teacher has little merit. I do not see the standardised teacher as the teacher that best serves the interests of pupils and students but that does not mean that this view will be shared by all. The standardised teacher may have value to the organisation if that means that such teachers become interchangeable. This contributes to the idea of business efficiency but efficiency is not the same as effectiveness. I have long heard the mantra "if you can teach, you can teach anything", I am yet to be convinced that it is valid. If education is to be fit for purpose, then there is a need to be very cautious about the way in which standardisation has become established across all sectors or levels of education.

9.3 WICKED ASSESSMENT AND THE PLACE OF LEARNING OUTCOMES

A concern with standardised approaches to assessment has already been established, and we can see within assessment just how particular practices such as teaching and assessing in a way that is aligned with learning outcomes can be counterproductive. Assessment then is obviously important in respect of an understanding of how education can be tame or wicked. The move towards assessment for learning, as it originally emerged within the schools sector, shows the extent to which assessment practices shape learning. It would be easy to dismiss a concern with assessment as being indicative of a utilitarian approach to education but it is the case that the mode of assessment that is adopted requires the development of particular skills. It should be self-evident that the use of examinations, as a form of assessment, will do more to encourage rote learning with a view to recall than will many other forms of assessment. Because of this, the ways in which assessment tasks are set up will push pupils and students to developing particular skills. At one level tame assessment can be seen as reflecting the rote learning of facts or pieces of information though it can also be seen in establishing what counts as learning also. Indeed, although it can be seen that there are clear benefits to some individuals in some roles being able to know certain things, such as formula, for some roles this is not sufficient at all. This returns us to the debate introduced earlier regarding the relative merits of education versus training. It also reflects the argument regarding the ways in which examinations promote surface learning but that what is really required is deep learning (Hargreaves and Fink 2006; Biggs 2003). Biggs does much to support the argument for depth in learning, if by deep learning we mean the development of understanding, but the focus on learning outcomes that is intrinsic to the solution offered by Biggs et al. (Biggs and Tang 2011, 2007; Biggs 2003, 1999; Biggs and Collis 1982) only contributes to tameness in spite of the authors' exhortations to accommodate unexpected learning as was discussed previously. For example, consider how arguments have been made to write learning outcomes that can be assessed and that teaching should be directed towards them (Kennedy 2008; Moon 2002).

In considering assessment it would be hard to argue that different students could be treated differently when it comes to assessing their learning but that still leaves a concern regarding how to accommodate creativity and originality. At the same time, it can be seen that individuals have different abilities or aptitudes and that possessing a range of abilities has benefits when it comes to being effective at work. What this suggests then is that adopting uniform approaches to the assessment of learning may be seen as being only partially effective if we want to assess the extent of learning or of change.

Although wickedity has tended to be presented as promoting creativity and originality, in a way that standardised approaches often fail to do, it can be argued that the benefits of wickedity are not restricted to this. Wicked assessment, for example, will also be fairer in giving students the opportunity to demonstrate their abilities to a greater extent and, as will be argued, may also contribute to fostering greater student engagement. However, it is also the case that adopting variable assessment as part of wicked education may conflict with concerns for accountability.

As such, achieving wickedity will rest upon accommodating a plurality of views with respect to how student work is assessed. The development and use of wicked assessment will be beneficial but failing to take the concerns of all parties into account is likely to lead to failure (Ney and Verweij 2014). Ney and Verweij refer to the clumsiness of solutions to wicked problems. There cannot be a tame strategy to achieving wickedity. So, because the drivers of tame assessment are plural, it should be recognised that changing this will not be straightforward.

It soon becomes apparent that the challenges to changing assessment are not uniform across education as a whole. In the primary sector within the UK, catering to children up to the age of 11, assessment is focused on Standard Assessment Tests (SATs). SATs, as a national form of assessment, are presented as a mechanism for providing evidence regarding children's progress, often on the grounds that parents will want to know this. They can also be understood as being driven by concerns with achieving regulation and accountability (Whetton 2009; Firestone 1998). Achieving a change to the existing system of SATs will involve political effort to reposition the professional judgement of teachers as valid. However, the driver behind the introduction of SATs was very much a political mistrust of professionalism as demonstrated by the third Thatcher government rather than for real educational purposes (Whetton **2009**). Because of this, and because SATs do not lead to public awards, there is probably greater scope for change with respect to SATs than there is for higher levels of the compulsory schooling sector where national public examinations lead to particular awards.

At secondary level, assessment within the UK is dominated by public examinations such as the GCSE. The scope of this assessment may make change from an examination approach very difficult but the history of assessment within England demonstrates that it is possible to incorporate coursework into the process. Again, the obstacle to changing this is generally political and, as with SATs, accountability plays a significant part in the GCSE system.

Within the Higher Education sector though, the relative independence of Higher Education Institutions affords much greater scope for wicked assessment. Although there are regulatory and accountability pressures resulting from the remit of the QAA for Higher Education, there is much greater scope for flexibility and creativity within Higher Education than in other sectors of education.

For change to be achieved though, to move towards wicked education, it is important that staff involved in assessment, not just teachers, be open to the possibility. For example, in the research reported on above, in Chap. 7, it could be argued that amongst the two staff groups, Quality Officers and teaching staff, there was little sense of an understanding that assessment within Higher Education could and should promote creativity and that assessment could be wicked. It was clear that some teaching staff expressed concern regarding the consequences of standardisation but it was more a sense of being critical of such approaches than of promoting a creative alternative. In other words, there was little sense that a wicked approach to assessment within Higher Education was something to strive for. This was most evident in the discussions about learning outcomes.

Although it should be obvious that I have a number of concerns for the ways in which education is developing, for me it is learning outcomes which stand out as the epitome of the way in which education comes to be seen as a process, and it is the ways in which learning outcomes are often used which does the most to tame education. This generally applies to Higher Education as at other levels it is public examinations which act to establish whether or not pupils or students have successfully learnt what was intended. That is not to say that learning outcomes have no impact upon other levels of education. They do, especially in relation to how good teaching sessions came to be scripted as starting with aims and objectives and with an explicit focus upon identifying how the learning outcomes were being addressed.

This should not be taken as a total rejection of learning outcomes. It would be easy to reach the conclusion that the factors which have led to changes within education have created systems and approaches which all need to be rejected, that we should give carte blanche to teachers with respect to what they do. As was said earlier, there are benefits to be gained from imposing structure onto education. When it comes to learning outcomes, we can see that they provide some benefits to the process of planning within education. In turn this can be seen to enhance how we approach teaching. The issue then is how we use learning outcomes, especially with how teachers use learning outcomes in either a hard or soft way when it comes to assessment. We might consider that in one sense the difference is between teachers using learning outcomes or learning outcomes restricting what teachers do.

An adoption of learning outcomes as soft can be achieved by establishing learning outcomes as intended or indicative. This approach will contribute to accommodating wickedity. In this approach learning outcomes may be established as part of planning and can contribute to discussions regarding what is being aimed for. It is what the teacher intends to be the outcome of study or what would indicate learning, but as the learning outcomes are only designated as intended or indicative, there is scope for the student to demonstrate a greater extent of their learning. In this approach we see an ability to reward the demonstration of what Hussey and Smith (2010) refer to as unintended or congruent learning outcomes. As the learning outcomes are not being established as a threshold, the student who produces a good piece of work can be rewarded for what they have done, rather than being penalised for what they have failed to do. This provides for a more positive, not to be confused with a positivist (!), approach to assessment which can be seen as being appreciative. This appreciative approach can be contrasted with what is essentially a deficit model as is intrinsic to using learning outcomes as hard. In the hard approach, learning outcomes are seen as having to be met because the first thing that any teacher must ask of an assignment submitted under a hard regime is "have the learning outcomes been met?"

An adoption of learning outcomes as hard means that they are established as thresholds which students are required to meet as indicated above. In this position we can see that learning outcomes become manifest as a bureaucratic, techno-rational device. They can act to dissuade teachers from appreciating what the student has done by narrowing the focus of assessment. Adopting learning outcomes as hard has the consequence that they are significantly more likely to act to tame the social process of assessment, with the danger that education is impoverished because of the inability to accommodate creativity and originality. In this position, as has been shown, it is possible for a student to submit a good assignment yet still be awarded a fail mark if the assignment is not able to demonstrate that one or more of the learning outcomes had been met. This was something that was reported upon in Chap. 7. Of course, within this position an assignment that does not demonstrate that some learning outcomes have been met would not be seen as good. This illustrates to an extent the way in which policies and procedures can come to shape the epistemological position adopted by teachers. At the same time, if we have a situation whereby teachers approach learning outcomes differently, then there is scope for problems to arise as this is a potential source for differential practice which can be understood as providing for inequitable practices.

The adoption of hard learning outcomes within assessment reflects a tame approach because of the way that the learning outcomes establish not only what the student will learn but also acts to invalidate other learning. This is because this approach generally restricts the student to producing work which is tied to demonstrating the learning outcomes. They may well have learnt other things as part of their studies, but there is likely to be little value in demonstrating this if it means that they do so at the expense of demonstrating that they have also met a learning outcome that is the focus of that assessment task. In such a system creativity and originality are less likely to be rewarded. A wicked approach to assessment would more easily accommodate a demonstration of learning which is not captured by the learning outcomes but which is made clear and explicit by the student. A wicked approach to assessment then would be able to accommodate and reward a student who is able to demonstrate creativity or originality.

That said, all educational institutions are subject to some form of quality assurance. Institutions such as schools and colleges, offering courses leading to public examinations, are subject to having their work assured through Ofsted inspections and moderation of examination entries by awarding bodies. This is not the same for Higher Education Institutions. There is little oversight by external bodies of standards with respect to the awards that are made. It is the case that Higher Education Institutions are obliged to assure the QAA that they have robust quality systems in place and that these provide for equity, and it can be argued that to cease using learning outcomes completely may create problems. However, it should be possible to revise how learning outcomes are used in a way which reflects the idea presented earlier above; how they may be seen as hard or soft.

One approach to the problematic nature of learning outcomes within Higher Education would be to use assessment to demonstrate that programme-level learning outcomes are met. This acts to move programmes within Higher Education towards the model adopted with GCE A levels to an extent by being focused on the programme as a whole, such as a BA/Sc (Hons) or FD as is analogous to an A level overall. This means that different contents may be covered in a way that modules within a FD or BA/Sc equate to a curriculum. If learning outcomes at programme level are treated as hard, in that they exist as threshold statements, it becomes possible for a university to satisfy the QAA that programmes reflect subject benchmarks. As such, students must demonstrate that they have met them. However, learning outcomes at module level could be treated as soft. In this way, learning outcomes at module level become guides rather than thresholds. Within Higher Education it is not unusual for both programme, and module-level learning outcomes to be established at validation, but then in practice, it is only module-level learning outcomes which are assessed. There is an assumption then that completing modules within a programme means that a student has achieved programme-level learning outcomes. This adds a level of complication which does not exist with GCE A levels.

In this way programme-level learning outcomes provide for quality assurance systems relating to subject benchmark statements and have to be demonstrated but a greater degree of flexibility is provided in terms of how students achieve the threshold at each level. Given that it is marks awarded at module level which contribute to the overall degree classification, the establishment of soft learning outcomes at module level (presented as intended learning outcomes and which are used to guide what students and teaching staff are likely to do within a module) provides greater scope for students to be rewarded for creative and original work.

As part of the move towards wicked education, a review of learning outcomes is likely to be a task that is achievable and is more realistic than an attempt to remove their use. Continuing to use learning outcomes as hard however may well reinforce the tameness that can be seen in some

Higher Education courses. Starting to use learning outcomes as soft will provide advantages. The aim will be to evaluate the extent to which creativity and originality can be encouraged, supported and rewarded. Where learning outcomes are identified as being restrictive, or where they do little to promote and accommodate creativity and originality, they should be considered as being in need of change.

9.4   CRITICAL REFLECTION

As part of the move towards achieving wickedity within education then, it should be apparent that many aspects of practice that have been established for good reason, or which are simply taken for granted, must be opened up to scrutiny. Because of this achieving wickedity means that there is also a need to change the epistemological positions held by those stakeholder groups who work within education. Central to this is the development of critically reflective practice, with a focus on creativity and originality. Within the Higher Education sector, the role of research has a prominent position, and for many teaching staff, it is engagement with the subject discipline that motivates them to become academic staff. The relevance of this is that many staff may be less concerned with understanding the practice of teaching than they are in their subject discipline. In schools and colleges, it may be the case that staff are more concerned with the practice of teaching than they are with research but the move towards seeing teaching as a practical activity rather than an intellectual or academic activity is something which is less likely to equip teachers for wickedity and is something which is very likely to undermine the experience of being a teacher.

The tension between those who see teachers as autonomous professionals and those who see them as branded technicians (Bottery 2008) can also be seen as a tension between those who may be more amenable to wicked education compared to those who seek tameness. What is evident is that how we train teachers is important in establishing their own understanding of what education can be and their role within it. As teachers we all have a need to cope with the classroom situation, no matter what level we work at and because of this, there is an element of seductiveness to training rather than education. The danger though is that the trained technician becomes less able to move teaching forward. In the same ways that it was said that education policy has become depoliticised, educational practice becomes de-theorised. The consequence of this is that challenges come to be viewed as being possible to tame through the adoption of particular routines or strategies. In such a scenario, the image of education as a process is reinforced. In this scenario the successful teacher is the teacher who employs the right tactics or practices, and in doing so their pupils or students learn and then demonstrate this learning by passing whatever form of assessment is being used to verify such learning.

One response to this is the promotion of the value of critical reflection with respect to teaching practices, and with regard to the policy and practice of institutions, especially with regard to how this contributes to the taming of education. In many ways I am wary of the rise of reflective practice, seeing it as a further way in which responsibility is in danger of being individualised. Academics such as Moon (2004, 1999) have successfully promoted the idea of reflective practice and it does fit well with the idea of professionals as empowered but this can overlook the conditions under which professionals work. There is an assumption within reflective practice that professionals are able to improve practice overall by changing what they do. Such a view takes little notice of the ways in which structural conditions, such as the policy framework of an organisation, may act as an obstacle to professional practice. The problem with reflection then lies in the capacity to end up as an instrument of blame in line with the concepts of governmentality and performativity (Macfarlane 2017; Ball 2013; Ball 2003).

The basic premise of reflective practice, something that has become endemic across a range of services and professions over recent decades, is that professionals take time to reflect upon why their efforts are not achieving the desired outcomes or how their practice may be enhanced. In this way reflective practice may be seen as an integral part of professionalism. There is the potential for problems however which can be seen when reflective practice is decontextualised, when the professional is brought to the fore at the expense of the structural and ideological context within which they are working. When this happens reflective practice may ultimately be disheartening and depressing.

For example, between 2010 and 2017 in England, professional practice as a whole, not just in education, has been subject to policies developed within a discourse of austerity. The claim from the governments during this time (a Conservative-Liberal coalition from 2010 to 2015, and a Conservative Government led by David Cameron from 2015 to June 2016) was that the UK was living beyond its means in running a budget deficit and that public spending needed to be significantly reduced because of this. The reduction in public spending saw reduced levels of funding for public services. The consequences for public sector workers have been more difficult working conditions as workloads rose because of staff cuts and an increased demand on many services. The reflective practitioner may recognise the changed conditions and seek to change their practice but it is important to acknowledge that they are only able to change so much. It is important that they do not internalise failure and start to see themselves as the problem, the source of weakness when, in fact, the problem is external to them.

For example, if we consider education as social provision that is being carried out within a context of neoliberalism in terms of social and public policies, where reductions in funding and the ideology of New Public Management require efficiency savings, we can start to see how changed conditions may impact upon teachers. One problem for management within educational organisations is how to accommodate funding reductions. One approach that has been adopted is to reduce the number of teaching hours allocated to any particular course. So, an A level course which may have been allocated six teaching hours per week in 1991 now has three hours per week allocated to it. The teacher still has to meet the same syllabus requirements but has less time in which to do this. However, because it is necessary to ensure that the teacher is teaching to their contractual hours, they are able to teach two A level classes where previously they only had to teach one. This intensifies their work and increases their workload in a manner that appears to be economically efficient. From a naïve reflective perspective though, if results start to fall, because the teacher now has much more work and less time for each class, the teacher will focus upon their own practice.

This is why it is important that reflection is critical. Reflection needs to extend beyond a consideration of what the teacher is able to do and start to recognise that teachers always work within a context over which they have increasingly had little control or influence. In the scenario presented above, it would not be surprising that the pressures of work make tame education welcome. The need to cope in a highly pressured environment lends itself to welcoming tameness.

Teachers will often be very comfortable with the idea of being critical within their own discipline; a much broader scope with respect to critical appreciation is required though to enhance professional activity. If we have a concern to promote wickedity within education, then promoting critical reflection of education as a whole will contribute to achieving this.

This is not to argue that all existing practices are in need of changing, rather it is to recognise that existing practices may not necessarily be based upon developing creativity and originality and so support tameness rather than wickedity. Critical reflection may be seen though as requiring professional confidence and the situation within England is such that teachers have been subject to political criticism for a long time. To foster critical reflection, it will be beneficial for teachers to recognise that when it comes to matters of education, it is worth reiterating that is they who are the experts, not politicians.

In making the claim that it is teachers, rather than politicians, who are experts, there is the basis of a more democratic approach towards education. An approach wherein those individuals who are charged with actually educating others regain some understanding of their own ability, based upon both theory and practice, to shape how education is carried out. In twenty-first-century England though, it seems as though teachers, at all levels, are viewed as resources to be used for the benefit of an organisation, rather than being viewed as individuals within their own right. At the same time that teachers across all sectors are being seen in a way which devalues them as individuals, we have seen how viewing pupils and students as consumers has also changed how they are seen. In the case of pupils and students, especially in post-compulsory and Higher Education, there has been a growing concern with how they experience education, whilst at the same time how teachers experience their role as teachers appears to be valued much less. How we value those who are engaged in education is obviously important.

9.5   VALUES

A key starting point then with regard to moving away from tameness and towards wickedity is the need for those working within education to work towards the adoption of an agreed view of what education is and what it is for. The issue of values is important in this respect as values will shape what we see as, and how we provide for, education. The discussion of learning, and of the therapeutic turn, has shown how values can shape education but in ways which may actually undermine the practice of teaching and contribute to tame education. Another way in which values can shape education is with respect to establishing what counts as quality. There is a danger that in a context where targets have become important, and where regulatory systems have been established, the result is that educational providers get drawn into being focused upon the production of data because data has become the measure of quality (Roberts-Holmes 2015). The consequence is that, as illustrated previously, quality is viewed as a measure of following a bureaucratic or administrative system rather than in terms of academic outcomes. Effort is diverted from providing education, to providing data. In this way both teachers and students can end up being drawn into the milieu of performativity as they seek to counter the prevailing value of mistrust by showing what they have done (Macfarlane 2017; Ball 2013).

What we should be considering is that the real measure of a quality assurance system is the extent to which it provides for outcomes that are desired. Although Chap. 4 demonstrated the ways in which economic aims have been important in recent decades, I would want to argue that the measure of quality within education is the extent to which creativity and originality are nurtured and rewarded. This reflects the arguments presented previously by Bottery (2004) and Hargreaves (2003), both of whom point to the importance of innovation within contemporary economic activities. This is because the role of individuals who can innovate plays a significant part in achieving economic advantage. It may be seen as odd that neoliberalism is generally understood as being an economistic ideology but that it seems to offer little in respect of understanding how education might underpin future economies. There seems to be a short-term view that is intrinsic to neoliberalism which places more emphasis upon establishing the value of market principles or justifying inequalities than it does to securing long-term economic advantages.

Much of Chaps. 3 and 4 could be understood as being underpinned by values, whether that was with respect to the values of self-interest that are said to be exhibited by groups involved in education or in the value of economic principles which is seen by many as overriding other concerns. It is probably clear by this point that my values do not correspond to the way in which, within a neoliberal perspective, individuals come to be seen as a means to an end, as epitomised by the term human resources, nor do they correspond with seeing individuals as automatons. Although the economy can be seen as being of importance and that fostering creativity and originality will have economic advantages, I would add to this that through fostering creativity and originality, we also provide scope for personal development and that this is equally important.

In assessing how values underpin Higher Education, Maughan Brown (2016) draws attention to the importance placed by the Dearing report with respect to establishing truth. It is hard to argue against this ideal but scrutiny of the idea of truth may be undermined somewhat by the post-modern turn within social science. There is not enough space to rehearse the arguments of post-modernity here, other than to point to the way in which post-modern theories have set out to refute the grand narratives of classical social theory and, in their place, have set out an argument based upon truths rather than truth (Detmer 2003; Bauman 1997; Lyotard 1984). In the theoretical approach taken by post-modernists, there can be no ultimate claim to truth. Truth becomes understood as relative and the possibility of competing truths is taken as inevitable. In some ways post-modern theories have their attractions. In particular they may be seen as being more able to accommodate the complexity of contemporary society in recognising that social life may be the product of a range of intersecting factors. There is a degree of wickedity evident within post-modern theories because of their accommodation of complexity.

However, within the contemporary political arena, the complexity that supports a plurality of truths appears to be overtaken by moves towards simple messages which appeal to emotions rather than rationality. Although it may be argued that post-modernism begins a move away from truth as unitary, it still rests, to some extent, on the notion of truth, even though this recognises competition between truths. Because of this there is still some semblance of truth as having value. Within contemporary politics, at least within the UK and the USA, it seems as though the link between truth and values has been broken and that truth is being ignored in the pursuit of political aims. It seems absurd to claim that a society has left a concern with truth behind, but some of the messages presented, as part of both the Brexit Leave campaign in the UK and as part of the presidential campaigns undertaken in the run-up to the 2016 presidential elections in the USA, illustrate the presentation of statements which are patently untrue and these support the argument that we have arrived at a society that can be defined as post-truth (Ellerton 2016; Jaser 2016). In making this claim, it is important to note these are not examples of competing truths as in the post-modern perspective nor are they examples of political rhetoric. Politicians have always engaged in rhetoric as is illustrated in calls to re-establish Grammar schools as a means to provide for social mobility.

What the Brexit Leave and the presidential campaigners in the USA demonstrate is that in two advanced Western societies, some politicians or their staff are willing to voice untruths for the purpose of achieving their political goals and ambitions. Such behaviour does not auger well for democracy if the democratic process is understood as relying upon citizens making political decisions based upon what they know about candidates and parties. This is because if a candidate makes a pitch for election based upon the promotion of arguments and evidence which they know to be untrue, then no reasoned choice can be made.

Such a situation demonstrates why values are important in any assessment of the provision of education as a whole. The examples referred to above may be of an extreme position but it is an extreme position that has been taken as part of a democratic process. In a more general sense then, the existence of educational provision within societies suggests that education is for something. The question as to what education is for suggests that values can act to shape education, and although it is evident that values can always be understood as being contested and dynamic, it does appear to be the case that in England it is economic values that are currently shaping education (Maughan Brown 2016). This results in education becoming subservient to economic needs in a manner which can be seen as anti-democratic (Shaker and Heilman 2008). This is because education comes to be established to serve the interests of economic enterprises rather than society.

The dominance of economic values within education supports the argument made earlier regarding the way in which education has come to be seen, and managed, as a process. In adopting this perspective of education, the focus is shifted from what education can do for society to a view of education wherein its success is measured in what it can produce, usually on an annual basis. As has been argued above though, the concern with outputs can shape how we provide and experience education. In this way values can be seen as being bound up with the taming of education. If both managers and teachers come to see pupils and students solely in terms of what they can achieve, then this will reinforce an understanding of education as a process and reinforce a move towards the taming of education so as to make outputs more certain.

9.6   STARTING TO CHANGE

Although arguments have been presented which suggest that making education wicked will be beneficial, it is inevitable that this will pose a challenge and it has to be acknowledged that there is little likelihood of a simple solution. To take one example, it has been argued that there are strong forces which act against wickedity, and for tameness, originating in those parties who promote standardisation and accountability on the grounds of equity. These are difficult claims to counter but accepting tameness on the grounds that demonstrating equity within a wicked system is challenging is not a justification for it. It seems then that establishing wickedity will involve convincing stakeholder groups of both the benefits of wickedity and the dangers of tameness.

Importantly, moves towards tameness are not the outcome of the efforts of one particular group or of one particular argument, they are complex, but if we are serious about the claim that we are living in a knowledge economy, then we cannot afford to allow education to be impoverished through tameness. This does not mean that wicked education only exists as part of a utilitarian approach to education which exists within a context of economisation. If we reject the basic claims that education should only exist to serve the economy, a claim that underpins the idea of a knowledge economy, then we are likely to adopt the humanist argument regarding the value of education: that it serves to enable us to lead richer and fuller lives and that it provides the basis of inclusion. If so, the response is the same. Tame education, the type of education which produces automatons, capable of rote learning information and passing assessments but without any real capacity for creativity, can be seen to impoverish society. So, what seems evident is that as it exists, tame education benefits neither society nor the economy. It maybe only seems to serve the interests of those who claim to be improving standards and/or achievements by pointing to comparative statistics relating to the awards being made. On a superficial level, this may appear good but those awards must be fit for purpose; they should not be an end in themselves.

If education continues to be changed in ways which increase control and remove uncertainty, there is no doubt that the illusion of improvements can be held up as evidence of a successful strategy and that some educational managers and politicians will no doubt use this as evidence of their own success. However, tame education will be an impoverished education and, as such, there is a need to establish education as a sector which embraces wickedity and which resists tameness. In essence wickedity is integral to education; it is not a problem to be tamed. If we want to ensure that we can accommodate creativity and originality, there is a need to work towards wickedity throughout education.

Recognising the wicked nature of many contemporary problems though can also mean recognising that sometimes there is no perfect, enduring solution. This applies very well to the case of education at all levels. A wicked problem is a messy problem (Ney and Verweij 2014). Indeed, if we accept the idea that a wicked problem is a messy problem, then we can see that a wicked problem is not a problem that can have a tame solution. There can be no "silver bullet" that will cure education of its tameness; no strategy which encapsulates an easily identifiable solution. Indeed, the formulation of a perfect, tame, strategy may fit with a problem that is tame, but, as has been argued throughout this book, education is neither tame nor is tameness desirable. What has been argued is that education exists within a dynamic landscape wherein numerous factors exert greater or lesser force, influencing what happens within each level and each sector. In place of the silver bullet then, more success may be achieved in the use of silver buckshot (Ney and Verweij 2014), wherein a number of changes are enacted which accommodates a range of views. As such, what is required is not an approach which will solve the problem per se, but rather an approach which is vigilant to it, an approach which emphasises the risks of education becoming tame and which recognises the benefits of wickedity.

As was indicated above though, this may be easier to achieve in some sectors than others. For example, in Higher Education there is greater scope to invoke the independence of those institutions which have the power to make awards. This is because in general there is less intervention by the State with respect to the awarding of qualifications within the Higher Education sector than there is in other sectors. That does not mean that there is none. It has already been shown how the State can increase regulatory control through the imposition of such as the QAA for Higher Education and both the Research Excellence Framework and the new Teaching Excellence Framework. The Teaching Excellence Framework employs the sort of phrase which is hard to critique. Who, working in education, would not want to see pupils and students receiving excellent teaching? However, whilst I support the argument that all students should experience teaching of a high quality, the use of metrics within the Teaching Excellence Framework which are not in any way a measurement of teaching, such as what sort of job a student takes, seems to be a clear indication that the TEF has aims that are not quite so obvious (Ashwin 2016).

Part of this change then must include recognition that bureaucratic procedures cannot be seen to constitute an adequate replacement for trust or professional judgements. Their function should be to support such qualities. As such the quality systems employed must be responsive to the concept of wickedity and recognise that in terms of employability we will provide a better service to our pupils and students if we do not tame them. There is a danger that in establishing quality procedures, for perfectly legitimate reasons, education becomes tamed as a consequence of such quality systems being seen as being of greater importance than learning and development.

For staff employed in roles that are focused on quality matters in particular, there is a need to recognise that the characteristics of both education and learning mean that wickedity is intrinsic. This means that achieving wicked education will be challenging. The purpose or role of education is unlikely to be agreed upon by different stakeholder groups and this in itself undermines the possibility of tameness being achieved in a manner that preserves the integrity of the educational system. In this way education is the epitome of the wicked problem.

9.7   A Manifesto for Wicked Education

In drawing to a close then, it seems more appropriate to eschew the aim of providing a tidy ending as this would fly in the face of the concept of wickedity, providing, as it does, a degree of tameness. Instead, I will conclude by promoting the value of wickedity as a manifesto for wickedity.

A manifesto is a document that aims to preface action. It is a document which sets out to establish change for purpose. In presenting a manifesto for wicked education, there is a need to resist developments which establish education as a process and developments which seek to remove uncertainty and which emphasises learning but which have done so in a way which decouples learning from teaching. In one sense this brings the individual back in, but not just the teacher. It can be seen that the focus on learning has muted the teacher but it has also changed the individual who is meant to be learning. As has already been alluded to previously, it is not sufficient to enter education and not engage. Students can be seen to have been called students because they study; studying implies some level of engagement. The move to recasting students as learners may appear to be a minor semantic shift but it can have significant implications with respect to the individual's self-identity.

It doesn't matter if we take a utilitarian view of education as existing to meet the needs of the economy or an idealistic view of education as providing for self-development. From both positions and from those more pragmatic positions that may fall in between, we must appreciate that tame education is not fit for purpose. Because of this we must look forward and consider the ways in which we can provide education that prepares individuals for an uncertain future. For this reason education must be wicked.

So, as a move towards resisting tameness and establishing wickedity, there is a need to do, or achieve, the following:

1. Establish the purpose and values of education.

   To establish what education is for is not as simple as it first sounds for it may have multiple purposes. It is important to recognise that in a complex society, we cannot hope to reduce our understanding of education to being its value. To suggest that there is a particular value of education is to demonstrate tameness for such a value would be more telling in what was not included than in what was. To identify "the" value of education would adopt a narrow perspective in a way that silenced many voices and concerns. For this reason wicked education will be an education system that accommodates the plurality that exists within society and, in doing so, recognises that education serves a number of interests. It becomes tame, and impoverished, when we seek to privilege one purpose and elevate one value at the expense of others.

2. Resist standardisation.

   In many ways standardisation is the epitome of tameness. It is found in the routinised practices of teachers following scripts and going through the motions in ways that are determined by leadership teams who only see the value in results. Standardisation can be wrapped up in claims regarding equity and fairness but they carry with them a sense in which teachers are not trusted to manage themselves. There is a real need to evaluate the ways in which parts of the education system come to be standardised so that we might reject standardisation for its own sake. Where a standardised system provides benefits to pupils and students, it may be accepted, but where the aim is simply to make managing the system easier or to achieve accountability, there are grounds for resistance.

3. Treat learning outcomes as soft, not hard.

   We must appreciate that the outcome of learning may not be the outcomes that we intend and that when we come to see learning outcomes as targets rather than intentions, we run the risk of stifling creativity and originality. The use of learning outcomes should give real cause for concern if they are used as hard and where the focus on learning outcomes comes to dominate approaches towards teaching and assessment.

4. Take risks.

   The pressures of targets inevitably lead to risk-averse cultures forming, but if we resist trying anything new, it is almost inevitable that education will stagnate and become detached from social life. We must recognise that entering education is always risky but resist those voices which seek to remove all risks. Risks may be managed but they are essential for development.

5. Support professionalism.

   Professionalism can be seen as the basis of teacher autonomy where it privileges decision-making by teachers. This requires a reiteration of the need for teacher education rather than teacher training and a valuing of the expertise that teachers have.

6. Recognise that being educated is not the same as being processed.

   We want anyone who enters education to be changed by the experience but we should not want the outcomes of that change to be uniform. We must stop seeing education as a process that can be controlled and acknowledge that teachers, pupils and students are not automatons.

7. Seek wickedity and resist tameness.

   Establish the concept of wicked and tame as a guiding principle wherein wickedity is sought and tameness is to be avoided. Recognise the benefits of creativity and originality but be concerned about the ways that tameness impoverishes education; aim for education that is wicked.

There is nothing fixed about the future of education, or about society. Our education practices and provision have been different in the past and will inevitably be different in the future. How it will differ will, in some ways, be the responsibility of those who are engaged in education. It will not only be down to these individuals though. As we have seen, there are a number of factors which shape education. Some are internal, but others are external. In ending this book, my concern would be that we do not follow the path that is increasingly taming education and that we are aware of the forces that increase tameness and reduce wickedity. As has been argued, the increasing complexity of the world that we live in means that it is more likely that tame education is education that is impoverished, that it is an education that is not fit for purpose. For that reason we should seek to resist tameness and aspire to providing education that is wicked.

REFERENCES

Ashwin, Paul. 2016. 'Bizarre' TEF Metrics Overlook So Much About Teaching Excellence. *Times Higher Education Supplement*. https://www.timeshighered-ucation.com/blog/bizarre-tef-metrics-overlook-so-much-about-teaching-excellence

Ball, Stephen J. 2003. The Teacher's Soul and the Terrors of Performativity. *Journal of Education Policy*. 18 (2): 215–228.

———. 2013. Foucault, Power and Education. In *Key Ideas in Education*, ed. Greg Dimitriardis and Bob Lingard. Abingdon: Routledge.

———. 2015. Education, Governance and the Tyranny of Numbers. *Journal of Education Policy* 30 (3): 299–301. doi:10.1080/02680939.2015.1013271.

Bauman, Zygmunt. 1997. *Postmodernity and Its Discontents*. Cambridge: Polity Press.

Beck, U. 1992. *Risk Society: Towards a New Modernity*. London: Sage.

Biesta, Gert. 2013. *The Beautiful Risk of Education*. Boulder, CO: Paradigm Publishers.

Biggs, John B. 1999. *Teaching for Quality Learning in University*. Buckingham: Society for Research in Higher Education and Open University Press.

———. 2003. *Teaching for Quality Learning at University*. 2nd ed. Maidenhead: Open University Press.

Biggs, John B., and K.F. Collis. 1982. *Evaluating the Quality of Learning*. New York: Academic Press.

Biggs, John B., and Catherine Tang. 2007. *Teaching for Quality Learning at University: What the Student Does*. 3rd ed. Maidenhead: McGraw-Hill/Society for Research into Higher Education & Open University Press.

———. 2011. *Teaching for Quality Learning at University: What the Student Does*. 4th ed. Maidenhead: Society for Research into Higher Education & Open University Press.

Bloom, A. 2017. Ofsted Launches Investigation into 'Scandal' of Schools Gaming the System. *Times Educational Supplement*. https://www.tes.com/news/school-news/breaking-news/ofsted-launches-investigation-scandal-schools-gaming-system

Bottery, M. 2004. *The Challenges of Educational Leadership*. London: Sage.

———. 2008. Critical Professional or Branded Technician: Changing Conceptions of the Education Worker. In *NZEALS International Educational Leadership*, Auckland, NZ.

Coffield, Frank, and Bill Williamson. 2011. *From Exam Factories to Communities of Discovery: The Democratic Route*. In *Bedford Way Papers*. London: Institute of Education.

Detmer, David. 2003. *Challenging Postmodernism: Philosophy and the Politics of Truth*. Amherst, NY: Humanity Books.

Ellerton, Peter. 2017/2016. *Post-Truth Politics and the US Election: Why the Narrative Trumps the Facts* [Cited 5 March 2017]. http://theconversation.com/post-truth-politics-and-the-us-election-why-the-narrative-trumps-the-facts-66480

Firestone, William A. 1998. A Tale of Two Tests: Tensions in Assessment Policy. *Assessment in Education: Principles, Policy & Practice* 5 (2): 175–191. doi:10.1080/0969594980050203.

Hargreaves, A. 2003. *Teaching in the Knowledge Society: Education in the Age of Insecurity*. New York: Teachers College Press.

Hargreaves, Andy, and Dean Fink. 2006. *Sustainable Leadership*. San Francisco, CA: Jossey-Bass/Wiley.

Hurst, G. 2013. Exam Reform Will Damage Creativity, Dyson Claims. *The Times*, June 17, p. 8.

Hussey, Trevor, and Patrick Smith. 2010. *The Trouble with Higher Education*. Abingdon: Routledge.

Jaser, Zahira. 2017/2016. *Post-Truth Leaders Are All About Their Followers* [Cited 5 March 2017]. http://theconversation.com/post-truth-leaders-are-all-about-their-followers-69020

Kennedy, Declan. 2008. Linking Learning Outcomes and Assessment of Learning of Student Science Teachers. *Science Education International* 19 (4): 387–397.

Lyotard, Jean-Francois. 1984. *The Postmodern Condition: A Report on Knowledge*. Manchester: Manchester University Press.

Macfarlane, B. 2017. *Freedom to Learn: The Threat to Student Academic Freedom and Why It Needs to Be Reclaimed*. Abingdon: Routledge.

Maughan Brown, D. 2016. Values in Higher Education: Articulation and Action. In *Values and Virtues in Higher Education Research*, ed. J. McNiff. Abingdon: Routledge.

Moon, Jennifer A. 1999. *Reflection in Learning and Professional Development: Theory and Practice*. London: Kogan Page.

Moon, Jenny. 2002. *The Module and Programme Development Handbook*. London: Kogan Page.

Moon, Jennifer A. 2004. *A Handbook of Reflective and Experiential Learning: Theory and Practice*. London: RoutledgeFalmer.

Ney, Steven M., and Marco Verweij. 2014. Messy Institutions for Wicked Problems: How to Generate Clumsy Solutions. http://ssrn.com/abstract=2382191

Ofsted, and A. Spielman. 2017. Amanda Spielman's Speech at the ASCL Annual Conference. HM Govt [Cited 24 March 2017]. https://www.gov.uk/government/speeches/amanda-spielmans-speech-at-the-ascl-annual-conference

Roberts-Holmes, Guy. 2015. The 'Datafication' of Early Years Pedagogy: If the Teaching Is Good, the Data Should Be Good and If There's Bad Teaching, There Is Bad Data. *Journal of Education Policy* 30 (3): 302–315. doi:10.1080/02680939.2014.924561.

Shaker, P., and E. Heilman. 2008. *Reclaiming Education for Democracy: Thinking Beyond No Child Left Behind*. New York: Routledge.

Whetton, Chris. 2009. A Brief History of a Testing Time: National Curriculum Assessment in England 1989–2008. *Educational Research* 51 (2): 137–159. doi:10.1080/00131880902891222.

REFERENCES

Adam, S. 2004. Using Learning Outcomes: A Consideration of the Nature, Role, Application and Implications for European Education of Employing Ëlearning Outcomesí at the Local, National and International Levels. In *UK Bolgna Seminar*. Edinburgh: Heriot-Watt University.

Adams, R. 2016. Schools Under Scrutiny on Crackdown on League Table 'Gaming'. *The Guardian*.

Adams, Richard, and Sally Weale. 2016. A*-C Grades in Dramatic Decline as GCSE Results are Published. *The Guardian*.

Ainley, P. 1994. *Degrees of Difference: Higher Education in the 1990s*. London: Lawrence & Wishart.

Amable, Bruno. 2011. Morals and Politics in the Ideology of Neo-Liberalism. *Socio-Economic Review* 9 (1): 3–30. doi:10.1093/ser/mwq015.

Andrews, Jon, Jo Hutchinson, and Rebecca Johnes. 2016. *Grammar Schools and Social Mobility*. London: Education Policy Institute.

AoC (Association of Colleges). 2016a. College Higher Education. [Cited 2 July 2016]. https://www.aoc.co.uk/term/college-higher-education

———. 2016b. *Progress Through Practice: The Future of Higher Education*. London: Association of Colleges.

Ashwin, Paul. 2016. 'Bizarre' TEF Metrics Overlook So Much About Teaching Excellence. *Times Higher Education Supplement*. https://www.timeshighereducation.com/blog/bizarre-tef-metrics-overlook-so-much-about-teaching-excellence

Attewell, Paul. 1990. What Is Skill? *Work and Occupations* 17 (4): 26.

Au, Wayne. 2011. Teaching Under the New Taylorism: High-Stakes Testing and the Standardization of the 21st Century Curriculum. *Journal of Curriculum Studies* 43 (1): 25–45.

© The Author(s) 2018

R. Creasy, *The Taming of Education*,

DOI 10.1007/978-3-319-62247-7

Avis, James, and Kevin Orr. 2016. HE in FE: Vocationalism, Class and Social Justice. *Research in Post-Compulsory Education* 21 (1–2): 49–65. doi:10.1080/13596748.2015.1125666.

Bahous, R., and N. Nabhani. 2011. Assessing Education Programme Learning Outcomes. *Educational Assessment, Evaluation and Accountability* 23 (1): 21–39.

Ball, Stephen J. 2003. The Teacher's Soul and the Terrors of Performativity. *Journal of Education Policy.* 18 (2): 215–228.

———. 2013. Foucault, Power and Education. In *Key Ideas in Education*, ed. Greg Dimitriardis and Bob Lingard. Abingdon: Routledge.

———. 2015. Education, Governance and the Tyranny of Numbers. *Journal of Education Policy* 30 (3): 299–301. doi:10.1080/02680939.2015.1013271.

———. 2016. Neoliberal Education? Confronting the Slouching Beast. *Policy Futures in Education* 14 (8): 13.

Ball, Stephen J., and Antonio Olmedo. 2013. Care of the Self, Resistance and Subjectivity Under Neoliberal Governmentalities. *Critical Studies in Education* 54 (1): 85–96.

Barnett, R. 1990. *The Idea of Higher Education.* Buckingham: SRHE & Open University Press.

———. 2000. *Realizing the University in an Age of Supercomplexity.* Buckingham: SRHE/Open University Press.

———. 2003. *Beyond all Reason: Living with Ideology in the University.* Buckingham: Open University Press with Society for Research into Higher Education.

———. 2005. *Reshaping the University: New Relationships Between Research, Scholarship and Teaching.* Maidenhead: Open University Press.

———. 2011. *Being a University.* Abingdon: Routledge.

Bassey, Michael. 1999. *Case Study Research in Educational Settings.* Maidenhead: Open University Press.

———. 2001. A Solution to the Problem of Generalisation in Educational Research: Fuzzy Prediction. *Oxford Review of Education* 27 (1): 5–22. doi:10.1080/3054980020030574.

Bauman, Zygmunt. 1997. *Postmodernity and Its Discontents.* Cambridge: Polity Press.

Beach, P. 2015. GCSE Marking and Grading. *The Ofqual Blog.*

Beard, R. 2000. Research and the National Literacy Strategy. *Oxford Review of Education* 26 (3–4): 15.

Beard, R.M., F.G. Healey, and P.J. Holloway. 1968. *Objectives in Higher Education.* London: Society for Research into Higher Education.

Becher, T. 1999. *Professional Practices: Commitment and Capability in a Changing Environment.* New Brunswick, NJ: Transaction Publishers.

Becher, T., and P. Trowler. 2001. *Academic Tribes and Territories: Intellectual Enquiry and the Cultures of Disciplines.* Buckingham: Open University Press.

Beck, U. 1992. *Risk Society: Towards a New Modernity.* London: Sage.

Bell, D. 1976. *The Coming of Post-Industrial Society.* New York: Basic Books.

Biesta, Gert. 2009. Good Education in an Age of Measurement: On the Need to Reconnect with the Question of Purpose in Education. *Educational Assessment, Evaluation & Accountability* 21 (1): 33–46. doi:10.1007/s11092-008-9064-9.

———. 2010. Learner, Student, Speaker: Why It Matters How We Call Those We Teach. *Educational Philosophy & Theory* 42 (5–6): 540–552. doi:10.1111/j.1469-5812.2010.00684.x.

———. 2012. Giving Teaching Back to Education: Responding to the Disappearance of the Teacher. *Phenomenology & Practice* 6 (2): 14.

———. 2013. *The Beautiful Risk of Education.* Boulder, CO: Paradigm Publishers.

Biggs, John B. 1999. *Teaching for Quality Learning in University.* Buckingham: Society for Research in Higher Education and Open University Press.

———. 2003. *Teaching for Quality Learning at University.* 2nd ed. Maidenhead: Open University Press.

Biggs, John B., and K.F. Collis. 1982. *Evaluating the Quality of Learning.* New York: Academic Press.

Biggs, John B., and Catherine Tang. 2007. *Teaching for Quality Learning at University: What the Student Does.* 3rd ed. Maidenhead: McGraw-Hill/Society for Research into Higher Education & Open University Press.

———. 2011. *Teaching for Quality Learning at University: What the Student Does.* 4th ed. Maidenhead: Society for Research into Higher Education & Open University Press.

Blacker, D.J. 2013. *The Falling Rate of Learning and the Neoliberal Endgame.* Winchester: Zero Books.

Blackman, T., E. Elliott, A. Greene, B. Harrington, D. Hunter, L. Marks, L. McKee, and G. Williams. 2006. Performance Assessment and Wicked Problems: The Case of Health Inequalities. *Public Policy and Administration* 21 (2): 66–80.

Bloom, A. 2017. Ofsted Launches Investigation into 'Scandal' of Schools Gaming the System. *Times Educational Supplement.* https://www.tes.com/news/school-news/breaking-news/ofsted-launches-investigation-scandal-schools-gaming-system

Bore, Anne, and Nigel Wright. 2009. The Wicked and Complex in Education: Developing a Transdisciplinary Perspective for Policy Formulation, Implementation and Professional Practice. *Journal of Education for Teaching* 35 (3): 241–256. doi:10.1080/02607470903091286.

Bottery, M. 2000. *Education, Policy and Ethics.* London: Continuum.

Bottery, Mike. 2003. The Management and Mismanagement of Trust. *Educational Management Administration & Leadership* 31 (3): 245–261.

Bottery, M. 2004. *The Challenges of Educational Leadership*. London: Sage.

Bottery, Mike. 2006. Education and Globalization: Redefining the Role of the Educational Professional. *Educational Review* 58 (1): 95–113.

Bottery, M. 2008. Critical Professional or Branded Technician: Changing Conceptions of the Education Worker. In *NZEALS International Educational Leadership*, Auckland, NZ.

———. 2016. *Educational Leadership for a More Sustainable World*. London: Bloomsbury.

Braverman, H. 1974. *Labour and Monopoly Capital*. New York: Monthly Review Press.

Brew, Angela. 2001. *The Nature of Research: Inquiry in Academic Contexts*. London: Routledge.

Brookfield, S. 1995. *Becoming a Critically Reflective Teacher*. San Francisco, CA: Jossey-Bass.

Brown, S. 2007. A Critique of Generic Learning Outcomes. *Journal of Learning Design* 2 (2): 8.

Brown, R., and H. Carasson. 2013. *Everything for Sale? The Marketisation of UK Higher Education*. Abingdon: Routledge/Society for Research into Higher Education.

Browne, J. 2010. Securing a Sustainable Future for Higher Education: An Independent Review of Higher Education Funding and Student Finance. http://hereview.independent.gov.uk/hereview/

Browne, Liz, and Jay Reid. 2012. Changing Localities for Teacher Training: The Potential Impact on Professional Formation and the University Sector Response. *Journal of Education for Teaching* 38 (4): 497–508. doi:10.1080/0 2607476.2012.709747.

Bryan, J., and D. Hayes. 2007. The McDonaldization of Further Education. In *A Lecturer's Guide to Further Education*, ed. D. Hayes, T. Marshall, and A. Turner. Maidenhead: Open University Press.

Busch, B. 2016. Four Neuromyths that are still Prevalent in Schools – Debunked. *The Guardian*.

Buyruk, Halil. 2014. "Professionalization" or "Proletarianization": Which Concept Defines the Changes in Teachers' Work? *Procedia—Social and Behavioral Sciences* 116: 1709–1714. doi:10.1016/j.sbspro.2014.01.460.

Camillus, J.C. 2008. Strategy as a Wicked Problem. *Harvard Business Review* 86 (5): 96–105.

Chakrabortty, A. 2016. Think Only Low–Paid Workers Get the Sports Direct treatment? You're Wrong. *The Guardian*.

Chakrabortty, A., and S. Weale. 2016. Universities Accused of 'Importing Sports Direct Model' for Lecturers' Pay. *The Guardian*.

Child, Sue. 2009. Differing Relationships to Research in Higher and Further Education in the UK: A Reflective Account from a Practitioner Perspective. *Research in Post-Compulsory Education* 14 (3): 333–343. doi:10.1080/13596740903139453.

Chitty, Clyde. 2014. *Education Policy in Britain*. 3rd ed. Basingstoke: Palgrave Macmillan.

Chitty, C., and B. Simon. 1993. *Education Answers Back: Critical Responses to Government Policy*. London: Lawrence & Wishart.

Clarke, John. 2010. After Neo-Liberalism? *Cultural Studies* 24 (3): 375–394. doi:10.1080/09502381003750310.

Clarke, Matthew. 2012. The (Absent) Politics of Neo-Liberal Education Policy. *Critical Studies in Education* 53 (3): 297–310. doi:10.1080/17508487.2012.703139.

Clarke, J., and J. Newman. 1997. *The Managerial State: Power, Politics and Ideology in the Remaking of Social Welfare*. London: Sage.

Clarke, M., and A. Phelan. 2017. *Teacher Education and the Political: The Power of Negative Thinking*. London: Routledge.

Clarke, J., S. Gewirtz, and E. McLaughlin. 2000. *New Managerialism, New Welfare?* London: Sage.

Cochran-Smith, Marilyn. 2005. The New Teacher Education: For Better or for Worse? *Educational Researcher* 34 (7): 3–17. doi:10.3102/0013189X034007003.

Coe, Robert, Karen Jones, Jeff Searle, Dimitra Kokotsaki, Azlina Mohd Kosnin, and Paul Skinner. 2008. *Evidence on the Effects of Selective Educational Systems*. Durham, NC: CEM Centre, Durham University.

Coffield, Frank. 2008. *Just Suppose Teaching and Learning Became the First Priority*. London: Learning and Skills Network. Edited by Learning and Skills Network.

Coffield, Frank, and Bill Williamson. 2011. *From Exam Factories to Communities of Discovery: The Democratic Route*. In *Bedford Way Papers*. London: Institute of Education.

Copnell, Graham. 2010. Modernising Allied Health Professions Careers: Attacking the Foundations of the Professions? *Journal of Interprofessional Care* 24 (1): 63–69. doi:10.3109/13561820902946115.

Cowan, John, and Diane Cherry. 2012. The learner's Role in Assessing Higher Level Abilities. *Practitioner Research in Higher Education* 6 (1): 12–22.

Creasy, Rob. 2013. HE Lite: Exploring the Problematic Position of HE in FECs. *Journal of Further and Higher Education* 37 (1): 38–53. doi:10.1080/0309877x.2011.644772.

Cripps, Sandy. 2002. *Further Education, Government's Discourse Policy and Practice: Killing a Paradigm Softly*. Aldershot: Ashgate.

Crozier, Gill., D. Reay, J. Clayton, L. Colliander, and J. Grinstead. 2008. Different Strokes for Different Folks: Diverse Students in Diverse Institutions—Experiences of Higher Education. *Research Papers in Education* 23: 167–177.

Curtis, B. 2012. How the Ofsted Chief got His Maths Wrong on Sats. *The Guardian*.

Daugherty, Richard, Paul Black, Kathryn Ecclestone, Mary James, and Paul Newton. 2008. Alternative Perspectives on Learning Outcomes: Challenges for Assessment. *Curriculum Journal* 19 (4): 243–254. doi:10.1080/09585170802509831.

Davies, W. 2014. *The Limits of Neoliberalism: Authority, Sovereignty and the Logic of Competition*. London: Sage.

DBIS. 2016. *Success as a Knowledge Economy: Teaching Excellence, Social Mobility and Student Choice*. London: DBIS. Edited by Department of Business Innovation & Skills.

Dean, Mitchell. 2014. Rethinking Neoliberalism. *Journal of Sociology* 50 (2): 13.

Dearing, Ron. 1997. *Higher Education in the Learning Society*. Norwich: HMSO. National Committee of Inquiry into Higher Education.

Deem, Rosemary. 1998. 'New Managerialism' and Higher Education: The Management of Performances and Cultures in Universities in the United Kingdom. *International Studies in Sociology of Education* 8 (1): 47–70. doi:10.1080/0962021980020014.

Deem, Rosemary, and Kevin J. Brehony. 2005. Management as Ideology: The Case of 'New Managerialism' in Higher Education. *Oxford Review of Education* 31 (2): 217–235. doi:10.1080/03054980500117827.

Denzin, Norman K., and Yvonna S. Lincoln. 2008. Introduction: The Discipline and Practice of Qualitative Research. In *Strategies of Qualitative Enquiry*, ed. Norman K. Denzin and Yvonna S. Lincoln. London: Sage.

Department for Business, Innovation and Skills (DBIS). 2009. Higher Ambitions: The Future of Universities in a Knowledge Economy. http://www.bis.gov.uk/wp-content/uploads/publications/Higher-Ambitions.pdf

Department for Education and Skills. 2002. *Building on Improvement. The National Literacy and Numeracy Strategies*. London: Department for Education and Skills. p. 18.

Detmer, David. 2003. *Challenging Postmodernism: Philosophy and the Politics of Truth*. Amherst, NY: Humanity Books.

DfE. 2010. *The Importance of Teaching: The Schools White Paper*. Norwich: The Stationary Office. Edited by Department for Education.

———. 2016. *Teaching Excellence Framework: Year Two Specification*. London: HM Govt. Edited by Department for Education.

———. 2017. *Policy Paper, 2010 to 2015 Government Policy: Young People*. London: HM Government. 2015 [Cited 3 March 2017]. https://www.gov.uk/government/publications/2010-to-2015-government-policy-young-people/2010-to-2015-government-policy-young-people

DfES. 2001. *Schools Achieving Success.* Annesley: DfES. Edited by Dept for Education and Skills.

———. 2003. *The Future of Higher Education.* Norwich: HMSC. Edited by Dept For Education and Skills.

Dhillon, Jaswinder K., and Jon Bentley. 2016. Governor and Course Leaders' Reflections on HE in FE: Strategic Ambition and Curriculum Practice in Two Large Colleges in England. *Research in Post-Compulsory Education* 21 (1–2): 137–150. doi:10.1080/13596748.2015.1125668.

Dunleavy, P., and C. Hood. 1994. From Old Public Administration to New Public Management. *Public Money & Management* 14 (3): 9–16.

Ecclestone, K., and D. Hayes. 2009. *The Dangerous Rise of Therapeutic Education.* London: Routledge.

Edwards, C. 2000. Assessing What We Value and Valuing What We Assess? Constraints and Opportunities for Promoting Lifelong Learning with Postgraduate Professionals. *Studies in Continuing Education* 22 (2): 201–217.

Ellerton, Peter. 2017/2016. *Post-Truth Politics and the US Election: Why the Narrative Trumps the Facts* [Cited 5 March 2017]. http://theconversation.com/post-truth-politics-and-the-us-election-why-the-narrative-trumps-the-facts-66480

Ellis, Viv, Melissa Glackin, Deb Heighes, Mel Norman, Sandra Nicol, Kath Norris, Ingrid Spencer, and Jane McNicholl. 2013. A Difficult Realisation: The Proletarianisation of Higher Education-Based Teacher Educators. *Journal of Education for Teaching* 39 (3): 266–280. doi:10.1080/02607476.2013.799845.

Ellis, Viv, Jane McNicholl, Allan Blake, and Jim McNally. 2014. Academic Work and Proletarianisation: A Study of Higher Education-Based Teacher Educators. *Teaching and Teacher Education* 40: 33–43. doi:10.1016/j.tate.2014.01.008.

Exworthy, M., and S. Halford. 1999. Professionals and Managers in a Changing Public Sector: Conflict, Compromise and Collaboration. In *Professionals and the New Managerialism in the Public Sector*, ed. M. Exworthy and S. Halford. Buckingham: Open University Press.

Feather, Denis. 2016. Organisational Culture of Further Education Colleges Delivering Higher Education Business Programmes: Developing a Culture of 'HEness'—What Next? *Research in Post-Compulsory Education* 21 (1–2): 98–115. doi:10.1080/13596748.2015.1125669.

Finn, Mike. 2015a. Education Beyond the Gove Legacy. In *The Gove Legacy*, ed. Mike Finn, 14. Basingstoke: Palgrave Macmillan.

———. 2015b. The Gove Legacy and the Politics of Education After 2015 (2). In *The Gove Legacy*, ed. Mike Finn, 10. Basingstoke: Palgrave Macmillan.

Firestone, William A. 1998. A Tale of Two Tests: Tensions in Assessment Policy. *Assessment in Education: Principles, Policy & Practice* 5 (2): 175–191. doi:10.1080/0969594980050203.

Fischman, Gustavo. 2008. Introduction. In *Contesting Neoliberal Education: Public Resistance and Collective Advance*, ed. Dave Hill. Abingdon: Routledge.

Flint, Nerilee Ra, and Bruce Johnson. 2011. *Towards Fairer University Assessment: Recognizing the Concerns of Students*. Abingdon: Routledge.

Furedi, F. 2002. The Bureaucratization of the British University. In *The McDonaldization of Higher Education*, ed. D. Hayes and R. Wynyard. Westport, CT: Bergin & Garvey.

Gage, N. 2007. The Paradigm Wars and their Aftermath: A 'Historical' Sketch of Research on Teaching Since 1989. In *Educational Research and Evidence-Based Practice*, ed. M. Hammersley. London: Sage.

Gerth, H.H., and C. Wright-Mills. 1948. *From Max Weber: Essays in Sociology*. London: Routledge & Kegan Paul.

Gillborn, D., and Deborah Youdell. 1999. *Rationing Education: Policy, Practice, Reform and Equity*. Buckingham: Open University Press.

Gleeson, Denis. 2001. Style and Substance in Education Leadership: Further Education (FE) as a Case in Point. *Journal of Education Policy* 16 (3): 181–196. doi:10.1080/02680930110041015.

Goodhew, Gwen. 2009. *Meeting the Needs of Gifted and Talented Students*. London: Network Continuum.

Goodlad, S. 1976. *Conflict and Consensus in Higher Education*. London: Hodder and Stoughton.

Gopal, P. 2012. A New Kind of Class Warfare. *The Guardian* [Cited 28 June 2016]. https://www.theguardian.com/commentisfree/2012/apr/03/new-kind-of-class-warfare

Gorard, Stephen, and Chris Taylor. 2001. The Composition of Specialist Schools in England: Track Record and Future Prospect. *School Leadership & Management* 21 (4): 365–381. doi:10.1080/13632430120108916.

Graham, G. 2008. *Universities: The Recovery of an Idea*. Exeter: Imprint Academic.

Gudanescu, N., and A. Cristea. 2009. Education and Life Long Learning: Argument for the Development of Knowledge Based Economy and Society. *Lex et Scientia* 16 (1): 430–441.

Habermas, J. 1984. *The Theory of Communicative Action, Vol. 1, Reason and the Rationalization of Society*. Trans. Thomas McCarthy. Cambridge: Polity.

Halsey, A.H. 1982. The Decline of Donnish Dominion. *Oxford Review of Education* 8 (3): 215–219.

Hammersley, Martin. 2007. *Educational Research and Evidence-Based Practice*. London: Sage/The Open University.

Hardy, Ian. 2015. A Logic of Enumeration: The Nature and Effects of National Literacy and Numeracy Testing in Australia. *Journal of Education Policy* 30 (3): 335–362. doi:10.1080/02680939.2014.945964.

Hargreaves, A. 2003. *Teaching in the Knowledge Society: Education in the Age of Insecurity*. New York: Teachers College Press.

Hargreaves, D.H. 2007. Teaching as a Research-Based Profession: Possibilities and Prospects. In *Educational Research and Evidence-Based Practice*, ed. Martin Hammersley. London: Sage.

Hargreaves, Andy, and Dean Fink. 2006. *Sustainable Leadership*. San Francisco, CA: Jossey-Bass/Wiley.

Hartog, Joop, and Henriëtte Maassen van den Brink. 2007. Epilogue: Some Reflections on Educational Policies. In *Human Capital: Advances in Theory and Evidence*, ed. Joop Hartog and Henriëtte Maassen van den Brink, 233–235. Cambridge: Cambridge University Press.

Hartog, Joop, and Hessel Oosterbeek. 2007. What Should You Know About the Private Returns to Education? In *Human Capital: Advances in Theory and Evidence*, ed. Joop Hartog and Henriëtte Maassen van den Brink, 7–20. Cambridge: Cambridge University Press.

Hayden, Carol, and Craig Jenkins. 2014. 'Troubled Families' Programme in England: 'Wicked Problems' and Policy-Based Evidence. *Policy Studies* 35 (6): 631–649. doi:10.1080/01442872.2014.971732.

Hayek, Frederik von. 2007/1960. *The Constitution of Liberty*. Abingdon: Routledge.

———. 2013/1973, 1976, 1979. *Law, Legislation and Liberty*. Abingdon: Routledge.

Hayes, D. 2003. Managerialism and Professionalism in Post-Compulsory Education. In *Working in Post-Compulsory Education*, ed. J. Lea, D. Hayes, A. Armitage, L. Lomas, and S. Markless. Maidenhead: Open University Press.

———. 2015. As They Compete to Lay on the Best Student Experience, Universities Mustn't Forget the Academic One Too. http://theconversation.com/as-they-compete-to-lay-on-the-best-student-experience-universities-mustnt-forget-the-academic-one-too-45197

Hayes, Dennis, Toby Marshall, and Alec Turner. 2007. *A Lecturer's Guide to Further Education*. Maidenhead: Open University Press.

Hefce. 2015. Institutions that HEFCE Funds. Bristol: Higher Education Funding Council for England. http://www.hefce.ac.uk/workprovide/unicoll/. Accessed 9 Aug 2017.

Held, D. 2002. *Globalisation and Anti-Globalisation*. Oxford: Polity.

Held, D., and A. McGrew. 2000. *The Global Transformations Reader*. Cambridge: Polity.

Hill, Jennifer, Helen Walkington, and Derek France. 2016. Graduate Attributes: Implications for Higher Education Practice and Policy. *Journal of Geography in Higher Education 40* (2): 155–163.

Hodgkinson, Peter John. 1990. *A Content-Theoretical Model of Educational Change: The Case of the New Vocationalism*. UCL Institute of Education (IOE).

Hood, C. 1991. A Public Administration for all Seasons? *Public Administration* 69 (Spring): 3–19.

———. 2000. Paradoxes of Public-Sector Managerialism, Old Public Management and Public Service Bargains. *International Public Management Journal* 3: 1–22.

House of Commons, Innovation, Universities Science and Skills Committee. 2008. *Withdrawal of Funding for Equivalent or Lower Level Qualifications (ELQs)*. London: The Staionary Office.

Hughes, P. 2007. Learning about Learning, or Learning to Learn (L2L). In *Learning, Teaching and Assessing in Higher Education: Developing Reflective Practice*, ed. A. Campbell and L. Norton. Exeter: Learning Matters.

Humfrey, C. 2011. The Long and Winding Road: A Review of the Policy, Practice and Development of the Internationalisation of Higher Education in the UK. *Teachers and Teaching: Theory and practice* 17 (6): 12.

Hurst, G. 2013. Exam Reform Will Damage Creativity, Dyson Claims. *The Times*, June 17, p. 8.

Hussey, Trevor, and Patrick Smith. 2008. Learning Outcomes: A Conceptual Analysis. *Teaching in Higher Education* 13 (1): 107–115. doi:10.1080/13562510701794159.

———. 2010. *The Trouble with Higher Education*. Abingdon: Routledge.

Hyland, Terry, and Barbara Merrill. 2003. *The Changing Face of Further Education: Lifelong Learning, Inclusion and Community Values in Further Education*. London: Routledge.

Irisdotter Aldenmyr, Sara, and Maria Olson. 2016. The Inward Turn in Therapeutic Education—An Individual Enterprise Promoted in the Name of the Common Good. *Pedagogy, Culture and Society* 24 (3): 387–400.

Jary, D., D. Gatley, and L. Broadbent. 1998. The US Community College: A Positive or Negative Model for UK Higher Education. In *The New Higher Education: Issues and Directions for the Post-Dearing University*, ed. D. Jary and M. Parker. Stoke-on-Trent: Staffordshire University Press.

Jary, D., and M. Parker. 1998. *The New Higher Education: Issues and Directions for the Post-Dearing University*. Stoke-on-Trent: Staffordshire University Press.

Jaser, Zahira. 2017/2016. *Post-Truth Leaders Are All About Their Followers* [Cited 5 March 2017]. http://theconversation.com/post-truth-leaders-are-all-about-their-followers-69020

Jenkins, Simon. 2006. *Thatcher & Sons: A Revolution in Three Acts*. London: Allen Lane.

Jentoft, S., and R. Chuenpagdee. 2009. Fisheries and Coastal Governance as a Wicked Problem. *Marine Policy* 33 (4): 553–560.

Jiang, N., and V. Carpenter. 2013. Faculty-Specific Factors of Degree of HE Internationalization: An Evaluation of Four Faculties of a Post-1992 University in the United Kingdom. *International Journal of Educational Management* 27 (3): 17.

Jones, K. 2003. *Education in Britain: 1944 to the Present*. Cambridge: Polity Press.

Jordan, Michelle E., Robert C. Kleinsasser, and Mary F. Roe. 2014. Wicked Problems: Inescapable Wickedity. *Journal of Education for Teaching* 40 (4): 415–430. doi:10.1080/02607476.2014.929381.

Kalfa, Senia, and Lucy Taksa. 2015. Cultural Capital in Business Higher Education: Reconsidering the Graduate Attributes Movement and the Focus on Employability. *Studies in Higher Education* 40 (4): 580–595.

Kennedy, Declan. 2008. Linking Learning Outcomes and Assessment of Learning of Student Science Teachers. *Science Education International* 19 (4): 387–397.

Kennedy, Aileen. 2015. What Do Professional learning Policies Say About Purposes of Teacher Education? *Asia-Pacific Journal of Teacher Education* 43 (3): 183–194. doi:10.1080/1359866x.2014.940279.

King, R. 2004. *The University in the Global Age*. Basingstoke: Palgrave Macmillan.

Knight, Peter, and C. Anna Page. 2007. *The Assessment of 'Wicked' Competences*. Milton Keynes: Open University Practice-Based Professional Learning Centre.

Knight, P.T., and M. Yorke. 2003. *Assessment, Learning and Employability*. Maidenhead: SRHE/Open University Press.

Knights, D., and H. Willmott. 1990. *Labour Process Theory*. Basingstoke: Palgrave Macmillan.

Kuhn, T. 1996. *The Structure of Scientific Revolutions*. 3rd ed. Chicago, IL: University of Chicago Press.

Le Grand, J., and W. Bartlett. 1993. *Quasi-Markets and Social Policy*. London: Macmillan.

Leach, Tony, and Ellie Lewis. 2013. Children's Experiences During Circle-Time: A Call for Research-Informed Debate. *Pastoral Care in Education* 31 (1): 43–52. doi:10.1080/02643944.2012.702781.

Light, G., and R. Cox. 2001. *Learning and Teaching in Higher Education: The Reflective Professional*. London: Sage.

Lorenz, Chris. 2012. If You're So Smart, Why Are You Under Surveillance? Universities, Neoliberalism, and New Public Management. *Critical Inquiry* 38 (3): 599–629. doi:10.1086/664553.

Lucas, Norman, and Norman Crowther. 2016. The Logic of the Incorporation of Further Education Colleges in England 1993–2015: Towards an Understanding of Marketisation, Change and Instability. *Journal of Education Policy 31* (5): 583–597.

Lumby, Jacky. 2007. 14- to 16-year-olds in Further Education Colleges: Lessons for Learning and Leadership. *Journal of Vocational Education & Training* 59 (1): 1–18. doi:10.1080/13636820601143031.

Lyotard, Jean-Francois. 1984. *The Postmodern Condition: A Report on Knowledge*. Manchester: Manchester University Press.

Maassen van den Brink, Henriëtte, and Joop Hartog. 2007. *Human Capital: Advances in Theory and Evidence*. Cambridge: Cambridge University Press.

Macfarlane, B. 2017. *Freedom to Learn: The Threat to Student Academic Freedom and Why It Needs to Be Reclaimed*. Abingdon: Routledge.

Mansell, W. 2016. *Ofqual's Apparent Use of Norm Referencing at GCSE*. NAHT 2012 [Cited 28 June 2016]. http://www.naht.org.uk/welcome/news-and-media/key-topics/assessment/ofquals-apparent-use-of-norm-referencing-at-gcse/

Marginson, Simon. 2009. Hayekian Neo-Liberalism and Academic Freedom. *Contemporary Readings in Law and Social Justice* 1 (1): 86.

Maringe, F. 2009. Strategies and Challenges of Internationalisation in HE: An Exploratory Study of UK Universities. *International Journal of Educational Management* 23 (7): 10.

Mather, Kim, Les Worrall, and Roger Seifert. 2007. Reforming Further Education: The Changing Labour Process for College Lecturers. *Personnel Review* 36 (1): 109–127. doi:10.1108/00483480710716740.

Mather, K., L. Worrall, and R. Seifert. 2009. The Changing Locus of Workplace Control in the English Further Education Sector. *Employee Relations* 31 (2): 139–157.

Maughan Brown, D. 2016. Values in Higher Education: Articulation and Action. In *Values and Virtues in Higher Education Research*, ed. J. McNiff. Abingdon: Routledge.

McGuigan, Jim. 2005. Neo-Liberalism, Culture and Policy. *International Journal of Cultural Policy* 11 (3): 229–241. doi:10.1080/10286630500411168.

Mirowski, P. 2014. The Political Movement that Dared Not Speak Its Own Name: The Neoliberal Thought Collective Under Erasure. https://www.ineteconomics.org/uploads/papers/WP23-Mirowski.pdf

Mirowski, P., and D. Plehwe. 2009. *The Road from Mont Pèlerin: The Making of the Neoliberal Thought Collective*. Cambridge, MA: Harvard University Press.

Moon, Jennifer A. 1999. *Reflection in Learning and Professional Development: Theory and Practice*. London: Kogan Page.

Moon, Jenny. 2002. *The Module and Programme Development Handbook*. London: Kogan Page.

Moon, Jennifer A. 2004. *A Handbook of Reflective and Experiential Learning: Theory and Practice*. London: RoutledgeFalmer.

Moore, Alex, and Matthew Clarke. 2016. 'Cruel Optimism': Teacher Attachment to Professionalism in an Era of Performativity. *Journal of Education Policy* 31 (5): 666–677. doi:10.1080/02680939.2016.1160293.

Nash, Ian. 2010. Widening Participation Will Be the First Victim of Funding Cuts: Funding Cuts Could Wipe Out Half of all the College Places That Are Linked with Universities. *The Guardian*.

Nash, Ian, Kathryn Eccleston, and Claire Fox. 2007. Symposium: The Future of Further Education. In *A Lecturers Guide to Further Education*, ed. Dennis Hayes, Toby Marshall, and Alec Turner. Maidenhead: Open University Press.

Neave, G. 1996. Higher Education in Transition: Twenty Five Years on. *Higher Education Management* 8 (1): 15–24.

Ney, Steven M., and Marco Verweij. 2014. Messy Institutions for Wicked Problems: How to Generate Clumsy Solutions. http://ssrn.com/abstract=2382191

Ofqual. 2016. *Grading the New GCSEs in 2017.* Ofqual 2014 [Cited 28 June 2016]. https://www.gov.uk/government/uploads/system/uploads/attachment_data/file/377768/2014-09-12-grading-the-new-gcses-in.pdf

———. n.d. *Grading New GCSEs from 2017* [Cited 18 October 2016]. https://www.gov.uk/government/uploads/system/uploads/attachment_data/file/537147/Postcard_-_Grading_New_GCSEs.pdf

Ofsted, and A. Spielman. 2017. Amanda Spielman's Speech at the ASCL Annual Conference. HM Govt [Cited 24 March 2017]. https://www.gov.uk/government/speeches/amanda-spielmans-speech-at-the-ascl-annual-conference

Olssen, Mark. 2016. Neoliberal Competition in Higher Education Today: Research, Accountability And Impact. *British Journal of Sociology of Education* 37 (1): 129–148.

Ozga, J. 1988. *Schoolwork: Approaches to the Labour Process of Teaching.* Maidenhead: Open University Press.

Pashler, H., M. McDaniel, D. Rohrer, and R. Bjork. 2008. Learning Styles: Concepts and Evidence. *Psychological Science in the Public Interest.* 9 (3): 15.

Peck, J. 2010. *Constructions of Neoliberal Reason.* Oxford: Oxford University Press.

Perraudin, F. 2016. Academy Trust Accused of Discriminating Against Disabled Pupils. *The Guardian.*

Peters, R.T. 2004. *In Search of the Good Life: The Ethics of Globalization.* London: Continuum.

Philips, Jane. 1999. Not Learning, But Coasting. *Checklist for School Governors in Great Britain* 4309: 30–30.

Plowright, David. 2011. *Using Mixed Methods: Frameworks for an Integrated Methodology.* London: Sage.

Power, Michael. 2003. Evaluating the Audit Explosion. *Law & Policy 25* (3): 185–202.

Preston, Susan, and Jordan Aslett. 2014. Resisting Neoliberalism from Within the Academy: Subversion Through an Activist Pedagogy. *Social Work Education 33* (4): 502–518.

Pring, Richard. 2004. *Philosophy of Education: Aims, Theory, Common Sense and Research.* London: Continuum.

Prøitz, Tine S. 2010. Learning Outcomes: What Are They? Who Defines Them? When and Where are They Defined? *Educational Assessment, Evaluation and Accountability* 22 (2): 119–137. doi:10.1007/s11092-010-9097-8.

QAA. 2014. *UK Quality Code for Higher Education. Part A: Setting and Maintaining Academic Standards*. Gloucester: QAA.

Raelin, J.A. 2007. Toward an Epistemology of Practice. *Academy Of Management Learning & Education* 6 (4): 495–519.

Ramsden, P. 2003. *Learning to Teach in Higher Education*. 2nd ed. Abingdon: RoutledgeFalmer.

Randle, Keith, and Norman Brady. 1997a. Further Education and the New Managerialism. *Journal of Further & Higher Education* 21 (2): 229.

———. 1997b. Managerialism and Professionalism in the 'Cinderella Service'. *Journal of Vocational Education & Training* 49 (1): 121–139. doi:10.1080/13636829700200007.

Rapley, Eve. 2014. Horses for Courses, or a Grumble in the Jungle? HE in FE Student Perceptions of the HE Experience in a Land-Based College. *Research in Post-Compulsory Education* 19 (2): 194–211. doi:10.1080/13596748.2014.897510.

Ravitch, D. 1998. What If Research Really Mattered? *Education Week* 18 (16): 33.

Reay, D., M. David, and S. Ball. 2005. *Degrees of Choice: Social Class, Race and Gender in Higher Education*. Stoke-on-Trent: Trentham Books.

Reay, Diane, Jacqueline Davies, Miriam David, and Stephen J. Ball. 2001. Choices of Degree or Degrees of Choice? Class, 'Race' and the Higher Education Choice Process. *Sociology* 35 (4): 855–874. doi:10.1177/0038038501035004004.

Regan, Bernard. 2008. Campaigning Against Neoliberal Education in Britain. In *Contesting neoliberal Education: Public Resistance and Collective Advance*, ed. Dave Hill. Abingdon: Routledge.

Reid, Ian C. 2009. The Contradictory Managerialism of University Quality Assurance. *Journal of Education Policy* 24 (5): 575–593. doi:10.1080/02680930903131242.

Richardson, William. 2007. In Search of the Further Education of Young People in Post-War England. *Journal of Vocational Education & Training* 59 (3): 385–418. doi:10.1080/13636820701551943.

Rittel, Horst W.J., and M. Melvin Webber. 1973. Dilemmas in a General Theory of Planning. *Policy Sciences* 4 (2): 155–169.

Ritzer, G. 2002. Enchanting McUniversity: Towards a Spectacularly Irrational University Quotidian. In *The McDonaldization of Higher Education*, ed. D. Hayes and R. Wynyard. Westport, CT: Bergin & Garvey.

———. 2011. *The McDonaldization of Society*. 6th ed. Los Angeles, CA: Pine Forge.

Roberts-Holmes, Guy. 2015. The 'Datafication' of Early Years Pedagogy: If the Teaching Is Good, the Data Should Be Good and If There's Bad Teaching, There Is Bad Data. *Journal of Education Policy* 30 (3): 302–315. doi:10.1080/02680939.2014.924561.

Robson, Sue. 2011. Internationalization: A Transformative Agenda for Higher Education? *Teachers and Teaching* 17 (6): 619–630. doi:10.1080/13540602.2011.625116.

Rochford, F. 2008. The Contested Product of a University Education. *Journal of Higher Education Policy & Management* 30 (1): 41–52.

Shaker, P., and E. Heilman. 2008. *Reclaiming Education for Democracy: Thinking Beyond No Child Left Behind.* New York: Routledge.

Singh, Mala. 2010. Quality Assurance in Higher Education: Which Pasts to Build on, What Futures to Contemplate? *Quality in Higher Education* 16 (2): 189–194. doi:10.1080/13538322.2010.485735.

Smith, C., D. Knights, and H. Willmott. 1991. *White-Collar Work: The Non-Manual Labour Process.* Basingstoke: Macmillan.

Stanton, G. 2009. A View from Within the English Further Education Sector on the Provision of Higher Education: Issues of Verticality and Agency. *Higher Education Quarterly* 63 (4): 419–433.

Stobart, Gordon. 2008. *Testing Times: The Uses and Abuses of Assessment.* Abingdon: Routledge.

———. 2014. *The Expert Learner: Challenging the Myth of Ability.* Maidenhead: Open University Press.

Stoller, Aaron. 2015. Taylorism and the Logic of Learning Outcomes. *Journal of Curriculum Studies* 47 (3): 317–333.

Sutherland, Margaret B. 2012. *Gifted and Talented in the Early Years: Practical Activities for Children Aged 3 to 6.* 2nd ed. London: SAGE.

Taylor, P.G. 1999. *Making Sense of Academic Life: Academics, Universities and Change.* Buckingham: SHRE and Open University Press.

Tharp, R.G., and R. Gallimore. 1988. *Rousing Minds to Life: Teaching, Learning, and Schooling in Social Context.* Cambridge: Cambridge University Press.

The Education and Training Foundation. 2016. *Further Education Workforce Data for England.* London: The Education and Training Foundation.

Tierny, W.G., and A. Rhoads. 1995. The Culture of Assessment. In *Academic Work*, ed. R. Smyth. Buckingham: SRHE and Open University Press.

Touraine, A. 1974. *The Post-Industrial Society.* London: Wildwood House.

Turner, R.S. 2011. *Neo-Liberal Ideology: History, Concepts and Policies.* Edinburgh: Edinburgh University Press.

Tysome, Tony. 2002. FE Crisis Hampers HE Growth. *Times Higher Education Supplement* 1559: 9.

University of Cambridge. 2014. Project Seeks Nation's Most Memorised Poems to Investigate Power of Poetry 'by Heart' [Cited 28 June 2016]. http://www.cam.ac.uk/research/news/project-seeks-nations-most-memorised-poems-to-investigate-power-of-poetry-by-heart

Vallas, Steven Peter. 1990. The Concept of Skill: A Critical Review. *Work and Occupations* 17 (4): 19.

Waters, Mick. 2015. The Gove Legacy. In *The Gove Legacy*, ed. Mike Finn, 12. Basingstoke: Palgrave Macmillan.

West, Anne. 2001. Choice and Diversity: The Case for Small Specialist Schools. *New Economy* 8 (4): 208.

Wexler, M. 2009. Exploring the Moral Dimension of Wicked Problems. *International Journal of Sociology and Social Policy* 29 (9–10): 531–542.

Whetton, Chris. 2009. A Brief History of a Testing Time: National Curriculum Assessment in England 1989–2008. *Educational Research* 51 (2): 137–159. doi:10.1080/00131880902891222.

Wiggins, K. 2015. 'Good' Schools May Be 'Coasting', Too. Times Educational Supplement. Times Supplements Ltd.

Wilson, Tom. 1991. The Proletarianisation of Academic Labour. *Industrial Relations Journal* 22 (4): 250–262.

Wolf, M. 2005. *Why Globalization Works*. London: Yale Nota Bene.

Wright, Nigel. 2011. Between 'Bastard' and 'Wicked' Leadership? School Leadership and the Emerging Policies of the UK Coalition Government. *Journal of Educational Administration and History* 43 (4): 17.

Wright, Katie. 2014. Student Wellbeing and the Therapeutic Turn in Education. *The Educational and Developmental Psychologist* 31 (2): 141–152. doi:10.1017/edp.2014.14.

Wrigley, T. 2009. Rethinking Education in the Era of Globalization. In *Contesting Neo-Liberal Education: Public Resistance and Collective Advance*, ed. D. Hill. Abingdon: Routledge.

Yorke, Mantze. 2008. *Grading Student Achievement in Higher Education: Signals and Shortcomings*. Abingdon: Routledge.

INDEX

© The Author(s) 2018
R. Creasy, *The Taming of Education*,
DOI 10.1007/978-3-319-62247-7

221

CPI Antony Rowe
Chippenham, UK
2017-09-18 10:21